Good Regulatory Practices to Support Small and Medium Enterprises in Southeast Asia

OECD
BETTER POLICIES FOR BETTER LIVES

Please cite this publication as:
OECD (2018), *Good Regulatory Practices to Support Small and Medium Enterprises in Southeast Asia*, OECD Publishing, Paris.
https://doi.org/10.1787/9789264305434-en

ISBN 978-92-64-30542-7 (print)
ISBN 978-92-64-30543-4 (pdf)

Photo credits: Cover © MuchMania / shutterstock.com

Corrigenda to OECD publications may be found on line at: *www.oecd.org/publishing/corrigenda*.

Foreword

Good regulatory practices (GRP) refer to the use of tools such as regulatory impact evaluation, stakeholder engagement and *ex post* evaluation to improve the quality of the regulatory environment for businesses, citizens and society. GRP tools are useful for identifying and reviewing which regulations are essential for achieving given outcomes, ultimately making regulatory compliance as straightforward and meaningful as possible.

For businesses, GRP facilitate a stable and enabling regulatory environment that can help boost investment, trade and entrepreneurship. While GRP benefits businesses of all sizes, they are especially helpful for small and medium-sized enterprises (SMEs). Compared with their larger counterparts, SMEs may be less adaptive to – and potentially disproportionately affected by – the stock and flow of regulations. In Southeast Asia, where the vast majority of businesses are SMEs, a regulatory environment ill-adapted to the needs and characteristics of SMEs can significantly undermine the health of the local economy as well as regional competitiveness.

Indeed, policy makers can help SMEs thrive in local communities as well as participate in global value chains by adopting GRP that make regulations easier to understand while simultaneously reducing the time and costs associated with compliance. This applies both to the national context, where SMEs may face a number of regulatory barriers to sustain operation or to grow larger, and to the international context, where SMEs may need additional support to meet varying regulatory requirements.

The OECD has published numerous guidelines and toolkits to help countries (central governments, sectoral ministries, regulatory and competition agencies) adopt regulatory policy, management and governance. These include the *OECD Guiding Principles for Regulatory Quality and Performance*, *APEC-OECD Integrated Checklist on Regulatory Reform* and the *Best Practice Principles for Regulatory Enforcement and Inspections*. The OECD has also worked with individual countries to improve regulatory delivery; for example, it undertook an evaluation of administrative simplification in Viet Nam.

This report presents the first stocktaking of GRP in all ten Association of Southeast Asian Nations (ASEAN) member countries. It highlights the efforts each government has taken to advance GRP in various areas, including cutting red tape, regulatory oversight, regulatory impact assessment, stakeholder engagement, *ex post* evaluation, e-government and appeals. As countries continue to move towards an ASEAN single market, co-ordinating GRP implementation will become increasingly important for improving regulatory oversight and reducing cross-border regulatory gaps.

Country-specific policy recommendations are proposed for improving regulatory design, co-ordination, implementation and impact assessment in Southeast Asia. Recommendations are intended to complement ongoing efforts to improve regulatory design and delivery to support the growth of SMEs in the region, in line with best practices.

This work supports the ASEAN Economic Community Blueprint, the Master Plan on ASEAN Connectivity and the ASEAN Strategic Action Plan for SME Development.

ASEAN government officials and the ASEAN Secretariat have provided significant inputs to this publication. It is part of the Canada-OECD Project on ASEAN SMEs (COPAS) funded by the Government of Canada. The report builds on the work on GRP conducted by the Regulatory Policy Division of the OECD Directorate of Public Governance. The Directorate's mission is to help government at all levels design and implement strategic, evidence-based and innovative policies that support sustainable economic and social development.

Acknowledgements

This report was co-ordinated and prepared by Shelly Hsieh and Winona Bolislis. Faisal Naru led the project and provided guidance on the analysis. The report benefitted from substantive inputs from Filippo Cavassini, Anna Pietikainen and Nick Malyshev, Head of the Regulatory Policy Division, with encouragement and support from Marcos Bonturi, Director of the Public Governance Directorate. Céline Kauffmann and Marianna Karttunen contributed to the initial phase of the analysis. Jennifer Stein co-ordinated the editorial process. Kate Lancaster and Andrea Uhrhammer provided editorial support.

Le Duy Binh from Economica Vietnam and Zoe Dayan provided essential data collection and advisory support for the country chapters for Cambodia, Lao PDR (Dayan) and Viet Nam (Binh).

This report has benefitted from extensive consultations with ASEAN government official, ministries and private sector representatives responsible for developing and implementing GRP. In particular, the authors would like to thank the following key country contacts for co-ordinating the consultations and data collection, providing in-depth feedback about regulatory policies and practices to support SMEs, and sharing insights on early findings: Mohamad Munawir Shazali Idris (Prime Minister's Office, Brunei) and Nadia Saiful Rizal (Ministry of Energy and Industry, Brunei); Sokha Pech (ECOSOCC, Cambodia); Diani Sadiawati and Ahmad Dading Gunadi (BAPPENAS, Indonesia), Destry Anna Sari (Ministry of Cooperative and SMEs, Indonesia), Sukarman (Coordinating Ministry for Economic Affairs, Indonesia), Tities Eka Agustine (KPPOD), Enny Nurbaningsih (Ministry of Law and Human Rights, Indonesia); Siti Norlailasari Binti Abdul Rahman (Ministry of International Trade and Industry, Malaysia), Roziana Othman (Malaysia Productivity Corporation), Intan Zanariah Hamdan (SME Corp. Malaysia); Aye Aye Win and Phyu Phyu Win (Department for SME Development, Myanmar), Aung Soe and Myat Soe Moe (Myanmar Trade Promotion Organisation), Aye Aye Win (Department of Customs, Myanmar), Minn Minn and Thandar Khin (Ministry of Commerce, Myanmar), Than Than Htay (Department of Agriculture, Myanmar), Mya Than and Kyaw Zin Lat (Department of Small Scale Industry, Myanmar), Aung Naing Oo (DICA/Myanmar Investment Commission); Carlos Bernardo Abad Santos and Thelma Manuel (National Economic Development Authority, Philippines) and Kenneth Francis Fernandez (Department of Trade and Industry, Philippines), Jun Han Wong and Geraldine Yeow (Enterprise Singapore); Pakorn Nilprapunt and Jaisai Wongpichet (Office of the Council of State, Thailand), Pimchanok Vonkorpon and Pattaranat Wuttiwai (Ministry of Commerce, Thailand), and Attanisa Changchaitum (Office of SME Promotion, Thailand). Aung Kyi Soe, Aung Thein and Maung Maung Lay (UMFCCI), Blaise Kilian (Eurocham Cambodia), Petra Schill (GIZ) and Peter Brimble (DaNa Facility) contributed valuable advice.

This report would not have been possible without support from the ASEAN Secretariat and the Government of Canada. Mark Steel and Julie Nind of the government of New Zealand also provided useful comments and support.

The analytical framework informing this report was initially discussed with the ASEAN-OECD Good Regulatory Practice Network (GRPN) at the 3rd GRPN in Iloilo, Philippines, in March 2017. Findings and recommendations were presented and discussed with the ASEAN Coordinating Committee on Micro, Small and Medium Enterprises (ACCMSME) in Luang Prabang, Lao PDR and the OECD Regulatory Policy Committee in April 2018. The report was presented to the GRPN at the 4th GRPN meeting in Kuala Lumpur, Malaysia, in October 2018.

Table of contents

Abbreviations and acronyms **13**

Executive summary **15**

Chapter 1. Good regulatory practices in Southeast Asia **19**

Improving regulatory environments with good regulatory practices (GRP) 20
Supporting small and medium enterprises (SMEs) with GRP 20
Good regulatory practice to enhance SME participation in the Global Value Chains 21
Applications of GRP in Southeast Asia 24
Notes 34
References 35

Chapter 2. Brunei Darussalam **37**

Regulatory context 38
Regulatory governance 39
Highlights of regulatory opportunities and challenges to support SMEs 42
Recommendations 51
References 52
Annex 2.A. 53

Chapter 3. Cambodia **55**

Regulatory context 56
Regulatory governance 58
Highlights of regulatory opportunities and challenges to support SMEs 64
Recommendations 73
References 74

Chapter 4. Indonesia **77**

Regulatory context 78
Regulatory governance 80
Highlights of regulatory opportunities and challenges to support SMEs 85
Recommendations 92
Notes 92
References 93

Chapter 5. Lao PDR **95**

Regulatory context 96
Regulatory governance 97
Highlights of regulatory opportunities and challenges to support SMEs 101
Recommendations 108
References 109

Chapter 6. Malaysia 111
Regulatory context 112
Regulatory governance 114
Highlights of regulatory opportunities and challenges to support SMEs 118
Recommendations 128
References 129

Chapter 7. Myanmar 131
Regulatory context 132
Regulatory governance 133
Highlights of regulatory opportunities and challenges to support SMEs 138
Recommendations 143
Notes 143
References 144

Chapter 8. Philippines 147
Regulatory context 148
Regulatory governance 151
Highlights of regulatory opportunities and challenges to support SMEs 156
Recommendations 168
Notes 169
References 170
Annex 8.A. 172

Chapter 9. Singapore 175
Regulatory context 176
Regulatory governance 177
Highlights of regulatory opportunities and challenges to support SMEs 179
Recommendations 198
Notes 198
References 199
Annex 9.A. 202

Chapter 10. Thailand 203
Regulatory context 204
Regulatory governance 205
Highlights of regulatory opportunities and challenges to support SMEs 208
Recommendations 222
Notes 222
References 223

Chapter 11. Viet Nam 225
Regulatory context 226
Regulatory governance 227
Highlights of regulatory opportunities and challenges to support SMEs 232
Recommendations 241
References 242

Tables

Table 1.1. Cutting red tape in Southeast Asia ... 26
Table 1.2. Regulatory oversight bodies in Southeast Asia and systematic adoption of good regulatory practice (GRP) tools ... 27
Table 1.3. Approaches to regulatory review ... 29
Table 1.4. Country progress towards integration with the ASEAN Single Window ... 32
Table 2.1. Institutional and regulatory setup in Brunei ... 39
Table 2.2. Classification of SMEs in Brunei ... 40
Table 2.3. Business-related laws and regulations in Brunei ... 40
Table 2.4. Registration requirements in Brunei ... 41
Table 2.5. Strengthening institutional development through the civil service in Brunei ... 42
Table 3.1. Institutional and regulatory setup in Cambodia ... 58
Table 3.2. Definition of SMEs in Cambodia ... 63
Table 3.3. Progressive tax rates for SMEs in Cambodia as of 1 January 2017 ... 63
Table 4.1. Targets for Ease of Doing Business (EoDB) in Indonesia ... 79
Table 4.2. Institutional and regulatory setup in Indonesia ... 80
Table 4.3. SME definition in Indonesia based on Law 20/2008 ... 83
Table 4.4. Ministries and agencies involved in SME policy and/or regulation ... 84
Table 5.1. Institutional and regulatory setup in Lao PDR ... 97
Table 5.2. Definition of SMEs in Lao PDR ... 100
Table 5.3. Policies and targets in the promotion of SMEs (Prime Minister's Decree 42) ... 101
Table 6.1. Institutional and regulatory setup ... 114
Table 6.2. Business-related laws and regulations in Malaysia ... 116
Table 6.3. SME definition in Malaysia ... 116
Table 6.4. Registration requirements in Malaysia ... 117
Table 6.5. Summary of administrative simplification activities and cost savings ... 120
Table 6.6. Capacity building programmes in Malaysia ... 127
Table 7.1. Definition of MSMEs in Myanmar ... 134
Table 7.2. Institutional and regulatory setup in Myanmar ... 135
Table 7.3. Good practices in SEZ policies in Myanmar ... 142
Table 8.1. Overall key performance indicators for the MSME Development Plan 2017-21 ... 149
Table 8.2. Institutional and regulatory setup ... 151
Table 8.3. Types of policies and regulations passed at the executive level ... 152
Table 8.4. Business-related laws and regulations in the Philippines ... 153
Table 8.5. MSME categories in the Philippines ... 154
Table 8.6. Registration requirements in the Philippines ... 156
Table 8.7. Industry clusters in the Philippines ... 166
Table 9.1. Institutional and regulatory setup ... 177
Table 10.1. Institutional and regulatory setup ... 205
Table 10.2. Definitions of MSMEs in Thailand ... 207
Table 10.3. Business-related laws and regulations in Thailand ... 207
Table 10.4. Registration requirements in Thailand ... 208
Table 10.5. Laws and decrees supporting e-commerce in Thailand ... 211
Table 10.6. Export promotion schemes in Thailand ... 220
Table 10.7. Agencies linked to the Thai National Single Window ... 221
Table 11.1. Institutional and regulatory setup in Viet Nam ... 227
Table 11.2. Definition of micro and SMEs in Viet Nam ... 230

Annex Table 2.A.1. Services provided by the Brunei Business Support Centre 53
Annex Table 8.A.1. Activities and fiscal incentives for registered enterprises in Philippine Economic Zones 172
Annex Table 9.A.1. Business-related laws in Singapore 202

Figures

Figure 1.1. Incidence of non-tariff measures by industry 22
Figure 1.2. Key dates on good regulatory practices in ASEAN 24
Figure 1.3. Scope and form of stakeholder engagement 30
Figure 2.1. Seven steps to a successful engagement in Brunei 49
Figure 3.1. Making laws, royal decrees and sub-decrees in Cambodia 61
Figure 4.1. Legislative process in Indonesia 81
Figure 5.1. Overview of the legislative process in Lao PDR 98
Figure 6.1. Framework for Modernising Business Regulation in Malaysia 112
Figure 6.2. Regulatory-making process in Malaysia 115
Figure 6.3. Roadmap to GRP implementation 122
Figure 6.4. Public consultation process in Malaysia 125
Figure 6.5. Framework for establishing a unified public consultation mechanism in Malaysia 126
Figure 7.1. Registration process for SMEs in Myanmar 137
Figure 8.1. Legislative process in the Philippines 153
Figure 8.2. Distribution of enterprises by size (left) and by employment (right) 155
Figure 9.1. Law-making process in Singapore 178
Figure 10.1. Legislative process in Thailand 206
Figure 11.1. Viet Nam's legislative process 229

Boxes

Box 1.1. What are good regulatory practices? 20
Box 1.2. Rising non-tariff barriers in ASEAN 22
Box 1.3. What are oversight bodies? 27
Box 1.4. Types of stakeholder engagement 30
Box 1.5. Regional halal certification standards 33
Box 2.1. Improving regulatory delivery in Brunei 43
Box 2.2. Improving the ease of doing business in Brunei 45
Box 2.3. Five types of public engagement in Brunei 48
Box 2.4. Reaching out to local businesses in Brunei 49
Box 3.1. Major public service reform programmes in Cambodia 57
Box 3.2. Administrative improvements in Cambodia's civil service 66
Box 3.3. Preliminary Assessment Statement (PAS) and Regulatory Impact Statement (RIS) 68
Box 3.4. Checklist of compliance costs for PAS/RIS 68
Box 3.5. Evaluation of Cambodia's One Window Service Office (OWSO) 69
Box 3.6. Results-based management in Cambodia's Public Financial Management Reform Programme (PFMRP) 70
Box 3.7. Government-private sector forum for tourism 70
Box 4.1. Economic policy packages in Indonesia 78
Box 4.2. Main principles and objectives of regulatory policies in Indonesia 82
Box 4.3. Regulatory simplification for licensing and investment in Indonesia 88
Box 4.4. National regulatory databases in Indonesia 90
Box 5.1. National plans emphasising SME development in Lao PDR 96

Box 5.2. Law on making legislation in Lao PDR, 2012 99
Box 5.3. One-stop service in Lao PDR's special economic zones 103
Box 5.4. Appeal process in the decision on food inspection No. 297/MOH 24/02/2012 105
Box 5.5. Criteria for investing outside of Lao PDR 107
Box 6.1. Identifying regulatory burden in Malaysia 118
Box 6.2. Improving business licensing in Malaysia 119
Box 6.3. Case study: Reducing Unnecessary Regulatory Burden on private hospitals 120
Box 6.4. Adopting e-payment for SMEs in Malaysia 121
Box 6.5. Considering small businesses in the development of new regulations 123
Box 6.6. Features of Malaysia's National Single Window (NSW) 128
Box 8.1. Improving the ease of doing business in the Philippines 149
Box 8.2. Reducing the burden on businesses in the Philippines 157
Box 8.3. Modernising Government Regulations (MGR) programme 158
Box 8.4. *Go Negosyo* Centres: A one-stop shop for businesses in the Philippines 159
Box 8.5. Standards and Conformance (S&C) Portal in the Philippines 160
Box 8.6. Supporting product development in the Philippines 161
Box 8.7. Regulatory impact assessment (RIA) pilot tests in the Philippines 162
Box 8.8. Facilitating court appeals in the Philippines 164
Box 8.9. Improving MSME productivity through shared facilities in the Philippines 165
Box 8.10. Export-assistance schemes and programmes in the Philippines 167
Box 8.11. Improving customs procedures in the Philippines 168
Box 9.1. Industry Transformation Maps (ITMs) in Singapore 176
Box 9.2. Examples of online one-stop shops in Singapore 180
Box 9.3. Promoting access to finance in Singapore through regulatory simplification 180
Box 9.4. Avoiding duplications in testing and inspections for exported goods from Singapore 181
Box 9.5. Government applications in Singapore 182
Box 9.6. Encouraging the use of digital platforms for SMEs 183
Box 9.7. Regulatory sandbox: Flexible regulations in Singapore 184
Box 9.8. Shared standards building in Singapore 185
Box 9.9. Strengthening intellectual property for SMEs in Singapore 186
Box 9.10. Various Approaches to regulatory enforcement in Singapore 188
Box 9.11. Improving transparency and ease of doing business in Singapore through stakeholder consultation 190
Box 9.12. Strengthening citizen engagement in Singapore 191
Box 9.13. Making legislation simple and accessible in Singapore 192
Box 9.14. Government initiatives to improve public-private collaboration 193
Box 9.15. Strengthening the labour market in Singapore 195
Box 9.16. Plug and Play Network (PPN) Singapore: Helping SMEs expand overseas quickly 196
Box 9.17. Customs initiatives in Singapore 197
Box 10.1. Improving licensing procedures in Thailand 209
Box 10.2. One-stop shops in Thailand 210
Box 10.3. Fostering e-commerce in Thailand 211
Box 10.4. Thailand's online platforms for SMEs 212
Box 10.5. Guidelines for drafting legislation in Thailand 213
Box 10.6. Doing business reform programme in Thailand 214
Box 10.7. Consultation process for draft legislation in Thailand 215
Box 10.8. Improving service delivery in Thailand 216
Box 10.9. Promoting intellectual property in Thailand 217
Box 10.10. Highlights of the Thailand 4.0 strategy 218
Box 10.11. Improving customs procedures in Thailand 221

Box 11.1. Viet Nam Government Action Plan on SME Development 2011-15 227
Box 11.2. Priorities of the Viet Nam SME Support Law 2017 and its prevailing regulatory policies 231
Box 11.3. Law on the Making of Laws and Legal Normative Documents (Law on laws) 232
Box 11.4. Principles of risk management in customs operations in Viet Nam.................................... 234
Box 11.5. One-stop shops in Viet Nam 235
Box 11.6. Regulatory simplification process and outcomes from Project 30...................................... 235
Box 11.7. RIA of proposed regulatory policies as stipulated in Article 35 of the Law on the Promulgation of Legal Normative Documents, 2015 237
Box 11.8. Online databases for regulations in Viet Nam.. 237
Box 11.9. Appeal process for regulatory decisions in Viet Nam.. 240

Abbreviations and acronyms

ACCSQ	ASEAN Consultative Committee on Standards and Quality
ADB	Asian Development Bank
AEC	ASEAN Economic Community
APEC	Asia-Pacific Economic Co-operation
APLAC	Asia-Pacific Laboratory Accreditation Co-operation
AQI	Audit Quality Indicator
ASEAN	Association of Southeast Asian Nations
ASPEC	ASEAN Patent Examination Co-operation
ASW	ASEAN Single Window
ASYCUDA	Automated System for Customs Data
ATIGA	ASEAN Trade-in-Goods Agreement
C/O	Certificate of Origin
CBA	Cost-Benefit Analysis
eCoSys	Electronic Certificate of Origin System
EEC	Eastern Economic Corridor
ePG	E-Payment Gateway
EV	Electric Vehicle
FAO	Food and Agriculture Organization
FDI	Foreign Direct Investment
FTA	Free Trade Agreement
GDP	Gross Domestic Product
GLC	Government-Linked Company
GRP	Good Regulatory Practices
GST	Goods and Services Tax
GVC	Global Value Chain
IEC	International Electrotechnical Commission
IFRS	International Financial Reporting Standards
ILO	International Labour Organization
IoT	Internet of Things
IP	Intellectual Property
IPR	Intellectual Property Right
ISO	International Standards Organisation
JICA	Japan International Co-operation Agency
KPI	Key Performance Indicator
MLA	Multi-lateral Recognition Agreements
MNE	Multi-National Enterprise
MOU	Memorandum of Understanding
MPAC	Masterplan on ASEAN Connectivity
MRA	Mutual Recognition Agreements
MSME	Micro, Small, and Medium Enterprise
NSW	National Single Window
NTB	Non-Tariff Barrier
NTM	Non-Tariff Measure
OECD	Organisation for Economic Co-operation and Development
PMO	Prime Minister's Office

R&D	Research and Development
RBC	Responsible Business Conduct
RMS	Regulatory Management System
SEC	Securities and Exchange Commission
SEZ	Special Economic Zone
SME	Small and Medium Enterprise
SOE	State-owned Enterprises
SOM-AMAF	Senior Officials Meeting – ASEAN Ministers of Agriculture and Forestry
SPS	Sanitary and Phytosanitary Standards
SSF	Shared Service Facilities
TBT	Technical Barriers to Trade
WIPO	World Intellectual Property Organization
WTO	World Trade Organization

Executive summary

Southeast Asian governments have been actively promoting trade and investment linkages between domestic firms and international markets, with the aim to unlock business opportunities and bolster national productivity and competitiveness. In Southeast Asia, participation in global value chains (GVCs) has contributed significantly to economic development and employment generation as Association of Southeast Asian Nations (ASEAN) countries gain a foothold in the manufacturing and supply chain hub dubbed “Factory Asia”. Nevertheless, ASEAN governments recognise that most ‘big business’ is driven by a limited number of large firms, while small and medium-sized enterprises (SMEs) operate at a local scale. Given that SMEs account for over 90% of all businesses and the bulk of local employment, their success is important not only for boosting gross domestic product (GDP) but also for improving socio-economic equity.

A fair, sensible and transparent regulatory environment helps SMEs thrive locally and internationally. Yet, even as regulations level the playing field among companies and protect social and environmental interests, compliance remains a challenge. Indeed, compared with large companies, SMEs are often disproportionately affected by the increasing stock and flow of regulations as they tend to have weaker adaptive capacity to comply with complex or changing regulations.

Adopting good regulatory practices (GRP) is thus more important than ever. This goes for businesses of all sizes, but especially for SMEs. GRP use tools in the regulatory cycle – such as administrative simplification, impact assessments, and stakeholder engagement – to improve the quality of the regulatory environment for everyone.

This report is the first comprehensive stocktaking of developments in implementing GRP to support SMEs in ASEAN countries.

ASEAN governments recognise the importance of good regulatory practices (GRP)

The report finds that ASEAN countries by and large recognise the importance of GRP and are increasingly streamlining its tools and methodologies into regulatory design and delivery. Almost all countries in the region have initiated some kind of administrative burden reduction programme, and all countries practice stakeholder engagement, as well as offer at least a few regulatory processes that can be completed online.

Some countries have introduced regulatory policies targeted at SMEs, while others have opted to level the regulatory playing field for businesses of all sizes. A dedicated SME regulatory policy may not be necessary as long as the general regulatory environment is fair, transparent, clear and effective. The diversity of the ten ASEAN countries means that governments necessarily tailor the use of GRP to their unique regulatory contexts.

While all ten ASEAN countries apply GRP, the consistency and quality of their implementation are seldom monitored or evaluated. Even when GRP is intended to be applied to all government agencies and arm's-length bodies, this may not be the case in practice. Very few countries conduct *ex post* evaluations of regulations.

Key recommendations:

- The purpose and impact of regulations – both existing and proposed – should be clearly set out, justified and expressly communicated to the public via systematic and targeted stakeholder consultations.
- *Ex ante* regulatory evaluation, including regulatory impact evaluations, should be followed by *ex post* evaluation to ensure continuous relevance.
- Regulatory enforcement is crucial for improving overall regulatory compliance. Penalties for non-compliance should be proportional and calibrated to facilitate compliance.

SMEs are highly heterogeneous and have different needs for regulatory support

SMEs are highly heterogeneous: some prefer to serve domestic demand while others target international markets; some are bound by local resources while others rely on imports; some sell products and services directly to their neighbours; others trade entirely on line. As a result, some SMEs want governments to help them do business locally, while others want support for accessing international trade. Governments will continue to be challenged to devise regulatory policies and approaches that can serve a wide and likely increasingly complex range of SME needs in both local and international contexts.

Key recommendations:

- Policy makers must continuously update their understanding of SMEs' needs, which are more dynamic than ever and may cut across sectors or jurisdictions.
- Regulatory interventions should be tailored to the sector(s) in which SMEs operate and the tools that they use, rather than administered according to simple employee count or revenue.
- Encourage SMEs to participate in and contribute to government policies and programmes by putting more emphasis on serving SMEs, which will also help build trust.

The diversity of ASEAN governance structures requires adaptable and forward-looking GRP tools and approaches

ASEAN countries vary greatly in terms of governance, institutional organisation and development priorities as well as levels of economic development and integration. Correspondingly, government approaches to setting regulatory policy and using GRP also differ from country to country. Yet, the region's aspiration to achieve a single market means that, at some point, national regulatory policies will need to be complementary, if not standardised across countries. As ASEAN advances towards regional integration, further challenges lie ahead for regulatory co-ordination and implementation.

Key recommendations:

- More co-operation on regulatory harmonisation is required to unlock the full potential of an inclusive, connected ASEAN economic community. Regulations may not be uniform, but they should be complementary.
- Anticipate regional regulatory requirements in the development and application of national regulations – whether on processes or standards – to help smooth the learning curve between local and international trade.
- Take advantage of digital technologies to deliver smarter policies, regulations and services.

Chapter 1. Good regulatory practices in Southeast Asia

Governments of the Association of Southeast Asian Nations (ASEAN) recognise the importance of Good Regulatory Practices (GRP) - the use of regulatory impact evaluation, stakeholder engagement and ex post *evaluation - for improving the quality of the regulatory environment for businesses, citizens and society. By applying GRP, policymakers can help maintain a stable and enabling regulatory environment that promotes investment, trade and entrepreneurship while limiting or even eliminating unnecessary administrative burden for businesses of all sizes – especially for small and medium enterprises (SMEs) that tend to have weaker adaptive capacity to adapt to changing or complex regulations. To support local businesses in growing and integrating into global value chains, ASEAN governments have initiated various GRP tools and measures aimed at simplifying regulations, reducing compliance costs, assessing regulatory impacts, migrating administrative procedures online, conducting stakeholder consultation and streamlining regulatory requirements. This chapter highlights uses of GRP across the Southeast Asia region.*

Improving regulatory environments with good regulatory practices (GRP)

Governments use laws and regulations as a key lever to achieve policy objectives and outcomes; for example, as a way to promote inclusive and sustainable growth, stimulate competition and productivity, improve social welfare and increase environmental protection. Different forms of regulations exist, with legal restrictions as the most common form used by governments. Other forms include: norm-setting; certification; accreditation; standard setting; market regulation, among others.

The net benefit created by regulations should be positive, and regulation must be fit-for-purpose to achieve its intended objectives (OECD/Korea Development Institute, 2017[1]). Regulations should be built on evidence and they should reflect the needs and objectives of regulated entities and citizens alike. This would also help ensure acceptance, effective implementation and compliance. By extension, regulatory processes should include efforts to minimise the costs and burden associated with regulatory compliance.

Governments around the world have adopted good regulatory practices (GRP) aimed at systematically improving the quality and delivery of regulations. GRP uses key tools in the regulatory cycle – such as administrative simplification, impact assessments, stakeholder engagement, e-government and appeals – to improve the quality of the regulatory environment for everyone.

Box 1.1. What are good regulatory practices?

Good regulatory practices (GRP) are internationally recognised processes, systems, tools and methods for improving the quality of regulations. GRP systematically implements public consultation and stakeholder engagement, as well as impact analysis of government proposals before they are implemented to make sure they are fit-for-purpose and will deliver what they are set to achieve.

Supporting small and medium enterprises (SMEs) with GRP

For businesses, GRP facilitate a stable and enabling regulatory environment that can help boost investment, trade, and entrepreneurship. While GRP benefits businesses of all sizes, they are especially helpful for small and medium-sized enterprises (SMEs). Compared with their larger counterparts, SMEs are often disproportionately affected by the increasing stock and flow of regulations and may, in turn, lack the adaptive capacity vis-à-vis large enterprise to cope and comply with the regulations. A burdensome regulatory environment may irritate a larger enterprise but cripple an SME, shrinking the latter's already limited resources and inhibiting its creativity to succeed.

The key challenges for SMEs in coping with regulatory requirements tend to be associated with: their *size*, which restricts access to economies of scale; and *resource constraints*, meaning issues like access to finance for new investment, information asymmetry, and access to technology. SMEs also face higher obstacles in navigating the legal landscape compared with larger firms that have a greater ability and more resources to address the various regulatory requirements, particularly those in global or regional value chains. Moreover, not only does the burden of regulatory compliance tend to fall more heavily on smaller firms as compared to larger ones – but business procedures themselves are also more likely to be accelerated for large and well-connected local companies, multi-nationals, or investors in priority sectors.

At the same time, SMEs account for the vast majority of businesses and the largest share of employment in Southeast Asia. Although the definitions of SMEs vary across member states and criteria changes over the years, micro and SMEs are found to make up between 70%-98% of all businesses in almost all Association of South East Asian Nations (ASEAN) countries, according to this study.[1] Yet, SMEs account for only a minority share – less than 30% – of value added or exports in the region, meaning that despite their numbers, their economic performance still lags far behind larger enterprises.

Given the large presence of SMEs in Southeast Asia, a regulatory environment ill-adapted to their particular needs and characteristics could significantly undermine the health of the local economy as well as regional competitiveness. Therefore, improving regulatory policy and delivery to support the development of SMEs is a clear priority for governments in the region. The extent to which GRP is implemented to achieve these goals could also reveal important opportunities and challenges for good governance and economic growth at the regional, national and subnational levels.

GRP contributions to structural reforms have been found to promote economic growth and development as well as contribute to societal well-being (OECD, 2011[2]). Improving regulatory policy supports the rule of law, improvements to appeal systems, social cohesion, enhanced transparency and reduced red tape for citizens and businesses alike. There is also a growing body of research linking regulatory performance with economic growth, which has found a positive relationship between the openness of regulatory systems and the growth rate for various economic indicators (OECD, 2011[2]). Additionally, for many countries, strengthening regulatory policy is also a means to minimise opportunities for corruption and its negative impacts on economic and social development.

Much of the literature on regulatory policy and governance confirms that poorly designed regulations could stifle economic activity or gains. However, good regulatory governance and sound institutional frameworks could help mitigate the damaging effects of bad regulation. As regulatory governance and institutional frameworks are context-specific, there is value in examining country-specific case study evidence in the policy process, in addition to trying to quantify the benefits of regulatory policy changes on economic outcomes (Parker and Kirkpatrick, 2012[3]).

Good regulatory practice to enhance SME participation in the Global Value Chains

In Southeast Asia, participation in global value chains (GVCs) has contributed significantly to local economic development and employment generation as ASEAN countries gain a foothold in the manufacturing and supply chain hub dubbed "Factory Asia" (Lopez Gonzalez, 2016[4]). Nevertheless, ASEAN governments recognise that most participation in GVCs to date has been driven by a small number of large firms, while SMEs continue to operate primarily at a local scale.

Box 1.2. Rising non-tariff barriers in ASEAN

While tariff barriers are being reduced and phased out over time, ASEAN countries have been struggling with rising non-tariff measures (NTMs) (ASEAN Secretariat, 2017[5]). Non-tariff measures are defined as measures other than normal tariffs, which have the effect of restricting trade between nations (OECD, 2018[6]). When NTMs become barriers for many companies, they can hinder the progress of ASEAN countries in further integrating as a regional trading bloc.

Figure 1.1. Incidence of non-tariff measures by industry

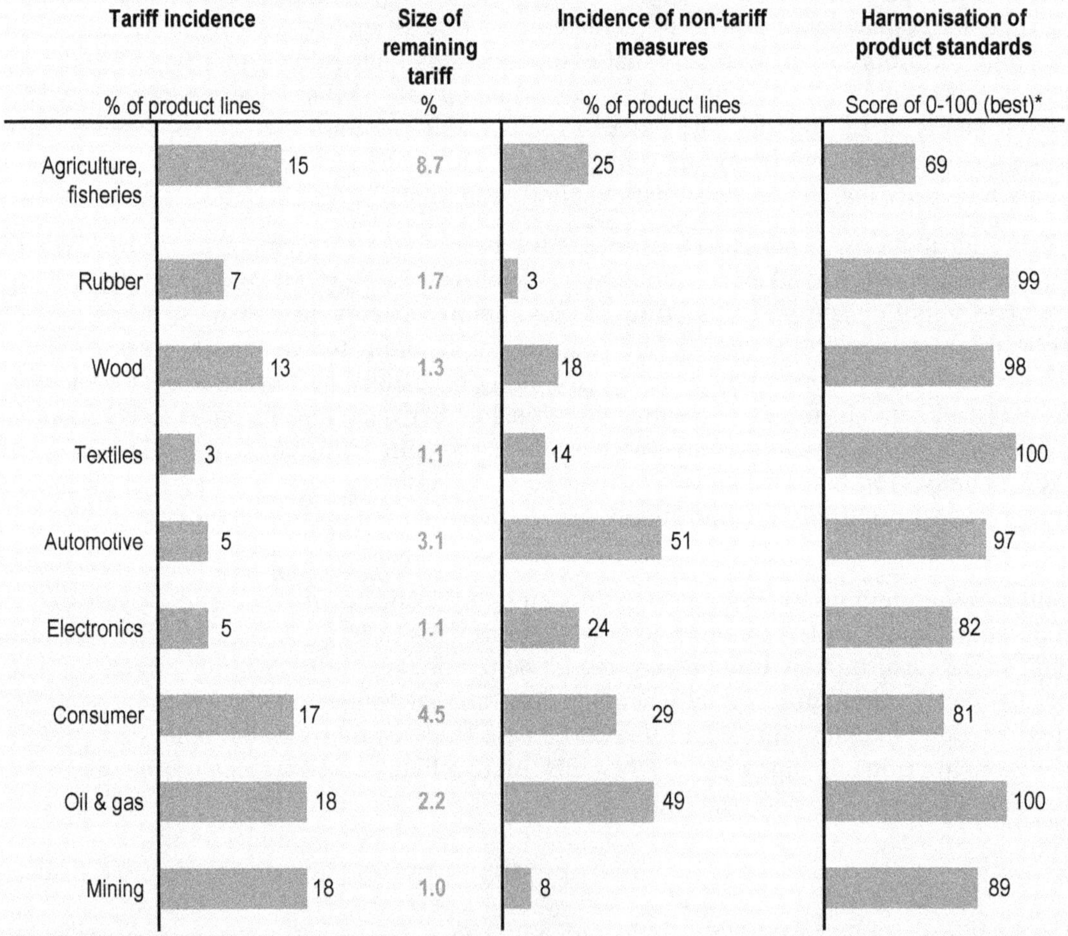

* Assessed based on incidence of standards and technical regulations, and non-tariff measures. Benchmarked against Singapore which has the least of such measures.

Note: Incidence of tariffs and non-tariff measures is based on average across ASEAN member states within sector.

Source: ASEAN Secretariat (2017), *Master Plan on ASEAN Connectivity*, ASEAN Secretariat, Jakarta, p. 59; OECD (2018), *Non-Tariff Measures*, http://www.oecd.org/tad/ntm/.

Increasing SME participation in GVCs can be an opportunity to expand or tap into diverse markets, as well as encourage broader socio-economic growth. However, successfully integrating SMEs into GVCs can be particularly challenging if SMEs must meet unfamiliar or additional trading or operational requirements issued by other jurisdictions, on top of domestic regulations. SMEs may also have limited access to information that helps them stay abreast of international opportunities or identify points of entries into GVCs. The complexity of tariffs, regulations and non-tariff barriers, as well as their applications from country to country, can further add to the challenge.

It is also important to recognise that not all SMEs in Southeast Asia want to grow or sell to international markets. SMEs are highly heterogeneous. Some may be perfectly content to supply goods and services to their neighbours or the domestic market. Some may be bound by local resources. A lack of interest in participating in GVCs could indeed be because SMEs truly prefer to operate locally, but it could also stem from various reasons that are in fact related to capacity to respond to the regulatory environment. For example, many SMEs in Southeast Asia are family businesses which may not have sufficient human or financial resources to scale up their operations and may not necessarily know where to obtain support or be eligible even if they did. Others may find it troublesome to understand and comply with licensing, reporting and taxation requirements associated with becoming bigger and therefore more visible companies – certainly, a very large share of SMEs in Southeast Asia operate informally, completely outside of any regulatory jurisdiction.

In almost all ASEAN countries, policymakers widely acknowledge that there is a significant percentage of SMEs that never register their businesses at all and rather prefer to operate informally. Policymakers also doubt whether limited government capacity to give small loans or training can sufficiently entice SMEs to formalise just to file more paperwork and start paying taxes.

All the same, weak participation by SMEs in the formal market, low SME growth, and limited participation in GVCs could be regarded as lost opportunities, not only for the companies themselves but for the growth of the national and regional economies. Going forward, adopting GRP that make regulations easier to understand and less burdensome to comply with can help SMEs formalise and grow in local communities as well as integrate more easily in global value chains (GVCs). It is important to recognise that GRP can support SMEs to overcome local regulatory barriers to sustaining operation or growing larger and international regulatory barriers where SMEs may need additional support to meet cross-border requirements. It is important that, in developing or updating national regulatory frameworks, governments continue to facilitate the bridge from local to international commerce by aligning national regulatory standards and procedures with international ones where appropriate.

Increasing the use of digital technology can help improve trade and regulatory connectivity for businesses and government alike. Today, the digital economy offers unprecedented opportunities for SMEs to participate in GVCs whether they grow larger or not; the internet can enable even a single-person enterprise to exports through e-commerce or social media transactions. Likewise, for governments, taking advantage of digital technologies can help policymakers deliver smarter policies, regulations and services to its citizens and businesses.

Recognising the importance of using digital technologies for better governance, the Master Plan on ASEAN Connectivity (MPAC) aims to "achieve a seamlessly and comprehensively connected and integrated ASEAN that will promote competitiveness, inclusiveness, and a greater sense of community" (ASEAN Secretariat, 2015, p. 9[7]). The MPAC focuses on three linkages: physical connectivity; people-to-people connectivity; and institutional connectivity. Regulatory excellence is deemed a strategic area in the MPAC as a way for policymakers to support improvements in both physical and people-to-people connectivity.

Applications of GRP in Southeast Asia

One of the first collaborations between the OECD and Southeast Asian countries on GRP was a joint initiative between the OECD and the Asia Pacific Economic Community (APEC) where many Southeast Asian countries are also members.[2] In 2000, APEC and OECD launched the *APEC-OECD Co-operative Initiative on Regulatory Reform*, which stemmed from a strong willingness on the part of APEC to improve the quality of regulation across APEC member economies. As part of this initiative, APEC and OECD started developing an integrated checklist for regulatory reform in 2002, which served as a guide for economies to conduct a voluntary self-assessment on their progress in developing regulatory policy, competition, and market openness. The checklist was subsequently approved and endorsed in 2005 by the respective executive bodies of APEC and the OECD (APEC-OECD, 2005[8]).

Since then, the Association of Southeast Asian Nations (ASEAN) has continued to develop and mainstream good regulatory practices at the regional level. The ASEAN Economic Community Blueprint 2025 recognises the importance of "Effective, Efficient, Coherent and Responsive Regulations and Good Regulatory Practice" in achieving "a Competitive, Innovative and Dynamic ASEAN" (ASEAN Secretariat, 2015[7]). This builds upon previous regional declarations, such as the Putrajaya Declaration by the ASEAN Heads of Civil Service issued in December 2015 and the Nay Pyi Taw Declaration issued by the Heads of State or Governments in November 2015, both of which underscore the importance of GRP. More recently, ASEAN Heads of State or Government have also endorsed an ASEAN Work Plan on Good Regulatory Practice (2016-2025), which aims to further advance the work on embedding good regulatory practices in national and ASEAN contexts.

Figure 1.2. Key dates on good regulatory practices in ASEAN

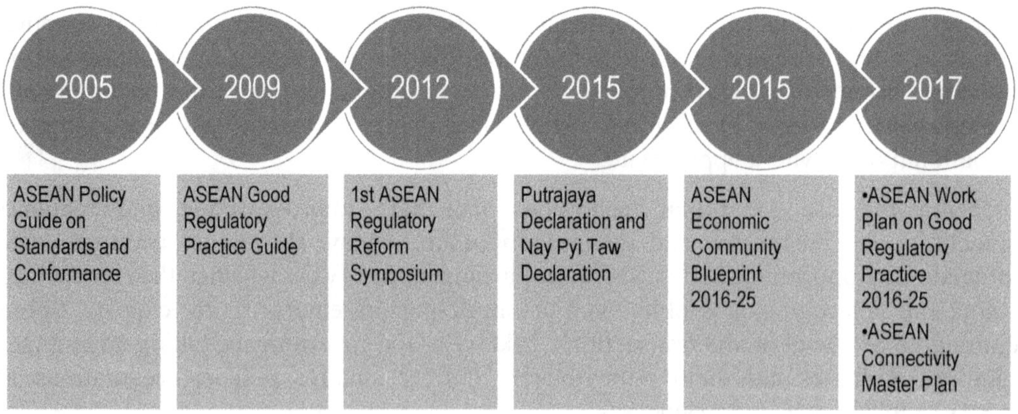

Individual ASEAN countries have also made progress to implement GRP to varying extents. In Malaysia, for example, Malaysia's the country's Vision2020 has underscored the need for "productive deregulation" to minimise the cost and maximise benefits of regulation in the country since 1991 (OECD, 2015[9]). A National Policy on the Development and Implementation of Regulations (NPDIR) subsequently introduced in 2013 has laid the foundations for future improvements in the area of GRP in Malaysia.

Other ASEAN countries have also introduced specific laws to support the use of GRP including: Cambodia (Government Decision No. 132, 2016); Indonesia (Law No. 12, 2011); Lao PDR (Law on Making Legislation, 2012); Thailand (Article 77 of the 2017 Constitution); and Viet Nam (Law on Promulgation of Legal Normative Documents, 2008).

Administrative burden reduction

Much of the attention on GRP in the region has stemmed from the need for governments to reduce administrative burden, lower compliance costs and simplify regulations. Cutting red tape has come to be an important method by which policymakers seek to stimulate entrepreneurship, encourage investments, and improve the welfare of citizens. Almost all countries in the region have initiated some kind of administrative burden reduction programme.

Administrative burden reduction programmes seek to make administrative processes more responsive, transparent, and efficient. It aims to provide services and access to services quicker and more effectively. As efforts to reduce administrative burden tend to require reviewing and consolidating laws and regulations, a "whole-of-government" approach is commonly taken. This can be done through a number of way including reviews of the stock of regulation, multi-level co-ordination, one-stop shops or e-services. In fact, many ASEAN countries have taken exactly such measures to reduce administrative burden.

Some ASEAN countries have introduced regulatory policies targeted specifically to SMEs, while others have opted to level the regulatory playing field for businesses of all sizes. For example, Cambodia and Viet Nam both offer simplified taxation schemes for SMEs, allowing them to file taxes less frequently than their larger counterparts, or even exempting certain qualifying SMEs from taxes entirely. Singapore, by contrast, has no SME-specific policies or regulations; all business-related policies and regulations aim to improve the business environment for everyone. It is not a given that a dedicated SME regulatory policy is needed, as long as the general regulatory environment is fair, transparent, clear and effective. The diversity of ASEAN countries means that governments necessarily tailor their regulatory policies and use of GRP to their unique regulatory contexts.

Still, there are some methods to reduce the administrative burden for businesses that have been enthusiastically adopted by all countries – the one-stop shop being a popular example. All ten ASEAN countries have introduced one-stop shops as a single-entry point for registering businesses and obtaining information or certification and permits. One-stop shops can be classified as informational or transactional. The former is used only for gathering information on a wide range of business process other than registration e.g. growing a business and closing a business, while the latter allows you to obtain necessary documents such as permits or business registration. One-stop shops can also be made available on line or off line. Brunei and Singapore are among the countries that have made all business registration activities online; while the rest of the countries offer both online and offline services or solely offline through locally-based offices. Viet Nam is a front-runner, having stipulated the implementation of one-stop shops in its Public

Administration Reform Programme as early as 2001, and today has one-stop shops at just about every district level and nearly as many at the commune level. Myanmar has set up more than 70 one-stop shops across the country to deliver transparent and efficient government administrative services closer to its citizens. Lao PDR has also introduced the one-stop service concept in its special economic zones and Cambodia is in the process of establishing its first one-stop shop to facilitate regulatory compliance from SMEs.

Table 1.1. Cutting red tape in Southeast Asia

	One-stop shop	Type	Availability
Brunei	Business Support Centre	Informational and Transactional	Online
Cambodia	One-stop shop for registration	Informational and Transactional	In progress
Indonesia	• One-Stop Shop • BKPM One-Stop Investment Centre	Informational and Transactional	Online and Offline
Lao PDR	Small Administrative-Wider Society Office	Informational and Transactional	Offline in Special Economic Zones (SEZs) only
Malaysia	• Companies Commission of Malaysia • SME Hub	Informational and Transactional	Online and Offline
Myanmar	• DICA One-Stop Shop • KBZ One-Stop Shop for SMEs financing	Informational and Transactional	Offline
Philippines	• Philippine Business Registry • Negosyo Centres	• Transactional • Informational and Transactional	• Online • Offline
Singapore	BizFile+	Informational and Transactional	Online
Thailand	One-Stop Service Centre	Informational and Transactional	Offline
Viet Nam	One-Stop Shop	Informational and Transactional	Offline

Source: OECD compilation from country questionnaire responses.

A number of ASEAN countries also target the civil service as a way to improve administrative efficiency and instil GRP. This is done by transforming and improving management styles and integrating a "customer-centric" approach to the delivery of regulations. For example, Brunei has introduced a "*deliverology*" approach to improve the governance and management of the public sector. Viet Nam has undertaken a sweeping Public Administration Reform Master Programme spanning a decade to streamline government procedures. Meanwhile, Singapore and Thailand have introduced incentives such as awards to individuals or agencies that advocate the use of GRP or serve as benchmarks and best practices for other aspiring agencies.

Regulatory oversight

To monitor and assess the quality of regulatory delivery, ASEAN countries have assigned government ministries or set up dedicated regulatory oversight bodies. Given the varying extent to which good regulatory practice (GRP) tools are implemented in the ASEAN region, some countries can have a more centralised oversight body, which is responsible for co-ordinating the use of GRP tools, as it is in the case of Cambodia, Lao, Thailand and Viet Nam; whereas, others may have multiple bodies responsible for overseeing the implementation of GRP. However, in some cases, even with multiple bodies operating, there remains to be a co-ordinating body responsible for overseeing all these activities, as it is in the case of Malaysia Productivity Corporation (MPC) and the National Economic and Development Authority (NEDA) of the Philippines. Table 1.2 provides an overview of regulatory oversight bodies in Southeast Asia and whether countries have systematically adopted selected GRP tools.

Table 1.2. Regulatory oversight bodies in Southeast Asia and systematic adoption of good regulatory practice (GRP) tools

	Regulatory oversight body(ies)	Regulatory impact assessment	Stakeholder engagement	*Ex post* evaluation
Brunei	Management Services Department, Ease of Doing Business Steering Committee	No	Yes	Ad hoc basis
Cambodia	Economic, Social and Cultural Council (ECOSOCC)	Mandatory for new laws; partial implementation	Yes	Project-by-project basis
Indonesia	Ministry of Law and Human Rights; Ministry of Home Affairs	Mandatory for new laws; not implemented	Yes	Project-by-project basis
Lao PDR	Ministry of Justice	Partial	Yes, mandatory	Partial
Malaysia	PEMUDAH, Malaysia Productivity Corporation, Ministry of Trade and Industry	Full implementation	Yes	Partial
Myanmar	Directorate of Investment and Company Administration (responsible for investment oversight); Multiple	Partial	Yes, mandatory	Not implemented
Philippines	National Economic Development Authority; Department of Trade and Industry; National Competitiveness Council	Partial – pilots	Yes	Not implemented
Singapore	Ministry of Trade and Industry; Pro-Enterprise Panel	Ad hoc basis	Yes	Ad hoc basis
Thailand	Office of the Council of State	Mandatory, in implementation	Yes. mandatory	Mandatory, in implementation
Viet Nam	Ministry of Justice	Mandatory; in implementation	Yes, mandatory	Partial

Source: OECD compilation from country questionnaire responses.

Box 1.3. What are oversight bodies?

Oversight bodies are crucial in the implementation of regulatory policy tools and the improvement of the regulatory management system. According to the 2012 OECD Recommendation of the Council on Regulatory Policy and Governance, an oversight body is tasked with a number of functions and can include any of the following (OECD, 2012, p. 12[10]):

- Quality control through the review of the quality of impact assessments and returning proposed rules for which impact assessments are inadequate.

- Examining the potential for regulation to be more effective including promoting the consideration of regulatory measures in areas of policy where regulation is likely to be necessary.
- Contributing to the systematic improvement of the application of regulatory policy.
- Co-ordinating *ex post* evaluation for policy revision and for refinement of *ex ante* methods.
- Providing training and guidance on impact assessments and strategies for improving regulatory governance.

Evidently, it is possible to have more than one regulatory oversight body; nonetheless, there is no single structure that is considered the most appropriate way to oversee a country's regulatory framework (OECD/Korea Development Institute, 2017[1]).

Sources: OECD (2012), *Recommendation of the Council on Regulatory Policy and Governance*, http://dx.doi.org/10.1787/9789264209022-en; OECD (2017), *Improving Regulatory Governance: Trends, Practices and the Way Forward*, OECD Publishing, Paris, http://dx.doi.org/10.1787/9789264280366-en.

Regulatory impact analysis

One of the key areas under the purview of regulatory oversight bodies is regulatory impact analysis or assessment (RIA). RIA is a form of *ex ante* evaluation and is undertaken in the development of new laws or regulations to assess its impact before it is promulgated. RIA is defined as a "systematic process of identification and quantification of benefits and costs likely to flow from regulatory or non-regulatory options for a policy under consideration" (OECD, 2012, p. 25[10]). RIA is applied using a range of methods – from cost-benefit analysis to multi-criteria analysis – and is particularly important when pursuing evidence-based policy making.

Among the pioneering countries in Southeast Asia for implementing RIA is Malaysia, which has successfully embedded its use among ministries across the country since 2015 (OECD, 2015[9]). Most of the other ASEAN countries have also introduced RIA, although they are not always mandatory or fully implemented. Cambodia has made particularly notable progress in RIA implementation; after mandating its use, several follow-up activities have undertaken to sensitise different ministries on its application and to expand its use. Viet Nam has likewise required the completion of an impact assessment as part of its process for preparing new legislation, ordinances and decrees since its 2008 Law on the Promulgation of Legal Normative Documents (Law on Laws) (OECD, 2011[11]). More recently in 2017, Thailand has written RIA into its new Constitution, which stresses the importance of using evidence-based policy making when drafting new laws and regulations as well as when amending or repealing existing ones. Singapore conducts *ex ante* analysis, similar to RIA, although not through a standardised approach. Other countries have started to explore RIA on a pilot basis.

Ex post *evaluation*

After laws and regulations are introduced, they should be evaluated *ex post* for continuous effect, relevance and efficiency in achieving its targets and objectives (Australian Productivity Commission, 2011[12]). A majority of *ex post* evaluation activities are carried out on an ad hoc basis, often linked to administrative burden reduction programmes or used to address specific issues such as enabling competition.

Present uses of *ex post* evaluations in Southeast Asia are limited. Only a few countries such as Brunei, Malaysia, the Philippines and Singapore conduct some reviews of regulations after they are implemented, and most typically on an ad hoc or project-by-project basis. This may be linked to the resource-intensive nature of *ex post* evaluations and the need for more sophisticated tools to review entire sets of regulations more efficiently.

Table 1.3. Approaches to regulatory review

Type	Description	ASEAN country example
	Stock management approaches (have an ongoing role that can be regarded as "good housekeeping")	
Regulator-based strategies	Refer to how the regulators interpret and administer regulations within their responsibility e.g. monitoring performance indicators and complaints, with periodic reviews to address these problems	Brunei, Singapore
Stock-flow linkages	Constraining the flow (new regulations) vis-à-vis the existing stock of regulations e.g. regulatory budgeting or x-in, x-out approaches	-
Red tape reduction targets	Reducing compliance costs by a certain percentage or value within a specified period e.g. administrative burden reduction programmes	Indonesia, the Philippines, Thailand, Viet Nam
	Programmed review mechanisms (examine the performance of specific regulations at a specified time or when a well-defined situation arises)	
Sunsetting	Automatic annulment of a statutory act after a certain period (typically five to ten years), unless keeping the act in the books is explicitly justified	Thailand
Process failure post-implementation reviews	Rests on the principle that *ex post* evaluation should be performed on any regulation that would have required an *ex ante* impact assessment	-
Ex post review requirements in new regulation	Regulators outline how the regulation in question will be subsequently evaluated	Brunei
	Ad hoc and special purpose reviews (take place as the need arises)	
Stocktakes of burdens on business	Prompted or rely on business suggestions and complaints about regulation that impose excessive compliance costs or other problems	Brunei, Singapore, Malaysia
Principles-based review strategies	Apply a guiding principle being used to screen all regulation for reform, for instance, removal of all statutory provisions impending competition or the quest for policy integration	Malaysia
Benchmarking	Provide useful information on comparative performance, leading practices and models for reform across jurisdictions and levels of government	Malaysia, Singapore
In-depth reviews	Most effective when applied to evaluating major areas of regulation with wide-ranging effects that seek to assess the appropriateness, effectiveness and efficiency of regulation within a wider policy context	Malaysia

Sources: Australian Productivity Commission (2011), *Identifying and Evaluation Regulation Reform*, Research Report, Canberra; OECD (forthcoming), *Best Practice Principles on Stakeholder Engagement in Regulatory Policy*, OECD Publishing, Paris.

Stakeholder engagement

Stakeholder engagement is a key part of the regulatory process for raising public awareness and understanding of new laws and regulations, which also serves to garner their acceptance and compliance. A meaningful engagement process can help make regulatory policy making and governance more inclusive, accountable, and efficient by giving concerned users, citizens, and businesses the opportunity to provide their insights towards improving the quality and utility of regulations.

Box 1.4. Types of stakeholder engagement

There are different forms of stakeholder engagement, based on the extent to which stakeholders are involved in the process and how information is relayed (OECD, forthcoming[13]). A basic classification of stakeholder engagement is presented in the figure below.

Figure 1.3. Scope and form of stakeholder engagement

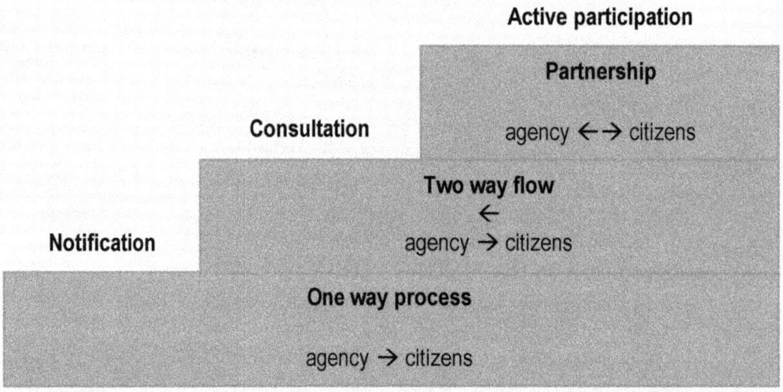

The first form of stakeholder engagement is **notification**, which is a one-way process from the agency to the citizens or the concerned stakeholder. Examples of this include circulation of regulatory proposals, e-notification, and public meetings during which stakeholders are informed of a new or amended regulation.

The second form involves **public consultation**, which is a two-way conversation between the agency and the stakeholder. This includes activities such as public hearings, feedback, public notice-and-comment, advisory bodies, and workshops. Some public consultation mechanisms are also carried online in the form of e-consultations or online petition systems.

Lastly, there is **active participation**, which is a partnership formed between the agency and stakeholder. This often concerns the formal involvement of stakeholders in the regulatory process; for example, in citizen juries, expert panels, focus groups, and working groups or government committees.

Source: OECD (forthcoming), *Best Practice Principles on Stakeholder Engagement in Regulatory Policy*, OECD Publishing, Paris.

ASEAN governments recognise the importance of stakeholder engagement, which is practised regularly in all countries, albeit to varying degrees and not always formally or systematically. Public consultation is the most common form of stakeholder engagement used in ASEAN countries. Across the countries, public consultations are most often undertaken in the form of open community consultations or business consultation meetings. Public consultation is mandatory in several ASEAN countries, including Lao PDR, Myanmar, Thailand and Viet Nam, although the process by which this is done is not prescribed. By contrast, Brunei, Malaysia, and Singapore have developed guidelines for stakeholder engagement throughout the regulatory process. Indonesia and the Philippines practice public consultation when developing new policies and programmes even though this is not mandated by law. Stakeholder engagement may happen before or after the notification of new regulations, although most consultations in Southeast Asia occur in the later stages of policy development.

Business sector engagement is a top priority in Cambodia and Viet Nam, where the Prime Ministers have been known to chair private-public sector fora to discuss with investors on how government could more effectively create an enabling business environment. In Indonesia, digitally-savvy citizens can participate in stakeholder consultations via online fora such as Hukum Online, in which legal experts also participate to respond to public inquiries. Singapore engages stakeholders through its reaching everyone for active citizenry @ home (REACH) and a Pro-Enterprise Panel (PEP).

Given the heterogeneity of SMEs in ASEAN countries, policymakers should continuously update their understanding of SMEs' needs, which are more dynamic than ever. SMEs today can operate across or even between sectors and jurisdictions, and it is no longer sufficient for policies and regulations to be defined on a purely localised or sectoral basis. Regulations must reflect the dynamism of SMEs and the contemporary business environment, and government support policies need to consider the needs of SMEs according to their diverse economic activities and means of conducting business. To date, many ASEAN countries continue to distinguish the support offered to SMEs according to their size – that is, the number of staff employed, or their annual turnover – but do not adequately reflect on other characteristics of SMEs' operations, such as whether they operate online or whether they trade in goods or services, which may, in fact, be more relevant factors for targeted regulatory interventions.

E-customs

ASEAN countries have been making significant advances in improving customs regulations and developing national customs databases – otherwise known as National Single Windows (NSW). The NSW aims to facilitate the import and export of goods by simplifying trade and administrative processes via an integrated electronic customs process (E-customs). E-customs allow government agencies, exporters and importers to conduct all customs-related transactions online, as well as reduce the need for paper documents and government visits.

Simultaneously, ASEAN countries are in the process of integrating their respective NSWs to establish an ASEAN Single Window (ASW). The ASW is a regional-wide initiative that aims to accelerate cargo clearance through electronic exchanges of border documents across ASEAN countries. As shown in Table 1.4, progress towards the ASW varies from country to country, since integration requires the development of accompanying legal frameworks to support cross-border exchanges of electronic data along with the standardisation of processes in the respective NSWs.

Table 1.4. Country progress towards integration with the ASEAN Single Window

	National Single Window	Status of integration with ASEAN
Brunei	Operational	Full integration/Partial
Cambodia	Operational	In progress
Indonesia	Operational	Integrated for C/O*
Lao PDR	In progress	Not in progress
Malaysia	Operational	Integrated for C/O*
Myanmar	In progress	Not in progress
Philippines	In progress	Integrated for C/O
Singapore	Operational	Integrated for C/O*
Thailand	Operational	Integrated for C/O*
Viet Nam	Operational	Integrated for C/O*

*ATIGA Form D
C/O = certificate of origin
Source: OECD compilation from country questionnaire responses.

At present, the implementation of ASW has been focused on the ASEAN Trade in Goods Agreement (ATIGA) Form D or the intra-ASEAN certificate of origin. As of January 2018, Indonesia, Malaysia, Singapore, Thailand and Viet Nam are participating in e-filing of ATIGA Form D. The remainder of the ASEAN countries are expected to follow suit. Other regional services that have not yet been integrated include a reference data service (RDS) application to serve as a master copy for regional references, a management information system (MIS), and a regional services portal.

Aligning standards and regulations

Standards and regulations are often designed in national contexts, resulting in heterogeneous regulatory environments across countries. Yet, the ASEAN community's aspiration to achieve a single market means that, at one point or another, national standards and regulations will need to be complementary, if not standardised, across countries. As ASEAN countries advance towards regional integration, further challenges lie ahead for regulatory co-operation and co-ordination.

ASEAN countries have already been making progress towards harmonising and aligning regulations, as well as adopting international standards, conformity assessment procedures, and other standardisation procedures in priority sectors. Since 2003, the ASEAN Consultative Committee on Standards and Quality (ACCSQ) has harmonised ASEAN standards in line with international standards via mechanisms such as mutual recognition arrangements. At present, all member countries have harmonised standards for 20 priority products (ASEAN Secretariat, n.d.[14]).

Individual ASEAN countries have also spearheaded regional standards and agreements in potential niche sectors. A notable example is Malaysia, which has proposed regional halal guidelines as a way to facilitate its halal exports within and outside the region. The guidelines are promoted through the ASEAN Working Group on Halal Food under the Senior Officials Meeting-ASEAN Ministers of Agriculture and Forestry (SOM-AMAF).

To better align local and international standards and regulations, the first step to take is to ensure that local, subnational and national regulations are not contradictory. Reviewing whether existing or planned domestic regulations could be integrated or scaled up to the regional level would also be helpful. Taking a forward-looking approach to regulatory policy development will pave to way to broader market access and economic integration, ultimately smoothing the learning curve for local companies aiming to expand from domestic to international trade.

Box 1.5. Regional halal certification standards

The halal industry poses a huge opportunity for the ASEAN region. The industry could undoubtedly evolve into more complex activities within the logistics, cosmetics and pharmaceutical, and tourism industry. With the increasing demand for halal products, interested countries in the ASEAN region can benefit from a more harmonised certification process. Malaysia envisions setting up an international halal authority board to help synchronise and align the various procedures in issuing halal certification for products and services. In addition to certification, Malaysia aims to achieve harmonised laboratory testing and accreditation schemes as a way to expedite the trade of manufactured halal goods and materials (Dube et al., 2016[15]).

Source: Dube, F. et al. (2016), "Halal certification system as a resource for firm internationalisation of China and Malaysia", *International Journal of Asia Pacific Studies*, pp. 125-141.

Special economic zones (SEZs) and industrial clusters

Special economic zones (SEZs) and industrial clusters have been introduced in every ASEAN country as a space to gather and incubate strategic or priority sectors. These special zones are typically located in strategic areas, such as borders or ports, to facilitate trade with other countries. Generally, SEZs are designed to level the playing field between local and international investors and otherwise offer the same incentives for operations. In countries such as Cambodia, the Philippines and Thailand, enterprises within SEZs are eligible for a range of financial incentives, including exemptions for profit tax, import and export duty, foreign exchange operations, and even more flexible labour mobility. SEZs and industrial clusters may provide an opportunity for SMEs to benefit from preferential policies and logistical support at the same level as larger enterprises. At present, ASEAN countries typically do not provide preferential allocation or additional benefits for SMEs in SEZs beyond those that are already offered to all accepted businesses.

Way forward

The OECD has published numerous guidelines and toolkits to help countries (central governments, sectoral ministries, regulatory and competition agencies) design and implement regulatory policy, management and governance. These include the OECD Guiding Principles for Regulatory Quality and Performance (OECD, 2005[16]), APEC-OECD Integrated Checklist on Regulatory Reform and the Best Practice Principles for Regulatory Enforcement and Inspections (OECD, 2014[17]). The OECD has also worked with individual countries to improve regulatory delivery, including in Southeast Asia.

This report takes into account the importance of context in regulatory policy development and implementation and focuses on country-specific approaches to regulatory delivery in supporting SMEs. Regulatory opportunities and challenges specific to each of the ten ASEAN member states are highlighted in the country chapters of this report.

Notes

[1] The ten countries that comprise the ASEAN of Southeast Asian Nations (ASEAN) are: Brunei Darussalam, Cambodia, Indonesia, Lao PDR, Malaysia, Myanmar, the Philippines, Singapore, Thailand, and Viet Nam.

[2] Southeast Asian countries that are also members of APEC are: Brunei Darussalam, Indonesia, Malaysia, the Philippines, Singapore, Thailand and Viet Nam.

References

APEC-OECD (2005), *APEC-OECD Integrated Checklist on Regulatory Reform.* [8]

ASEAN Secretariat (2017), *Master Plan on ASEAN Connectivity*, ASEAN Secretariat, Jakarta. [5]

ASEAN Secretariat (2015), *ASEAN Economic Community Blueprint*, ASEAN Secretariat, Jakarta. [7]

ASEAN Secretariat (n.d.), *ASEAN Cooperation on Standards and Conformance to Facilitate Trade in the Region*, http://asean.org/asean-economic-community/sectoral-bodies-under-the-purview-of-aem/standards-and-conformance/. [14]

Australian Productivity Commission (2011), *Identifying and Evaluating Regulation Reform*, Research Report. [12]

Dube, F. et al. (2016), "Halal certification system as a resource for firm internationalisation of China and Malaysia", *International Journal of Asia Pacific Studies*, pp. 125-141. [15]

Lopez Gonzalez, J. (2016), "Using Foreign Factors to Enhance Domestic Export Performance: A Focus on Southeast Asia", *OECD Trade Policy Papers*, No. 191, OECD Publishing, Paris, http://dx.doi.org/10.1787/5jlpq82v1jxw-en. [4]

OECD (2018), *Non-Tariff Measures*, http://www.oecd.org/tad/ntm/ (accessed on 10 August 2018). [6]

OECD (2017), *Improving Regulatory Governance: Trends, Practices and the Way Forward*, OECD Publishing, Paris, http://dx.doi.org/10.1787/9789264280366-en. [18]

OECD (2015), *Implementing Good Regulatory Practice in Malaysia*, OECD Publishing, Paris, http://dx.doi.org/10.1787/9789264230620-en. [9]

OECD (2014), *Best Practice Principles for Regulatory Enforcement and Inspections*, OECD, https://doi.org/10.1787/9789264208117-en. [17]

OECD (2012), *Recommendation of the Council on Regulatory Policy and Governance*, OECD Publishing, Paris, http://dx.doi.org/10.1787/9789264209022-en. [10]

OECD (2011), *Administrative Simplification in Vietnam: Supporting the Competitiveness of the Vietnamese Economy*, OECD Publishing, Paris. [11]

OECD (2011), *Regulatory Policy and Governance: Supporting Economic Growth and Serving the Public Interest*, OECD Publishing, Paris, http://dx.doi.org/10.1787/9789264116573-en. [2]

OECD (2005), *OECD Guidance Principles for Regulatory Quality and Performance*, OECD Publishing, Paris, http://www.oecd.org/fr/reformereg/34976533.pdf. [16]

OECD (forthcoming), *Best Practice Principles on Stakeholder Engagement in Regulatory Policy*, OECD Publishing, Paris. [13]

OECD/Korea Development Institute (2017), *Improving Regulatory Governance: Trends, Practices and the Way Forward*, OECD Publishing, Paris, http://dx.doi.org/10.1787/9789264280366-en. [1]

Parker, D. and C. Kirkpatrick (2012), *The Economic Impact of Regulatory Policy: A Literature Review of Quantitative Evidence*, OECD Publishing, Paris. [3]

Chapter 2. Brunei Darussalam

Brunei acknowledges the importance of regulatory reform in increasing its opportunities at home and abroad. It has also made significant efforts in recent years to make government services for small and medium-sized enterprises (SMEs) available and accessible through online one-stop shops. Regular review and evaluation of regulations are undertaken by the government to ensure that these do not deviate from pre-agreed targets or impose specific burdens on citizens or businesses. As a way to enhance regulatory effectiveness, Brunei has focused on improving its civil service by introducing a number of initiatives that aim to improve the governance and management of the public sector. The use of regulatory impact assessments (RIA) has not yet been formally practiced in Brunei; nonetheless, it has proactively used post-implementation reviews to improve the stock of regulations in the country and improve the country's business environment.

Regulatory context

Wawasan Brunei 2035, the country's national vision, aims to ensure that by 2035, Brunei Darussalam will be recognised globally for the accomplishments of its well-educated and highly skilled people, high quality of life, and dynamic and sustainable economy. In ensuring the achievement of these goals, the government has developed the *Wawasan Brunei 2035* framework, which articulates the national vision into national outcomes, key areas, and key performance indicators that measure the key areas identified. The framework provides guidance to government agencies and bodies in its implementation, including ensuring a modern, independent, accountable and impartial legal system, introducing regulatory frameworks aligned with international best practices, streamlining government procedures and other public services and broadening the participation of stakeholders in the planning and implementation of all aspects of development policies (Government of Brunei Darussalam, 2017[1]).

Within the context of the *Wawasan Brunei 2035* framework, support to the private sector in the country is emphasised through providing excellent service delivery and encouraging the use of technology to produce higher output. The growth of local businesses, notably SMEs, is therefore encouraged by improving access to finance, developing infrastructure and incubation centres, encouraging the use of local products and privatisation, and reducing the cost to doing business.

Brunei aims to create a more conducive environment for micro, small and medium enterprises (MSMEs) by improving the regulatory environment in which they operate. Recent efforts have been focused on improving the ease of doing business. This includes streamlining business processes (e.g. business registration, improving tax applications, etc.) and utilising online tools and websites to broaden the use and participation of these different government services.

Brunei has a favourable environment for trade and foreign investment. The Brunei Economic Development Board has been supporting current and potential foreign investors in navigating the regulatory environment in the country.

The recently established MSME central agency, Darussalam Enterprise (DARe), focuses on programmes and projects that promote enterprise growth and development. DARe serves as a facilitator for the different MSME initiatives across government agencies – creating a more co-ordinated approach to addressing specific issues faced by MSMEs.

Focus on improving the regulatory process has likewise been linked to strengthening the civil service through the Civil Service Framework (CSF). The government aims to reform the civil service towards one that is responsive to global change and public expectations.

Brunei has underscored its efforts to focus on new diversification measures to focus on downstream energy and non-oil sector. As an alternative, Brunei is currently focused on developing five industry clusters, namely: 1) halal; 2) innovative technology and creative industry; 3) business services; 4) tourism; and 5) downstream oil and gas. Brunei currently faces a number of issues in expanding its global value chain.

In line with this, the country seeks to strengthen its manufacturing and industrial exports as well as advance its legal and regulatory reform programmes to attract foreign investment and improve strategic industries.

Regulatory governance

Institutional and regulatory setup

Table 2.1. Institutional and regulatory setup in Brunei

	Government
State structure	Unitary state
Head of state	**Sultan**
Executive	The **Sultan** and **Yang Di-Pertuan** is the Head of State and the Prime Minister. The **Supreme executive** falls under the authority of the Sultan. The Sultan appoints any number of ministers or deputy ministers who shall be responsible solely to the Sultan for the exercise of executive authority and who shall assist and advise the Sultan in the discharge of the Sultan's executive authority. The Sultan is assisted and advised by six councils, namely: - **Council of ministers** handles executive matters. - **Privy council**, which advises on the appointment of persons to customary ranks, titles, honours and dignitaries. - **Religious council,** which advises on religious matters. - ***Adat Istiadat* council**, which advises on matters relating to state custom. - **Legislative council** handles legislative matters. - **Council of succession**, which is responsible for succession of the throne if the need arises.
Legislative	Legislative council with 33 appointed members, overseen by the Prime Minister
Legal system	Brunei Darussalam's legal system is based on the English Common law and Bruneians enjoy the benefit of an independent, fair, and efficient judiciary. The laws of Brunei Darussalam comprise of written judgments and legislation enacted by the Sultan and the legislative council. Judicial power is placed on the Sultan's privy council, the supreme court, the intermediate courts, the subordinate courts and the syariah courts. - The **Supreme court** comprises the High court and the court of Appeals and has competence over all criminal and civil matters, commercial matters such as bankruptcy and companies winding up, as well as other matters of personal status of non-Muslims. - The **Subordinate c**ourts comprise of the courts of magistrates. - The **Syariah courts** consist of the Syariah Appeals court, the Syariah high court, and the Syariah subordinate court. These courts have such jurisdiction, powers, duties and authority as are conferred by the Syariah courts cap (Cap 184) as well as any other written law. These courts have both criminal and civil jurisdiction, under any written law creating criminal offences relating to Islamic family law or conferring to the Syariah high court jurisdiction.
Administrative-territorial structure	4 districts (*daerahs)* and 38 subdistricts (*mukims)*
Ministry or agency responsible for SMEs or SME-related issues	Darussalam Enterprise (DARe)
Regulatory oversight body or bodies	**Management Services Department (MSD)** manages initiatives related to introducing innovation, reforms, and improvements in management and civil service and public service delivery. **Ease of Doing Business (EoDB) Steering Committee** aims to foster a pro-business environment conducive to economic growth and employment. The EoDB Steering Committee is chaired by the Minister of Energy and Industry and comprises of 14 champion groups from various agencies under the different ministries.
Other support structures within government on regulatory policy	**Registry of Companies and Business Names** of the Ministry of Finance (ROCBN) is responsible for all business registrations in the country. **Civil Service Reform Committee (JPPA)**[1] is responsible for ensuring a competent, effective innovative and responsible civil service sector. **Steering Committee for Public Service Delivery (JKPANDU)**[2] is aimed at addressing issues related to the delivery of public services and to facilitate the co-ordination among relevant agencies.

1. *Jawatankuasa Pembaharuan Perkhidmatan Awam*
2. *Jawantankuasa Pandu Pemberian Perkhidmatan Kepada Orang Ramai oleh Agensi-agensi Kerajaan*

Regulatory process

All laws can be drafted in three ways via the Sultan, the legislature, or the ministry or statutory body.

Each ministry is responsible for drafting their policy and the preparation of their legislation is prepared in co-ordination with the Attorney General's Chamber. The relevant ministry would also consult stakeholders for inputs on their policy considerations, where necessary. In all cases, the Sultan provides the final decision over any proposed legislation. Regulations related to SMEs also go through a similar process to other business regulations.

Business laws and regulations in Brunei

MSMEs comprise almost 97% of the private sector businesses in Brunei. MSMEs in Brunei are defined by the number of employees engaged in the enterprise, which are 100 employees or less. These are categorised accordingly:

Table 2.2. Classification of SMEs in Brunei

Size	Number of employees
Micro	1-4
Small	5-19
Medium	20-99

Source: Information provided by the Department of Economic Planning and Development (JPKE), Definition of MSMEs for Brunei Darussalam, 2015.

There is no single SME regulatory policy in Brunei. All SMEs are subject to business laws unless otherwise specified.

Table 2.3. Business-related laws and regulations in Brunei

Type	Description
Banking and Credit Laws	Banking Order 2006 Islamic Banking Order 2008
Bankruptcy and Collateral Laws	Insolvency Order 2016 Bankruptcy Act (Cap 67)
Commercial and Company Laws	Companies Act (Cap 39); amended 2017
Labour Law	Workmen's compensation Act (Cap 74); Trade Union Act (Cap 128); Trade Dispute Act (Cap 129); Employment Information (Cap 99), Employment Agencies Order 2004, Employment Order 2009
Land and Building Laws	Land Code (Cap 40); Building Control Order 2014
Securities Laws	Hire Purchase Order 2006
Customs Law	Customs Order 2006 Excise Duty Order 2006

Source: Information provided by the Government of Brunei Darussalam, 2018.

Business registration in Brunei can be carried out within a day through the Registry of Companies and Business Names of the Ministry of Finance (ROCBN) website. The Ministry of Finance provides a step-by-step guide on how to use the ROCBN system (Ministry of Finance Brunei, n.d.$_{[2]}$). Interested entrepreneurs or companies can register their account by filling out the application and uploading the relevant documents. There are minimum requirements for registering a business: for all types of business (sole proprietorship, partnership or company), the registrant must be at least 18 years of age and must not have been declared bankrupt, unless it has received court or official receiver's approval (Government of Brunei Darussalam, 2018[3]).

Table 2.4. Registration requirements in Brunei

	Sole proprietorship	Partnership	Company
Description	A business owned by one person Registered under Business Names Act, Chapter 92	A business firm or organisation with two or more business partners Registered under Business Names Act, Chapter 92	A legal entity, separate and distinct from its shareholders and directors Incorporated under Companies Act, Chapter 39
Registration requirements	• At least 18 years of age • Brunei citizens and permanent residents only • Undischarged bankrupts cannot manage a business without court or official receiver's approval		• At least 18 years of age • Minimum 2 directors (with at least one resident from Brunei) • At least 2 shareholders • Undischarged bankrupts cannot manage a business without court or official receiver's approval
Setup fee	BND 30 (registration fee)		BND 300 (incorporation fee)
Continuity of the business entity	As long as owners are alive and desire to continue the business	Subject to partnership agreement	Perpetual succession unless wound up
Closure of business	By owner's cessation	By partners' cessation or dissolution	Winding up or striking off

Source: Ministry of Finance Brunei (n.d.), *Register of Companies and Business Names: Frequently Asked Questions (FAQ) for the ROCBN System*, http://www.mof.gov.bn/Shared%20Documents/pdf/rocbn%20faqs_v1.0.pdf.

Once the application has been approved, the company or business will receive a certificate of registration (for business names) or certificate of incorporation (for companies) within one working day. Depending on the type of business activity, the entrepreneur or company would need to acquire specific licences or permits from other authorities or agencies, hire employees, acquire infrastructure for office space and continuing operations.

A recent reform undertaken by Brunei to simplify its business process is focused on the country's Companies Act, Chapter 39. Since 2014, the Registry of Companies and business names division of the Ministry of Finance has actively reviewed the act to further cater and adapt to the changing business needs and create an environment conducive to business and investment.

The Companies Act (Amendment) Order 2017 has made amendments to remove the requirements to upload a Notice of Situation of Registered Office form, as well as a Returns of Allotment of Shares, form during incorporation. The new amendments also removed the fee for name reservations (BND 5) and fixed the overall incorporation fee to BND 300.

The Stamp Act (Amendment) Order 2017 has also made changes to remove the requirement to stamp Memorandum and Articles of Association as well as share certificates for the purpose of incorporation.

Highlights of regulatory opportunities and challenges to support SMEs

Regulatory delivery

Civil Service Framework

There is a strong emphasis on regulatory delivery in the government and improving the way government officials carry out their tasks and provide public services.

The PMO has assigned the Management Services Department (MSD) as the focal point for handling complaints or grievances related to public service delivery. The main objectives are: 1) to enable the public to channel complaints on government services; 2) to enable the public to evaluate the effectiveness of the service recovery system and public complaints handled by respective government agencies; and 3) to ensure accountability of public services contribution towards the enhancement of integrity, credibility, and the government's image.

The Civil Service Framework (CSF) identifies the following themes, goals and strategies to strengthen the public sector's capacity to effectively deliver programmes and policies (bin Haji Mohd Daud, 2017[7]):

Table 2.5. Strengthening institutional development through the civil service in Brunei

Themes	Goals	Strategies
Leadership excellence	1A. Produce competent, capable and quality leaders that steer towards civil service excellence	S1. Developing and managing the future leaders of the civil service S2. Sharpening the performance and accountability of leaders
Organisational performance and productivity	2A. Ensure efficient and effective work processes that facilitate socio-economic development 2B. Ensure organisational manpower capability in supporting productivity delivery	S3. Implementing new models to deliver public services S4. Moving towards digital services S5. Improving work/project delivery S6. Fill skills gaps and match resources to government priorities S7. Promoting a culture of excellence and positive mind shift
Pro-business and public environment	3A. Implement policies and regulatory reforms that encourage economic activities 3B. Streamline government procedures and regulation to enable prompt decision making and provision of high-quality services 3C. Align policies towards a conducive private sector environment	S8. Conducive business and public environment S9. Improving efficiency and transparency S10. Enhancing labour mobility

Source: bin Haji Mohd Daud, A. (2017), *Sistem Pengurusan Prestasi Baru Perkhidmatan Awam Brunei Darussalam*, www.psd.gov.bn/shared%20documents/prestasi%202017/taklimat%20sistem%20pengurusan%20prestasi%20baru%2027%20mac%202017%20final%20editted.pdf.

In 2015, the organisational grading performance assessment programme through star ratings was introduced as a way to improve organisational performance within the government. This assessment acts as a diagnostic tool to identify the strengths and areas for improvement in managing the public service as well as to recognise government agencies through star rating. The prescriptive measures from this programme aim to assist in the improvement of the performance, quality and productivity among civil service agencies.

Government officials and agencies are also guided by a number of tools and guidelines, which are described in the following box:

Box 2.1. Improving regulatory delivery in Brunei

Brunei has developed a number of manuals and initiatives as a way to improve regulatory delivery in the country. Many of these emphasise on the importance of pursuing best practices to improve governance and management at the civil service level, which includes a civil service vision for the 21st century, *Rukun Akhlak* (moral pillars), work ethics, among others. However, the main tools and strategies used are outlined accordingly:

The implementation of Work Procedures Manual (WPM)

The Work Procedures Manual was originally an innovation created by a working committee from Public Service Department which joined the Civil Service Excellence Awards (*Anugerah Cemerlang Perkhidmatan Awam*, ACPA). A WPM is developed by each ministry or public agency that carries out and offers public services. The implementation of the WPM is monitored and facilitated continuously, such as through briefings, workshops, and consultations, by the Management Services Department (MSD) of the Prime Minister's Office (PMO).

The WPM document consists of eight main features: 1) background of a ministry or department; 2) objective of a ministry or department; 3) organisational chart of a ministry or department and unit or section; 4) core functions of a ministry or department; 5) work activity; 6) work process; 7) workflow chart; and 8) forms or referrals used as circulars or statutes.

Monitoring the achievement of *Tekad Pemedulian Orang Ramai* (TPOR) or the client's charter

The TPOR was officially introduced in September 1995. In May 1997, the Sultan mandated all ministries and departments to provide or formulate their own TPOR in accordance with the guidelines provided by the Management Services Department of the Prime Minister's Office. The TPOR is a statement or written commitment by a department on the service or product standard to be delivered to the public. It is a pledge of service delivery in line with the standard or capability of the department. The goal of the TPOR is to emphasise the importance of customer care and efforts to improve public service delivery.

Efforts that have been carried out to improve the quality of customer services through each ministry include:

- an audit according to the current client's charter
- publication of the client's charter and WPM guidelines book, and
- briefings/seminars/workshops/consultations on client's charter, WPM and business process re-engineering (BPR).

Streamlining processes through business process re-engineering (BPR)

The Business Process Re-engineering is one of the initiatives under the Civil Service Framework. BPR involves re-modelling and streamlining existing processes or procedures to improve the quality of provisions of services to the public or stakeholders. This is done by reviewing the different business processes and eliminating overly bureaucratic processes and any work duplications to improve the efficiency of a service and increase organisational productivity.

Improving frontline delivery through the Customer Focus Survey (*Kaji Selidik Tupian Pelanggan*, KSTP)

Introduced in 2002, KSTP aims to: 1) identify customer satisfaction levels; 2) know customer's perception towards the quality of service delivery in government agencies; and 3) gather feedback and solution on how to improve the quality and productivity in the service delivery.

Instilling the Delivery Approach

The Prime Minister's Office has practised and championed the delivery approach since its inception in 2014. The approach has been installed throughout all government ministries and key government-linked companies (GLCs) by advocating programmes such as the Brunei Top 100 Leaders (B100) Programme, which aims to develop the capacity of Brunei's future leaders in adopting the delivery approach towards achieving the Brunei Vision 2035 goals.

Furthermore, the delivery approach stresses the importance of setting targets and building trajectories utilising delivery plans to prioritise impactful actions; identifying delivery chains to map out lines of communication; implementing capacity reviews to assess a system's state of delivery; setting regular routines; and using data to monitor its performance against targets towards ensuring the irreversibility of the delivery culture in the system.

Source: Information provided by the Government of Brunei Darussalam, 2017.

Enforcement and inspections

There is currently no published cross-sectoral policy that guides enforcement and inspection in Brunei. Each ministry holds autonomous sanctioning powers and is responsible for their own inspection authorities, as guided by relevant order and acts.

Regulatory compliance

Compliance with intellectual property

Brunei has a strong and effective intellectual property rights (IPR) protection and enforcement system in place. Nonetheless, the government strives to improve the delivery of this service. Brunei has established its own independent patent system, which is in line with a number of international frameworks such as the patent co-operation treaty (PCT) and the Madrid protocol for the international registration of marks.

A number of legal protections are offered to help protect IPR, especially for SMEs in Brunei. Brunei's Intellectual Property Office is well connected with ASEAN's Intellectual Property portal and is active in the ASEAN Patent Examination Co-operation (ASPEC), which is a patent work-sharing programme among connected ASEAN member states.

The recent amendments to the Copyright Order 1999 have enhanced powers for enforcement of copyright as well as increased penalties for copyright offences. It further allows the Attorney General's fiat to allow private enforcement of copyright infringement.

Administrative simplification

Administrative simplification efforts can be carried out on an ad hoc basis by respective ministries or agencies. Between 2015 and 2017, Brunei Darussalam had implemented a total of 10 reforms focused on improving the ease of doing business (Box 2.2). These have been done in specific areas such as improving the amount of time and procedures to incorporating a company to obtaining a construction permit as well as providing alternative mediation for companies facing difficulties in meeting its financial obligations. The evaluation process is data-based and allows expedient re-alignment of any regulations or reforms should they deviate from or slow down the process of achieving pre-agreed targets.

Box 2.2. Improving the ease of doing business in Brunei

The EoDB steering committee, chaired by the Minister of Energy and Industry and composed of fourteen champion agencies from various relevant ministries, is responsible for identifying and monitoring the implementation of reform towards improving the country's business climate in line with international best practices and ensuring the reforms implemented by relevant ministries have benefited its end users. Each champion group within the committee is tasked with a specific reform or issue related to the different aspects of doing business.

The steering committee convenes every month and serves as a platform for each champion group to report the progress of their comprehensive reform agenda, including the status of their action plans, implementation, and performance of key business processes. It also provides them with the possibility to share their challenges and seek support from other champion groups. The evaluation of each group is backed by relevant data, statistics, and other direct feedback from agencies.

In March 2017, the Steering Committee further stepped up this engagement process by expanding its consultation to private individuals and professional associations comprising of legal practitioners, accountants, architects, contractors and logistics companies. The insights received from these stakeholders will be used as a basis to design the different reform strategies.

Once new reforms have been implemented, the EoDB steering committee conducts a dialogue session followed by the publication of a press release on their website and local newspapers to ensure that relevant stakeholders are informed and understand the objectives of the reform. These socialisation activities are regularly monitored by the EoDB secretariat, the Department of Energy and Industry.

Source: Information provided by the Government of Brunei Darussalam, 2017.

In 2015, a review on business licences and permits was conducted by the Prime Minister's Office and the Ministry of Home Affairs. As a result of this thorough review, selected low-risk businesses no longer require a licence to operate.

Furthermore, the Brunei Economic Development Board (BEDB), together with the Foreign Direct Investment (FDI) Action and Support Centre, offers a fast-track system that allows investors to obtain permits, licences, and approvals as well as undertake foreign labour recruitment. Each investor has a dedicated liaison officer that supports the investor in account management and all other inquiries and processes.

E-government

Darussalam Enterprise (DARe) and other government agencies have worked closely to set up the country's premier one-stop-shop for all businesses processes. The Business Support Centre (BSC) brings together 13 agencies providing various services and involved in the different steps of the business cycle: starting, growing, and running a business. The website offers information on both general services and specific services such as import and export, permit applications, and payment services (Annex 2.A) (Government of Brunei Darussalam, n.d.[5]). Interested businesses can also convey their feedback and inquiries to the centre and are addressed by a representative from DARe.

Brunei has made concerted efforts within the different ministries in the recent years to make government services available online as a way to improve or simplify the regulatory environment for businesses. For example, the central monetary authority of Brunei has been developing policies and plans to create an interoperable market infrastructure and system for electronic retail payments and other innovative payment instruments, as a way to shift from paper-based to electronic-based payments. Other examples of these online business processes include:

- An online registration of companies and business names through the Online Registry of Companies and Business names (www.roc.gov.bn).
- An online payment of contributions to an employee's government mandated trust fund (Employee's Trust Fund and Supplemental Contributory Pension Fund) (www.tap.com.bn).

- The Brunei Darussalam National Single Window, which allows forwarding agents and registered traders to apply for permits, declarations and other customs procedures.
- The establishment of an online tax filing system through the Systems for Tax Administration and Revenue Services (STARS) (www.stars.gov.bn).
- Online payment for government services through the centralised e-payment gateway (ePG).

Regulatory quality management

Performance monitoring

The costs and savings resulting from pursuing administrative reforms are monitored according to a performance-based budgeting system introduced by the Ministry of Finance. This system helps facilitate the measurement of administrative costs of policies as it allocates expenditure according to the "programmes" undertaken in the government.

Ex post *evaluation*

There is currently no dedicated or special agency in Brunei that is responsible for the oversight of regulatory reforms. That is, the agency responsible for undertaking reviews of the regulatory processes and the use of good regulatory practice tools within the whole-of-government. Nonetheless, regulatory reform efforts are often undertaken by specific agencies, committees or ministries within a particular jurisdiction.

Ex post and *ex ante* evaluations of regulations are conducted by respective ministries and agencies in the country. Regulations are reviewed prior to implementation and post-implementation by the Civil Service Reform Committee. Post-implementation reviews are done periodically, but some are also demand-driven. The latter type of review is conducted based on issues raised in the client's charter audit report, public complaints, findings from customer satisfaction survey reports and the public sector performance grading programme. Reviews can be undertaken for a single regulation or for a whole policy sector or area.

The Prime Minister's Office carries out periodic reviews on the performance of the different government agencies and the implementation of policies and programmes; for example, on improving the ease of doing business in the country. This is done in collaboration with the Ease of Doing Business Steering Committee.

As a way to further identify issues faced by businesses and citizens, the Prime Minister's Office (PMO) regularly convenes meetings with permanent secretaries from all ministries. These meetings provide the opportunity for ministries to raise any projects, reforms, or regulations in any stage of formulation or implementation for discussion and wider deliberation. This cross-sector and inter-ministry dialogue, therefore, provides the concerned ministry with possible solutions to be considered to improve effective implementation of a programme or policy.

A status report of the key performance indicators (KPI) of the national vision, *Wawasan* Brunei 2035, is permanently included in these regular meetings with the PMO, which allows for its continuous monitoring. Special sessions are also held periodically to provide an opportunity for more detailed discussion on efforts towards achieving the national vision: highly educated and skilled people, a high standard of living, and a dynamic and sustainable economy.

Regulatory impact assessment

Brunei acknowledges the importance of the use of evidence-based policy-making, including the use of regulatory impact assessments (RIA). RIA is not formally practised in Brunei and there is currently no regulatory oversight body implementing its application; nonetheless, the government has been very proactive in collecting feedback from different stakeholders in the public and private sphere to understand the impact of policies or reforms that have been implemented.

Regulatory database

The Attorney General's Office is responsible for consolidating all laws that have been passed. Since 2009, all consolidated documents have been made public through the Legislation Online website.

Stakeholder engagement

Public consultations have been carried out regularly, notably after an administrative reform has been passed, as a way for stakeholders to be informed and to provide feedback or ask questions concerning a specific reform. These exchanges are often documented and some findings or results are published or accessible online. At present, there are no mandatory requirements or unified frameworks for consultation. Each ministry or agency utilises its own tools and methods to undertake consultation exercises with relevant stakeholders. For example, recently in March 2017, the Ministry of Home Affairs sought feedback from different business owners affected by upcoming reforms on labour regulations.

Under the Civil Service Framework initiative, the Management Services Department (MSD) of the Prime Minister is finalising a set of guidelines for public engagement (Government of Brunei Darussalam, forthcoming[6]). The aim is to promote a more transparent and caring government in order to strengthen public confidence and encourage more engagement in future government activities. The guideline identifies five different types of public engagement, which are flexible and may be used at any stage of the regulatory-making process.

Box 2.3. Five types of public engagement in Brunei

1. Inform – the most limited form of engagement, which aims to provide the public with balanced and objective information.
2. Consult – aims to obtain public input and feedback on proposed policies, programmes, alternatives or decisions to improve outcomes.
3. Involve – the recommended form of engagement, which aims to work directly with the public to understand their views, opinions and concerns while sharing ideas of decision-makers.
4. Collaborate – the government works closely with the public to develop solutions or alternatives to address specific issues.
5. Empower – the highest level of engagement in which final decision is placed in the hands of the public.

Source: Government of Brunei Darussalam (forthcoming), *Guidelines on Public Engagement*, Government of Brunei Darussalam, Bandar Seri Begawa.

The guideline also aims to introduce a 7 step-by-step process to successful engagement:

Figure 2.1. Seven steps to a successful engagement in Brunei

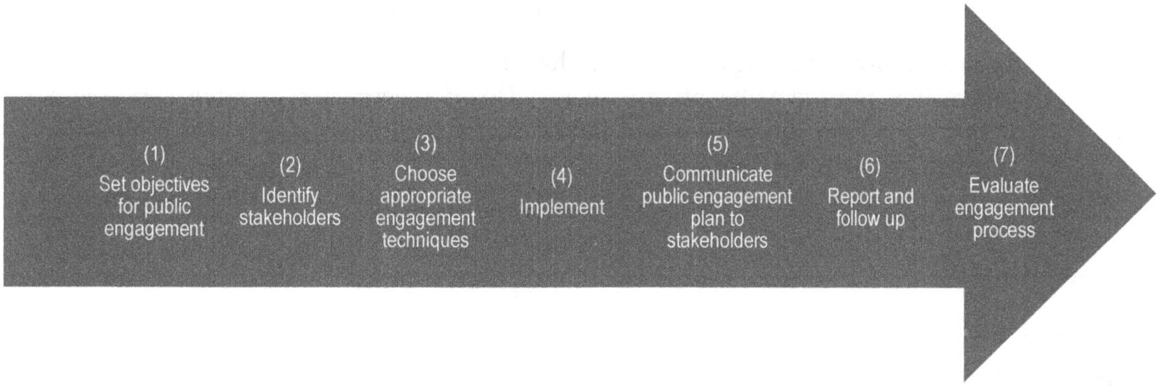

Source: Government of Brunei Darussalam (forthcoming), *Guidelines on Public Engagement*, Government of Brunei Darussalam, Bandar Seri Begawan.

Since March 2016, Darussalam Enterprise (DARe) has been organising regular dialogues with the local business community to better understand and collaborative address the challenges they face in business development or operation (Box 2.4).

Box 2.4. Reaching out to local businesses in Brunei

Darussalam Enterprise (DARe) regularly organises dialogues with the business community. DARe dialogues have covered a wide range of topics. These organised dialogues are categorised into three categories:

1. **Issue-based dialogues or focus** groups. These dialogues focus on a specific process or regulation that has an impact on the way an entrepreneur initiates or manages a business.
2. **Opportunity-based dialogues.** These dialogues share potential business opportunities in different industry sectors to current or aspiring entrepreneurs. Guest speakers from an industry or sector are invited to provide insights into their experiences.
3. **Group-based dialogues.** These dialogues invite specific groups from the business community or a particular organisation in order to understand the issues affecting them.

In addition to regular dialogues with the business community, Darussalam Enterprise (DARe) has also been using different platforms to engage with other government agencies and the private sector, including:

- **Focus group engagement sessions.** These sessions are organised with smaller groups of individuals from a specific industry or sector. These sessions allow for detailed discussions on issues faced within a specific industry and provide an opportunity for DARe and concerned government agencies to provide guidance and solutions.

- **Enterprise Open Day (EOD).** These are events run by DARe to help promote the Business Support Centre, including the Business Help Desk in which the local business community is able to log in any issues faced related to their businesses. In 2016, DARe has organised EODs in all four districts of the country.
- **Regular board meetings.** More than half of the individuals in DARe's board of governance represent the private sector. Board meetings also often serve as a platform for both the private and public sector to discuss issues concerning the local business environment.

Source: Information provided by the Government of Brunei Darussalam, 2017.

Appeals

In Brunei, each regulatory process has its own appeals process, as included in their relevant acts and orders. For example, the recently established Income Tax Board of Review, which is aimed at facilitating the administration and operation of taxation in the country, also introduces a new process of hearing, examining and settlement of objection for cases from companies against the income tax assessor. To ensure a transparent and fair system of administration, the case will be reviewed by an independent body and then considered by the board for resolution.

SME linkage policies

Engaging the private sector

DARe has a number of ongoing initiatives that are catered to accelerate the growth of small businesses and eventually prepare them for export. Among the different programmes available for MSMEs, include:

- A Boot Camp Programme, which is an intensive, targeted capacity building programme held over a period of one to three months where DARe brings mentors from different industries and sectors to share their experience and train participating MSMEs, including issues relating to regulations and other business processes. There are currently two boot camps available for MSMEs:
    - Start-up boot camp for businesses that can scale and export rapidly.
    - Microbusiness boot camp to help micro businesses remain sustainable.
- An Industry Business Academy (IBA), a learning platform for SMEs that offers a number of modules covering core aspects of running a business throughout different levels of complexity. The academy also offers specific modules and training for individuals on various business practices. A number of training sessions have been organised by IBA to help SMEs to be export ready, which include topics relevant to the implementation of product quality standards as well as specific steps and processes to follow in order to export.

Incubators

Part of developing key industries in Brunei is setting up new infrastructure that serves as incubation for new or emerging industries and start-ups. Brunei has recently initiated the first phase of a halal industrial park and the development of the bio-innovation corridor that aims to facilitate manufacturing and exporting of halal and non-halal products.

Launched in 2008, iCentre serves as Brunei's start-up incubation programme, which provides entrepreneurs with a co-working space and workshops and other knowledge development programmes to help raise the market value of SME products. Other programmes and activities under the iCentre include a capacity building development programme (industry business academy), a 100-day accelerator programme (start-up boot camp programme), sharing and networking sessions, and other events that showcase businesses and entrepreneurship (BEDB Brunei Darussalam, 2014[8]).

Customs

The government encourages MSMEs to grow and export by linking micro, small, and medium enterprises with potential partners and clients locally and abroad. Customs regulations in Brunei are compliant with the agreed World Trade Organization (WTO) valuation code. Inspection of imported goods mostly only occurs once the duties have been collected. The inspection of goods is also carried out with the presence of the importer or importer's agent. The importer or agent will be responsible for opening, weighting, sorting and marking the goods as directed by the customs officer. Examination is carried out to the satisfaction of the customs officer, who is also responsible for taking samples of goods if needed.

Brunei Darussalam's National Single Window (NSW) for Trade Facilitation has been in place since 2013. The country's common platform for electronic submission and exchange of customs data has been integrated into the ASEAN National Single Window (ASW) since 2017.

Recommendations

- **Introduce a systematic, whole-of-government review process**, building on the efforts undertaken from the ease of doing business exercise.
- **Maintain the development and implementation of e-government services**. Ensure that new business-related services offered online continue to be streamlined and linked to the platform.
- **Formalise the use of RIA and gradually introduce its use through pilot tests across government agencies**. Initial tests on the use and implementation of RIA can be applied in specific issues where the government and the public perceive the most burden e.g. specific industries or sectors.
- **Build capacity within the government to undertake evidence policy-making when drafting new regulations**. Align these capacity building efforts with existing activities focused on improving the quantity and quality of regulations, e.g. pre- and post-implementation reviews.
- **Ensure engagement of stakeholders throughout the whole regulatory process.** Encourage participation in the initial stages of the reform process, maintain a meaningful and dynamic engagement during the drafting and analysis process, and consider informing stakeholders as to how their feedback was reflected in the reform of a regulation.
- **Consider developing a framework and initiatives that improve inspection and enforcement**, as a way to strengthen regulatory delivery efforts.

References

BEDB Brunei Darussalam (2014), *Assistance Schemes for Business Start-ups and SMEs*, http://www.bedb.com.bn/images/pdf/e-guidebook/BEDB.SME.Guide.Book(2014).pdf. [8]

bin Haji Mohd Daud, A. (2017), *Sistem Pengurusan Prestasi Baru Perkhidmatan Awam Brunei Darussalam*, http://www.psd.gov.bn/Shared%20Documents/Prestasi%202017/Taklimat%20Sistem%20Pengurusan%20Prestasi%20Baru%2027%20Mac%202017%20FINAL%20EDITTED.pdf. [7]

Government of Brunei Darussalam (2018), *businessBN Portal - Register Your Business*, Government of Brunei Darussalam, http://www.business.gov.bn/SitePages/Register%20your%20business.aspx (accessed on 16 November 2017). [3]

Government of Brunei Darussalam (2017), *businessBN Portal - Wawasan Brunei 2035*, https://www.brunei.gov.bn/SitePages/Wawasan%20Brunei%202035.aspx (accessed on 16 November 2017). [1]

Government of Brunei Darussalam (n.d.), *businessBN Portal - Business Support Centre*, Government of Brunei Darussalam, http://www.business.gov.bn/SitePages/Business%20Support%20Centre.aspx (accessed on 3 October 2017). [5]

Government of Brunei Darussalam (forthcoming), *Guidelines on Public Engagement*, Government of Brunei Darussalam, Bandar Seri Begawan. [6]

Ministry of Finance Brunei (n.d.), *Register of Companies and Business Names: Frequently Asked Questions (FAQ) for the ROCBN System*, http://www.mof.gov.bn/Shared%20Documents/pdf/rocbn%20faqs_v1.0.pdf. [2]

Ministry of Finance Brunei (n.d.), *Website*, http://www.mof.gov.bn (accessed on 16 November 2017). [4]

Annex 2.A.

Annex Table 2.A.1. Services provided by the Brunei Business Support Centre

Service provided	Description of service provided	Responsible agency
	Starting a business	
Registration of a business	Advice on process relating to the registration of company and business names	Registry of Companies and Business Names, Ministry of Finance
Setting up a co-operative	1. Advice on the setup of co-operatives 2. Receive inquiries, feedback and issues with regard to co-operative	Cottage Industry and Co-operatives Division, Ministry of Energy and Industry
Beauty and Health Establishment Licence	1. Receive, review and renew licences for health and beauty establishments 2. Register e-Darussalam accounts 3. Update data on OneBiz system	Ministry of Home Affairs
Employing foreign workers	1. Receive and process applications for patent, trademark and industrial design 2. Advice on IP-related matters 3. Searches of the Register books	Brunei Intellectual Property Office
	Getting a location	
Planning permission	Advice on planning permission applications	Town and Country Planning, Ministry of Development
Construction, occupation and signage permits	Advise and assist on submission of applications for: 1. Approval plans of building works 2. Permit to carry out building works (Form C) 3. Occupation Permit (OP) 4. Billboard Signage	Authority for Building and Construction Industry (ABCi), Ministry of Development
Land Services via Land Application and Registration Information System (LARIS)	1. Transfer of land ownership 2. Change of land special conditions 3. Land charge 4. Land lease 5. Extend expired leased land	Land Department, Ministry of Development
Industrial land and industrial complexes	Advice and submission of applications for industrial land and complexes	Darussalam Enterprise (DARe)
Commercial electrical connection	1. Online application 2. Advice on how to get electricity connection	Department of Electrical Services, Ministry of Energy and Industry
Commercial water connection	Advice on how to apply for commercial water meter online	Department of Water Services, Ministry of Development

Service provided	Description of service provided	Responsible agency
	Running a business	
Trade fairs	1. Providing advisory on the online process for application of Trade Fairs 2. Processing and approval of licence to organise trade fairs (including road shows related to trade, local and international trade expos, garage or car boot sales, and wedding fairs)	International Affairs Division, Ministry of Energy and Industry
Certificate of Origin and Tariff Advisory	1. Advice on how to get tariff exemption or reduction under different Free Trade Agreements 2. Application for Certificate of Origin 3. Approval of Certificate of Origin issued or received	Certificate of Origin, Ministry of Foreign Affairs and Trade
Import and export	1. Advice on import and export procedures, tariff classification and other customs matters 2. Receiving, processing and approving customs declaration for preferential tariff treatment 3. Trade registration 4. Check on customs declaration status	Royal Customs and Excise Department, Ministry of Finance
	General services	
Business help desk	1. Log-in business-related issues and inquiries 2. Information on DARe events and activities 3. General advice on BSC 4. Receive industrial land applications 5. Activate e-Darussalam accounts	Darussalam Enterprise
Self-inquiry and dispute resolution	1. Self-inquiry reports 2. Dispute resolution service	Credit Bureau, Autoriti Monetari Brunei Darussalam
Miscellaneous online applications and payment of services	Receive and process payments for: 1. Health and Beauty establishment licence 2. Billboard signage 3. Carpark 4. Public Entertainment 5. Water 6. Electricity 7. Construction permit ba/form c/op/pp 8. Endorsement of Jawi Scripts 9. Investment incentives	OneBiz, Ministry of Energy and Industry

Source: Government of Brunei Darussalam (n.d.), *businessBN Portal - Business Support Centre*, Government of Brunei Darussalam, http://www.business.gov.bn/SitePages/Business%20Support%20Centre.aspx (accessed 3 October 2017).

Chapter 3. Cambodia

Cambodia has been undertaking regulatory reforms aimed at enhancing the competitiveness and diversity of Cambodian businesses since early 2004. It has introduced a number of policies and plans to improve the quality and efficiency of administrative services and public financial management, including systematic impact assessments and the use of information and communications technology (ICT). Recently, Cambodia has installed a central oversight and quality assurance body in its executive branch to oversee regulatory policymaking, making it among the first countries in the Association of Southeast Asian Nations (ASEAN) to do so. Cambodia has also embraced convergence with regional and national standards in formulating regulatory policies, including in tax collection and reporting. Support for micro- and small enterprises has been particularly highlighted in numerous national development plans and promoted at the highest level by the Prime Minister.

Regulatory context

The Cambodian government has committed broad support to small and medium-sized enterprises (SMEs) for more than a decade, with the Prime Minister emphasising the importance of SMEs to Cambodia's economy since the first Rectangular Strategy for Growth, Employment, Equity and Efficiency (2004). This strategy highlights the need to streamline licensing and registration procedures to reduce red tape, improve market access for SMEs through better trade facilitation and support linkages between SMEs and larger enterprises.

Subsequently, the SME Development Framework 2005-2010 has aimed to establish an enabling environment for SMEs through legal and regulatory reforms in the following areas:

- missing legislation on commercial enterprises, contracts, insolvency, dispute resolution (commercial arbitration and commercial courts)
- inadequate legislation for secured transactions and sharing of credit information between banks
- reformed business registration and link with Ministry of Economy and Finance (MEF) tax and value added tax (VAT) registration
- collateral system and land titling
- simplified accounting and taxation system for SMEs
- setup of a One Window Service for all business licences.

The government's efforts to support SMEs are progressing amidst a backdrop of three ongoing major public service reform programmes in Cambodia: the Public Financial Management Reform Programme (PFMRP); the National Programme for Administrative Reform (NPAR); and the Decentralisation and De-concentration Programme (D&D).

Simultaneously, economic developments such as Cambodia's accession to the World Trade Organization (WTO) also continue to shape both the introduction and reform of regulation.

The latest exposition in Cambodia's Industrial Development Plan 2015-25 (Ministry of Industry and Handicraft, 2016[1]) aims to "improve the regulatory framework" for trade facilitation, export promotion, industrial standards, property rights, tax payment, labour market development and industrial relations, among others. Under this broad mandate, the government has continued to support the improvement of customs systems and the rollout of Cambodia's One Window Service Offices. The government is also keen to level the playing field for all businesses by strengthening VAT enforcement in general.

According to the Industrial Development Plan, priority sectors for national development include: new and creative industries; SMEs in all sectors especially those involved in biomedical production, materials production and other industrial production; agro-industrial production; supporting industries for mainstay sectors such as agriculture, tourism and textiles; industries serving regional or international production chains; ICT and green technology.

An SME Policy has been in preparation since 2015, led by the Ministry of Industry and Handicraft. However, it has not yet been approved and issued. It is to be seen how or whether the general election planned for July 2018 may affect the progress of SME Policy development in Cambodia.

Box 3.1. Major public service reform programmes in Cambodia

Public Financial Management Reform Programme (PFMRP)

The Prime Minister launched a 10-year Public Financial Management Reform Programme (PFMRP) as part of the government's economic agenda in December 2004. Developed with the World Bank and other development partners, the four-stage programme aimed to strengthen realistic budgeting, effective financial accountability, an affordable policy agenda and programme management accountability. The PFMRP is currently in Stage 3. Evaluations of the PFMRP reveal that budgeting has improved, although public sector financial management and service delivery improvements require more work. The government recognises that a full rollout of the reform, including capacity building for line ministries, will take time and is committed to continuing to push forward with the PFMRP. Annual performance reviews of the programme since 2009, including key performance indicators, are available on the Ministry of Economy and Finance website (Ministry of Economy and Finance Cambodia, 2016[2]).

National Programme for Administrative Reform (NPAR)

The Public Administration Reform was highlighted as one of the key reforms necessary to achieving the Rectangular Strategy. In 2009, a four-year Public Administration Reform Programme (NPAR) was introduced by the Prime Minister to improve the transparency, quality, efficiency and accountability of civil service delivery, as well as develop human resource and management capacity. The NPAR has been renewed since, and the current programme runs from 2015-18 (Council for Administrative Reform, 2010[3]).

Decentralisation and De-concentration (D&D)

Decentralisation and De-concentration (D&D) in Cambodia have been in progress since the mid-1990s, eventually granting autonomy to *sangkats* (communes) in 2001 and passing of the Organic Law in 2008, which mandated the establishment of subnational structures and systems together with the appropriate functions and resources. As the D&D reform progresses, various provincial departments of different ministries are being brought under the management of the Governor, which may create potential for setting up integrated licensing arrangements (Niazi, 2011[4]).

Sources: Ministry of Economy and Finance Cambodia (2016), *Annual Performance Report on Public Financial Management Reform Program: Stage 3*, http://www.pfm.gov.kh/document/report/Annual%20Progress%20Report%202016%20English.pdf; Council for Administrative Reform (2010), *National Program for Administrative Reform*, http://www.cdc-crdb.gov.kh/cdc/twg_network/country_systems_cambodia/strengthening_national_systems/documents_for_reform/par/npar_programme_2010_en.pdf; Niazi (2011), *Deconcentration and Decentralisation Reforms in Cambodia: Recommendations for an Institutional Framework*, https://www.adb.org/sites/default/files/publication/28879/deconcentration-decentralization-cambodia.pdf.

According to the Federation of Association for Small- and Medium-sized Enterprises of Cambodia (FASMEC), there are an estimated 530 000 SMEs in the country (Phnom Penh Post, 2017[5]). However, low compliance with regulations and uneven regulatory enforcement has meant that only some 39 141 SMEs have registered with the Ministry of Industry and Handicraft at the end of 2016 (Ministry of Industry and Handicraft, 2016[6]).

Cambodia's industrial base remains narrow and uneven, with most of its activities concentrated in garment production and food processing. There is a "missing middle" in the industrial base, wherein a small percentage (0.6%) of large enterprises account for the majority of Cambodia's turnover at some 76% and 63% of employment while the most numerous micro-enterprises (97%) account for only 12% of turnover and 30% of employment (Ministry of Industry and Handicraft, 2016[1]). 80% of the large industrial enterprises manufacture garments, textiles and footwear and more than 63% of large manufacturers are foreign direct investment (FDI) and export-driven (Ministry of Industry and Handicraft, 2016[1]). The bulk of Cambodia's export revenues come from textiles at nearly 68% of total exports (World Bank, 2016[7]). By contrast, almost all micro- and small enterprises in Cambodia are locally-owned.

The number of informal businesses in Cambodia is very high. The informal sector is estimated to account for an overwhelming 98.6% of micro-enterprises, 62.8% of small enterprises, 28.6% of medium enterprises and 7.0% large enterprises (Ministry of Industry and Handicraft, 2016[1]). Given that micro-enterprises account for the vast majority of businesses in Cambodia, this means that a limited number of medium and large companies are formally registered and contributing the bulk of the government's revenue from taxes. Approximately 45% of Cambodian women are self-employed in the informal sector (Ministry of Industry and Handicraft, 2016[1]).

Overall, the Cambodian government is making steady progress towards adopting best practice in many areas which affect SMEs, within the context of trying to formalise and diversify the economy. Business registration and taxation procedures have been simplified and clarified and some service fees set out. WTO accession has, and still is, driving reform - as are the opportunities and challenges of ASEAN integration. In particular, Cambodia has made significant efforts to introduce regulatory impact assessments in a step-wise approach, with the aim to eventually fully implement mandatory regulatory impact assessment (RIA). Cambodia is also well on-track in creating its National Single Window towards convergence with the ASEAN Single Window project.

Regulatory governance

Institutional and regulatory setup

Table 3.1. Institutional and regulatory setup in Cambodia

	Government
State structure	Monarchy
Head of state	**King**
Executive	• The **Royal Government of Cambodia** (RGC) is formed by the party occupying the highest number of seats in the National Assembly following general election. The **executive power of the RGC is vested in the Prime Minister**, who is a member of the National Assembly appointed by the King upon the recommendation of the President and Vice Presidents of the Assembly. The Prime Minister is responsible for appointing its members. • The **Council of Ministers** is the central co-ordinating body working to link the executive and legislative branches, comparable to the Prime Minister's Office in other countries. Its meetings are chaired by the Prime Minister. • **Ministry of Economy and Finance** is responsible for approving the annual budget cycle and advising the executive on financial affairs. • **Line Ministries** are responsible for formulating annual and medium-term strategic frameworks and plans within the national strategies set out by the central government.

Legislative	Bicameral legislature • The **National Assembly** has at least 120 deputies elected every five years by general election. Its President and Vice President are elected by members. • The **Senate** comprises no less than half the number of deputies in the National Assembly.
Legal system	Cambodia's legal system is a hybrid of civil law (based on the French system) and common law (introduced with international aid and support to legal and judicial reform). • The **Supreme Court** is the highest judiciary power. The Supreme Court generally only rules on questions of law following an appeal from the Appeal Court. • The **Constitutional Council** is responsible for interpreting the Constitution (1972, Article 95), as well as overseeing the election of the President and Vice President of the Republic and deciding cases of contested elections of members of Parliament. Requests to review the constitutionality of any law may be made by the King, Prime Minister, one-fourth of the Senators or one-tenth of the members of the National Assembly. • The **High Court of Justice** holds the power to judge the President, Vice President, as well as members of the Cabinet, Constitutional Court and Supreme Court for crimes and offences committed in the execution of their functions (Constitution of 1972, Article 97). • An **Appeals Court** was created in 1992 following the arrival of the United Nations Conference on Trade and Development (UNCTAD), adding a third tier to Cambodia's court system: Supreme Court, Appeals Court, and courts of first instance. • A network of **courts of first instance** comprises lower courts extending to each of Cambodia's 24 provinces and municipalities, as well as the military court. The provincial and municipal courts cover their respective territorial jurisdictions, while the military court covers the whole country. Decisions by the courts of first instance may be appealed to the Appeal Court on questions of fact and law. • A **Supreme Council of Magistracy** was established in accordance with the 1993 Constitution. It is responsible for appointing judges and prosecutors of all levels, and for adjudicating disciplinary actions against them. The Supreme Council of Magistracy is chaired by the King and convenes under the chairmanship of the President of the Supreme Court or the General Prosecutor when adjudicating disciplinary cases.
Administrative-territorial structure	24 provinces and municipalities
Ministry or agency responsible for SMEs or SME-related issues	Ministry of Industry and Handicraft
Other support structures within government on regulatory policy	• **Inter-Ministerial SME Sub-Committee** leads the implementation of the SME Development Framework and provides policy co-ordination on behalf of SMEs. The sub-committee comprises 18 Line Ministries. • **Council for the Development of Cambodia (CDC)** is tasked with leading, co-ordinating and implementing the Industrial Development Plan, including monitoring performance. The CDC has traditionally been very involved in the relationship between the RGC and donors and trading partners. • **Cambodian Investment Board (CIB)** sits inside of the CDC and acts as the co-ordinating body of the government-private sector forum. • **Institute for Standards of Cambodia (ISC)** has a role in the adoption of standards for key products and potential exports (e.g. milled rice, fish, beverages, soy sauce, cement, additives and contaminants in food), adopted as voluntary standards by the private sector and codified by the RGC through the ISC. However, it is not the main regulation-making entity. • **National Bank of Cambodia** is the micro-finance and banking regulator. It issues regulations - Prakas, for instance, on the process of registration and licensing, under the Law on Banking and Financial Institutions. It is also leading the country's discussions on Fintech.

The Council of Ministers plays a key role in the preparation of laws, the central co-ordinating body. It works across all areas of government and serves as the link between the executive and legislative branches. This Council participates in the preparation of laws and serves as the final judge in administrative matters according to Article 104 of the Constitution of 1972. Meetings are chaired by the Prime Minister. Within the Council of Ministers sits two important players in preparing and reviewing regulatory policy:

- The *Economic, Social and Cultural Council (ECOSOCC)* sits within the Office of the Council of Ministers and is responsible for tracking the evolution of cultural, social and economic situations in Cambodia. It examines the assessment of the impact of various legal regulations done by proposed line ministries and also makes suggestions for some particular cases to the government. Within ECOSOCC, the *Regulatory Executive Team* (RET) serves as the central oversight and quality assurance stage in regulation making. RET, on the other hand, helps ministries prepare Preliminary Assessment Statements (PAS) for new legislation and any subsequent Regulatory Impact Statements (RIS) necessary. RET also advocates good regulatory practices, assist with training, and generally promote the rollout of RIA across government.
- The *Council of Jurists* helps ministries with drafting legal texts so as to harmonise them with the general principles governing the national legal order, and also checks proposed laws and regulations for the legality and quality of their drafts.

Figure 3.1 shows the lawmaking process in Cambodia. According to Principles 21 and National Assembly Internal Rules, a proposed law must include a "statement of cause", or reason for its introduction. Additionally, the new law cannot aim at reducing public revenue or increase the burden on the people.

Figure 3.1. Making laws, royal decrees and sub-decrees in Cambodia

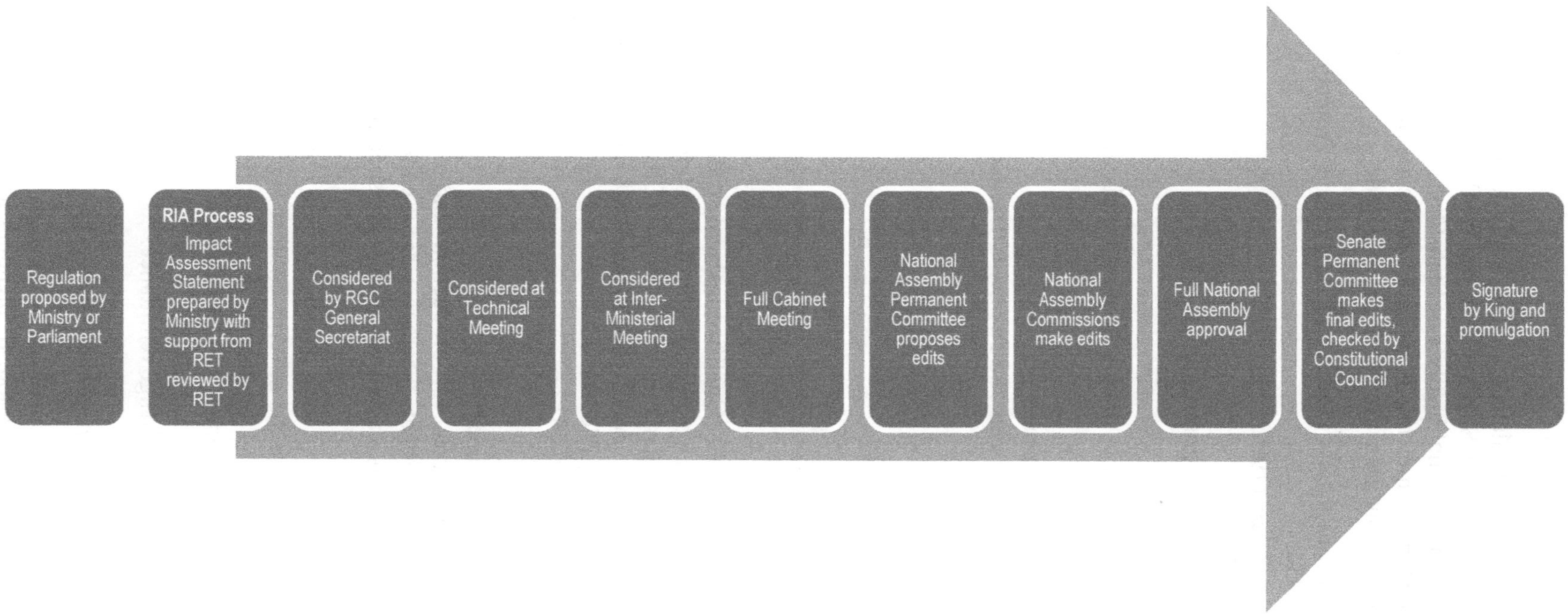

Note: While both the ministry and the parliament can create draft laws, in practice, the parliament rarely drafts laws. *Prakas*, directives and circulars may be approved directly by the minister after the RIA process.
Source: Information provided to the OECD by ECOSOCC, 2017.

Business laws and regulations in Cambodia

In Cambodia, general business regulatory policies apply to businesses of all sizes. There is no specific regulatory policy for SMEs. Given that SMEs account for more than 99% of businesses in Cambodia (National Institute of Statistics, 2016[8]), it can be said that the general business regulatory framework is *de facto* sufficient for capturing SMEs. The main business-related laws that are currently in place include:

- Cambodian Investment Law (1994) and Law on the Amendment to the Law on Investment (2003)
- Foreign Exchange Law (1997)
- Labour Law (1997)
- Law on Commercial Enterprise (2005)
- Law on Taxation (1997).

Several new laws have also been in draft following Cambodia's accession to the WTO. These include:

- Law on Commercial Enterprises
- Law on Negotiable Instruments and Payments Transactions
- Secured Transactions Law
- Securities Law
- Commercial Contract Law
- Commercial Arbitration Law
- Competition Law
- Consumer Protection Law
- E-commerce Law.

Investment projects that qualify as a "Qualified Investment Project" (QIP) can register its status as a project (rather than a company) with the Council for the Development of Cambodia (CDC) and the Cambodian Investment Board (CIB). The CDC and CIB jointly regulate QIPs. Special Economic Zones (SEZs) also fall under the category of QIPs. Registered QIP projects are eligible for a number of financial incentives including (Ministry of Commerce Cambodia, 2014[9]):

- Profit tax exemption.
- Special depreciation allowance.
- Exemption on import taxes for production and construction equipment and materials, and production inputs where they are used to produce exports.
- Exemption on export taxes, except where they are specifically applied for specific goods.
- QIPs inside SEZs are exempt from paying VAT on imports.
- Investment guarantees from the government that investors will be treated equally (with the exception of land ownership and specific investment opportunities); protection from nationalisation by the government; protection from price controls on products and services.
- No restriction on foreign exchange remittance.

SME-specific regulatory policies and processes

SMEs may register with the government online through the Ministry of Commerce, or with the relevant Department of Taxation. If intending to employ staff, SMEs may also register with the Ministry of Labour and Vocational Training. To encourage more SMEs to register their businesses, the government is offering a two-year tax holiday for SMEs that voluntarily registers with the General Department of Taxation (Phnom Penh Post, 2017[5]).

SMEs may benefit from reduced taxation or tax exemption, along with simplified reporting requirements. Eligible SMEs are defined according to one or more of the three criteria: number of employees; size of capital; and/or annual turnover. There is no consistent SME definition in Cambodia; different ministries may define SMEs according to their own purposes. For example, the Ministry of Industry and Handicraft (MIH) takes into account all three criteria to define SMEs, whereas the Ministry of Economy and Finance focus on taxation category according to annual turnover as the key criteria (Ministry of Economy and Finance Cambodia, 2017[10]; Ministry of Economy and Finance, 2014[11]; Government of Cambodia, 2005[12]).

Table 3.2. Definition of SMEs in Cambodia

	Employees	Assets excluding land (USD)	Annual turnover (KHR)
Micro	< 10	< 50 000	< 250 million
Small	11-50	50 000 - 250 000	250-700 million
Medium	51-100	250 000 – 500 000	700 million - 2 billion

Note: USD and KHR from different sources of documents as below, according to different ministries.
Sources: Government of Cambodia (2005), *Small and Medium Enterprise Development Framework*, https://wits.worldbank.org/CountrySnapshot/en/KHM; Ministry of Industry and Handicraft, No. 951 MIH/2014, 31 March 2014 (says 10-50 employees); Ministry of Economy and Finance (2014), No. 5278 MEF, July 22 (says 11-50 employees).

Depending on their categorisation, SMEs may be eligible for tax exemption or reduction as follows (Government of Cambodia, 2016[13]):

Table 3.3. Progressive tax rates for SMEs in Cambodia as of 1 January 2017

Annual taxable profit (KHR)	Tax rate on annual taxable profit (%)
< 12 million	Exempt
12 000 001 – 18 million	5
18 000 001 – 102 million	10
102 000 001 – 150 million	15
150 million and above	20

Note: A minimum tax of 1% on annual turnover is charged if businesses fail to keep proper accounts.
Source: Government of Cambodia (2016), *Law on Financial Management as promulgated by Royal Kram no. NS/RKM/1216/019*, Phnom Penh.

SMEs may file taxes according to International Financial Reporting Standards (IFRS) or Cambodian International Financial Reporting Standards (CIFRS).

The General Department of SMEs and Handicraft under the Ministry of Industry and Handicraft has the core mandate to develop and implement SME policies and action plans. It is also responsible for promoting SMEs, supporting business registration, and developing the draft SME Policy. This department is expected to be the home of any kind of SME Agency if one is to be established.

The Ministry of Industry, Mines, and Energy (MIME), on the other hand, leads efforts on regulatory reforms targeted at enhancing competitiveness and diversity of Cambodian businesses, as well as improving the business environment in general. MIME has been working on such regulatory reform issues since 2008, with support from the ADB and other international partners.

The Ministry of Interior is responsible for overseeing the One Window Service Office, which also offers small business registration support, among other services.

The Ministry of Commerce is mostly dedicated to trade policy, development and facilitation but is also responsible for business registration. Much of their work to improve import, export, and customs arrangements has significantly benefitted SMEs, although SMEs are not a strict focus for the ministry. SMEs may also register their businesses online with the Ministry of Commerce.

Highlights of regulatory opportunities and challenges to support SMEs

Regulatory clarity

The Industrial Development Plan 2015-25 provides a specific list of activities intended to expand and modernise SMEs in Cambodia as follows (Ministry of Industry and Handicraft, 2016[1]):

- Identify enterprises with good export potential and help them link to multinationals, connect to the value chain and regional production networks.
- Strengthen SME Development Framework, focusing on registration in the formal tax regime so RGC has better information, credit support policies and advice.
- Establish research and development (R&D) fund.
- Scholarships for engineers and technicians.
- Consider support for investment in machinery/production equipment.
- Promote formation of sub-sectoral associations.
- Build their capacity to help them deal better with large enterprises including in SEZs.
- Amend the Law on Corporate Accounts, Audit and Accounting Profession to introduce simplified accounting standards for SMEs.
- Use single window for registration and make registration criteria for incentives.
- Implement National Single Window Service for trade.
- Establish trade information centre online info on trade measures, tariffs and formal fees.
- Improve customs clearance for tax-exempt goods by strengthening co-operation, streamlining paperwork, facilitating procedures and eliminating informal payments.
- Reduce and abolish repetitive and non-transparent procedures.

The plan also sets targets to register 80% of SMEs by 2020 and for 50% of small companies to have financial accounts by 2025. There are no accompanying policies on monitoring the progress towards achieving the targets.

Regulatory delivery

Compliance with business registration

The vast majority of micro- and small enterprises are not registered. To encourage more companies to register, the government introduced a sub-decree in February 2017 offering a two-year tax holiday for any SME that voluntarily registers with the General Department of Taxation (GDT). There are also simplified accounting procedures for SMEs. Small companies with an annual turnover of under KHR 250 million (USD 6 425) are exempt from taxation.

Compliance with standards

Product testing capacity is currently weak and there is a lack of accredited laboratories and lack of knowledge of requirements.

Standards for key products have been developed by the national standards body, the Institute of Standards of Cambodia (ISC), based on international standards. These standards have been endorsed by the private sector. Accreditation of ISC by an international standards-setting body has been completed. However, compliance with Technical Barriers to Trade requirements is still in progress (World Bank, 2017$_{[14]}$).

As part of its WTO accession process, Cambodia has passed a Law on Standards of Cambodia ("Standards Law") to improve the quality of products, services, management, product efficiency and use, consumer protection and all activities related to standardisation and quality assurance in Cambodia. The first version of the law (promulgated in 2007) currently requires a revision.

As laws are being created to help Cambodia meet international standards, there are opportunities for these to be made SME-friendly the first time around. For example, Camcontrol, the import-export inspection and fraud repression department of the Ministry of Commerce, is preparing a modern Food Law with support from the United Nations Food and Agriculture Organization (FAO), which should supersede current requirements from both the Ministry of Health and the Ministry of Tourism. The Food Law is likely to include good practice such as public rating systems and should be aligned with regional standards. The current draft is being reviewed at FAO headquarters. However, there remain significant issues around the Law, including which should be the implementing institution.

Enforcement and inspection

Inspection and enforcement mechanisms vary depending on the ministry, department or inspectorate. Each one is responsible for the dissemination and delivery of its own regulations. Under the Trade Support Programme, for example, customs inspections have started to take a risk-based approach, effectively reducing inspections from 100% to below 25% for imports and below 5% for exports.

Non-compliance to regulations tends to be attributed to lack of knowledge and the most common government response is to deliver training workshops. There have been no studies to assess the effects of enforcement action on SME compliance, for example, and it may be worthwhile to pilot such exercises.

An independent telecommunication regulator implements policies and regulations issued by the Ministry of Post and Telecommunications. A regulator may also be created for tourism. It is not clear whether the potential SME Agency will have any regulatory role, for instance in relation to registration.

Administrative simplification

The government is carrying out a number of administrative reforms aimed at improving the efficiency and standard of government processes and services, including civil service registration and payment, public service standards and service feedback mechanisms. The main regulatory reduction initiatives in Cambodia since 2009 have stemmed from trade policy and trade facilitation efforts, which has led to a Trade Sector-Wide Approach to funding. Much of the business registration, customs automation and trade policy developments have happened with and through this programme. Each project has been successful; trade has increased and benefits of economic growth have accrued, although Cambodian SMEs are still largely lagging behind their neighbours.

Box 3.2. Administrative improvements in Cambodia's civil service

Under the Public Administrative Reform Programme (PARP), several significant civil service-wide administrative improvements are taking place. For example, civil servants are now registered and paid directly via the banking system. Ministries are also starting to install online HR Management Information Systems.

The current phase of the PARP (2015-18) focuses on public service standards. The RGC has adopted a Guide on Public Service Standards (2013 sub-decree), including a complaint and feedback mechanisms. The next focus will be on standardised job descriptions and performance assessments.

The National Public Service Evaluation Committee has been created and tasked with monitoring the administrative bodies that are responsible for public services and issuing warning letters to those that do not meet the appropriate standard. This was alongside publication of the correct fees for a range of services. It is early days but this can clearly apply to regulators (Government of Cambodia, 2015[15]).

Source: Government of Cambodia (2015), *National Program for Public Administrative Reform 2015-2018*, http://www.era.gov.kh/eadmin/data/2017/4/national_public_admin_reform_khmer_and_english.pdf.

Regulatory simplification is not a specific policy in Cambodia, but it is nonetheless implemented in a targeted way, driven by identified needs. In recent years, the government's regulatory simplification efforts have targeted customs clearance, business registration, among others. Regulatory simplification efforts are often combined with donor interest.

At present, SMEs have to liaise with as many as 18 ministries to register their business. A draft sub-decree for a one-stop shop for SME registration is under review. The Ministry of Industry and Handicraft would be responsible for overseeing the one-stop shop, while the other 17 ministries would provide support. It is hoped that this one-stop shop will improve registration compliance for some 450 000 SMEs that are estimated to be operating informally in Cambodia (Phnom Penh Post, 2015[16]).

The Trade Development Support Program administered by the Ministry of Commerce and supported by the World Bank has supported other "automation" in addition to business registration, including simplification in the issue of Certificate of Origin and trademark registration, and reduction of clearance times of cargoes at the General Department of Customs and Excise through the Automated System for Customs Data (ASYCUDA) (General Department of Customs and Excise of Cambodia, 2017[17]).

Getting VAT refunds on inputs to export sectors can take several years. Short-term import licences are expensive, uncertain and time consuming for renewal. Informal payments are common, so there is also competition with informal flows.

E-government

The government is increasingly using ICT to automate and simplify administrative processes, for example through online registration and online fee payments. However, public sector capacity (skills and willingness to budget) to maintain and develop websites is limited. In many cases, development partners support the development and installation of an online system; however, with no further capacity to sustain the system after the project has ended, it becomes outdated over time.

Cambodia has introduced several databases for regulations. For example, the ECOSOCC database should include laws, decrees and sub-decrees. However, it does not include legislation at the level of *Prakas* or below, which would mean that it omits a significant body of regulatory and procedural information. Some Ministries maintain good records of regulatory policies relevant to their duties, while others do not. It can be difficult to track when old regulations have been superseded by new ones, as many new regulations simply say that any older ones are overruled without naming them.

The Customs Department has implemented the ASYCUDA to automate customs in 54 major customs offices, covering nearly 87% of total trade volume (General Department of Customs and Excise of Cambodia, 2017[17]). It is also in progress to converge all import, export and transit-related regulatory requirements in a National Single Window by 2018. The Cambodia National Single Window (NSW) is intended to facilitate government-to-business, government-to-government and business-to-business trade, including towards convergence with the ASEAN Single Window (ASW).

Regulatory quality management

Regulatory impact assessment

All new laws need to be accompanied by a regulatory impact assessment (RIA). Following a Preliminary Assessment Statement (PAS) and a Regulatory Impact Statement (RIS) (Box 3.3), draft laws are considered at the Technical Meeting held by the Council of Ministers. Depending on whether agreement is reached, draft laws may be sent back or allowed to go forward to the full Cabinet meeting. Once the Cabinet approves, the draft law can proceed to the National Assembly and Senate and thereafter be signed into law by the King.

RIA is gradually being introduced across Ministries in a step-by-step approach, a number of ministries at a time and on a voluntary basis. Since 2016, Decision No. 132-SSR requires all line ministries and institutions to establish a Regulatory Impact Assessment Working Group. Each ministry appoints champions who get trained in RIA and who are responsible for writing the PAS/RIS. The scope of the RIA could potentially cover primary and subordinate regulation, such as laws, Royal decrees, sub-decrees and Prakas.

The execution of RIA is presently voluntary. The current focus of RIA is on capacity development.

Box 3.3. Preliminary Assessment Statement (PAS) and Regulatory Impact Statement (RIS)

Preliminary Assessment Statement

A Preliminary Assessment Statement (PAS) is the first step of the RIA process in Cambodia. It asks whether the proposed law is regulatory, advising that policymakers "consider all alternatives, noting that regulating should not be the first option" (Section 3 of the PAS template). The PAS should also identify the costs of the proposed regulation on businesses. If the proposed law is regulatory, and if it has a non-negligible impact on business, then the PAS will be followed by a Regulatory Impact Statement (RIS). There is no quantification of the cut-off that determines whether a PAS imposes a significant enough impact to require a RIS.

Regulatory Impact Statement

A Regulatory Impact Statement (RIS) asks policymakers to make a base case and then to identify and quantify costs and benefits where possible. It is expected that most cost-benefit estimates will be derived from existing research or simple calculations, applying the discount rate. When benefits cannot be quantified, then other measures such as break-even analysis or qualitative analysis may be used. The distributional impact of regulations should be considered. For example, there is a Gender Impact Statement template available for assessing the distributional impacts of regulations on women.

Source: OECD communications with the Government of Cambodia, 2017.

There is a methodology for measuring administrative burden in the PAS/RIS process, but this is not how areas for attention are identified. Those have come from international benchmarking (such as the Doing Business survey) or arisen from debate with development partners that support global best practice areas. There is a checklist of compliance costs, which includes costs for the government and costs for businesses.

Box 3.4. Checklist of compliance costs for PAS/RIS

Costs for the government

- Designing regulation*
- Consultation (notification, designing questionnaire).
- Training staff and stakeholders.
- Administrative arrangements such as checks and approvals.
- Equipment and services to administer and enforce (e.g. cars, buildings, legal advice).
- Record keeping – storing and maintaining records – filing time, server maintenance, paper copies.
- Printing and publishing documentation, websites, awareness workshops.
- Enforcement – wage-based costs for compliance officers, inspections, issuing fines, car rental.

Costs for businesses

- Consultation – time, transport.
- Training and keeping up to date with changes.
- Administrative costs – applying and seeking permission, licence fees, internal checking.
- Services or materials and equipment to comply.
- Record keeping.
- Printing (e.g. instructions, warning signs).
- Cost of co-operating with audits, inspections.

* Usually the cost of developing the regulation is included even though the bulk of the design would have been completed by the time the PAS is prepared.
Source: OECD communications with the Government of Cambodia, 2017.

Monitoring and evaluation of regulatory reduction initiatives have been undertaken on a project-by-project basis. There have been examples where progress monitoring has shown significant regulatory improvements resulting from the implementation of good regulatory practice, such as the One Window Service Office (Box 3.5). Monitoring mechanisms are also in place in the form of internal audits for the National Strategic Development Plan and the IDP.

Box 3.5. Evaluation of Cambodia's One Window Service Office (OWSO)

Analysis from a 2011 project to increase the use and capacity of Cambodia's One Window Service Offices (OWSOs) showed that use of this service resulted in a large decrease in administrative costs for businesses in the construction sector. Average spending decreased significantly from KHR 1.5 million (USD 378) to KHR 157 000 (USD 39) as people shifted from accessing services at line departments to the OWSOs. OWSOs were also shown to provide services faster than the line departments across three areas: tourism (4.6 days compared to 10.3 days); transportation (14.3 days compared to 24.8 days); and construction (22.4 days compared to 26.5 days) (Neb, 2017[18]).

There is potential for the OWSO to take on a wider SME-support role. This has been recommended in several ways, including by the Japan International Co-operation Agency (JICA)-supported SME Promotion Policy Formulation Project which proposes an SME Development Framework. They recommended that the OWSO becomes a gateway for consultation and an information centre for SMEs on import-export procedures, taxation, safety approval, technical assistance, business advice, etc. Some, or all, of these recommendations may appear in the SME Policy document when it is finally approved. However, given centralised views in the Ministry of Industry and Handicraft (MIH), these may be reserved for a proposed SME Agency first.

Source: Neb, S. (2017), "One window service offices: Improving government transparency and responsiveness", *Social Science Asia*, Vol. 3/2, pp. 12-24.

Overall, evidence-based regulatory policy preparation and evaluation is in its infancy in Cambodia. Some government programmes - such as the Public Financial Reform Programme (PFMRP) - have started to pilot results-based management (Box 3.6.). Regulatory reviews have also been undertaken in specific policy areas, driven by concerns that Cambodia's regulatory policies may be more burdensome than those of ASEAN neighbours or compared against international benchmarks. At present, the capacity to conduct monitoring and evaluation for regulatory policy is very limited in most ministries. Evaluations, where they exist, tend to be carried out for projects funded by development partners, who are proponents of international best practice.

Box 3.6. Results-based management in Cambodia's Public Financial Management Reform Programme (PFMRP)

The Public Financial Reform Programme in Cambodia is moving the government programme budgeting towards a more results-based approach, which could improve the environment for evaluation generally. The first two phases of budget credibility (Phase 1: 2004-08) and financial accountability (Phase 2: 2009-15) have created a public accounting system with some traceability and accountability. The programme is now rolling out programme-based budgeting (Phase 3: 2016-20) with some output and outcome indicators. As the focus moves to achieving results, the selection of indicators will become much more critical (Ministry of Economy and Finance Cambodia, 2018[19]).

Source: Ministry of Economy and Finance (2018), *Public Financial Management Reform Program*, www.pfm.gov.kh/index.php/en/.

Stakeholder engagement

The PAS/RIS process intends that the submitted documents may be used for public consultation. There is also a website for the publication of PAS/RIS, which includes a comment and feedback option. The website provides a mechanism for online consultation, although this is not yet common practice. It is worth noting that general computer ownership is low in Cambodia, so it may be that online feedback would be transmitted via representative organisations, which typically have web access.

There is a Government-Private Sector Forum with sectoral working groups, which helps carry out public consultations on regulatory issues. The tourism working group is the most developed to date. Across sectors overall, public consultations are neither formalised nor consistent.

Box 3.7. Government-private sector forum for tourism

The Government-Private Sector Forum for Tourism is overseen by a Joint Secretariat comprising the General Department of Tourism and EuroCham. The tourism forum includes nine thematic task forces as of January 2018, each of which comprises technical officials from the ministry as well as private sector representatives:

- Tourism Industry
- Training

- Cleanliness and Green Tourism
- Research and Development
- Domestic Marketing and Promotion
- International Marketing and Promotion
- Investment and Tourism Products Development
- China Ready
- Safety and Transportation.

These task forces meet regularly to discuss, identify, and address challenges in the tourism and hospitality industry, as well as to increase the efficiency of public-private co-operation to promote tourism in Cambodia. So far this public-private collaboration has helped improve law enforcement, safety for tourists, environmental awareness, and joint-promotion of Cambodia as a tourist destination.

The Cambodia Tourism Federation (CTF) has increasingly taken on responsibilities in co-ordinating the private sector, with support from EuroCham, whose ultimate objective is to hand over the Secretariat to the CTF.

Source: EuroCham correspondence with OECD, 2017.

Appeals

Formal appeals against a regulatory decision by an individual business – SME or not – is highly unusual. It is possible to take an appeal through the commercial court system, although this is uncommon.

The first systematic steps towards a local appeals process take place at the local authority level, at the District Ombudsman Office (DO, or the Citizen's Office) which is created alongside the One Window Service Office. The DO has the following duties:

- Receiving and resolving complaints or conflicts from citizens regarding the district administration.
- Overseeing that citizen concerns are served in line with laws and rulings.
- Fighting corruption.
- Building a good relation between businesspeople and the administration.

The Phnom Penh Municipal Court of First Instance is the court most frequented by commercial litigants. The lower courts preside over all types of legal matters including civil, criminal, insolvency and commercial disputes. An unsatisfied litigant may appeal a municipal court's decision at the Court of Appeal, which will review both questions of law and fact. A final appeal may be taken up to the Supreme Court, but generally only on questions of law.

For customs duty disputes, the procedures for challenge and settlement are clearly set out in *Prakas* no. 618 MEF.PR.CE dated 24 July 2009 on Customs Offence Mediation and *Prakas* no. 570 MEF.PR dated 19 August 2010 on Complaining Procedures against Customs Record.

For challenges relating to resolving overlapping competencies or disputes regarding responsibilities for rulemaking, the challenge has to be referred back to the relevant ministries for a change in the appropriate level of the law. The only resolution mechanism is debate at the Council of Ministers or the personal intervention of the Prime Minister.

SME linkage policies

The Industrial Development Plan 2015-25 highlights support for industries serving regional production chains linked with either global markets or global value chains in the form of forward linkages and backward linkages (Ministry of Industry and Handicraft, 2016[1]).

According to the IDP 2015, the government has also committed to developing industrial zones in provinces as hubs for SMEs, equipped with electricity, clean water, and logistics services. There are currently 22 special economic and industrial zones across Cambodia. The IDP 2015-25 intends to monitor and evaluate the plan, including industrial clusters.

Special Economic Zones (SEZs) were established in 2005 by Sub-decree No. 148 on the Establishment and Management of the SEZ. As of November 2015, Cambodia has 35 SEZs operating under the authority of the Cambodia Special Economic Zone Board, which sits in the Council for Development of Cambodia. The SEZs offer better infrastructure, tax breaks, as well as dedicated import and export support. As an SEZ also qualifies as a "Qualified Investment Project" (QIP), its developers and investors are eligible to receive preferential financial incentives including profit tax exemption for nine years, import duty exemption for construction materials, VAT exemption, guarantees against nationalisation and price fixing, and unrestricted foreign exchange (Ministry of Commerce Cambodia, 2014[9]). The SEZs are governed by the Law on Investment.

Cambodia has a very open financial framework for investors local or international. According to the 1997 Foreign Exchange Law, there are no restrictions on foreign exchange operations, including transfers. Investors are only required to report foreign transfers valued at USD 10 000 or more to customs, who would then report to the National Bank of Cambodia.

Cambodian law permits 100% foreign company ownership. By contrast, foreign investors cannot own land in Cambodia, although they may nonetheless exercise some control over land through a land-holding company.

Most government support for SEZs and industrial zones goes into financial incentives (as foregone revenue), while the bulk of the financial investment comes from donors, loans or foreign developers. Most frequently, government funding goes to salaries for officials while donors fund the activities.

Both local and foreign investors are also eligible for full import and export duty exemptions on projects that qualify as Quality Investment Projects (QIPs) by the Council of Development of Cambodia (CDC). Additionally, local and foreign investors alike are eligible to access one-stop services to process investment applications, tax and customs duty exemptions.

The Rice Export Policy is so far the only major effort to help SMEs integrate into global value chains. This policy aims to develop Cambodia's brand (new varieties) and milling capacity for higher-value exports. In addition to offering seed variety production and Sanitary and Phytosanitary Standards (SPS) arrangement support, the government also purchases and warehouses paddy at market price. The government is investing in the extension of agricultural techniques and basic marketing, together with piloting an online trading platform. The government has also continued to run a price dissemination system for vegetables by SMS messaging, a service that is available to farmers but predominantly used by traders. Cambodian Rice Federation, a nominally private sector organisation, has been authorised by *Prakas* as the only body that can represent the rice sector to the government. The Cambodia Rice Federation (CRF) is involved in policy dialogue, although it mainly represents large millers rather than smaller actors.

Recommendations

- **Consider unifying SME registration under one portal.** At present, SMEs may register in a number of places including the Ministry of Commerce, Labour and Vocation Training, and the General Department of Taxation. SMEs may register with the government online through the Ministry of Commerce, or with the relevant Department of Taxation.
- **Consider unifying online databases for regulations of all levels under one portal**, which will help track overlaps or outdated regulations between ministries. This could be done by building the existing ECOSOCC database, which already includes laws, decrees and sub-decrees but does not include legislation at the level of *Prakas* and below.
- As laws are being created to help Cambodia meet international standards, there are **opportunities for these to be made SME-friendly the first time around.**
- **Review targets for SMEs in regulatory policies** to set relevant indicators and measures for monitoring progress towards achievement.

References

Council for Administrative Reform (2010), *National Program for Administrative Reform*, http://www.cdc-crdb.gov.kh/cdc/twg_network/country_systems_cambodia/strengthening_national_systems/documents_for_reform/par/npar_programme_2010_en.pdf. [3]

General Department of Customs and Excise of Cambodia (2017), *ASYCUDA Project*, http://www.customs.gov.kh/trade-facilitation/customs-automation/. [17]

Government of Cambodia (2016), *Law on Financial Management as Promulgated by Royal Kram no. NS/RKM/1216/019*, Phnom Penh. [13]

Government of Cambodia (2015), *National Program for Public Administrative Reform 2015-2018*, Committee for Public Administrative Reform, http://www.era.gov.kh/eadmin/data/2017/4/national_public_admin_reform_khmer_and_english.pdf. [15]

Government of Cambodia (2005), *Small and Medium Enterprise Development Framework*, https://wits.worldbank.org/CountrySnapshot/en/KHM. [12]

Ministry of Commerce Cambodia (2014), *Cambodia Trade Integration Strategy 2014-2018*, http://www.kh.undp.org/content/dam/cambodia/docs/PovRed/Cambodia%20Trade%20Integration%20Strategy%202014-2018.pdf. [9]

Ministry of Economy and Finance (2014), *No. 5278.* [11]

Ministry of Economy and Finance Cambodia (2018), *Public Financial Management Reform Program*, http://www.pfm.gov.kh/index.php/en/ (accessed on 10 August 2018). [19]

Ministry of Economy and Finance Cambodia (2017), *Prakas No. 638 on the Criteria of Improper Accounting Records and Procedures for Paying Minimum Tax*, Ministry of Economy and Finance Cambodia. [10]

Ministry of Economy and Finance Cambodia (2016), *Annual Performance Report on Public Financial Management Reform Program: Stage 3*, Ministry of Economy and Finance Cambodia, Phnom Penh, http://www.pfm.gov.kh/document/report/Annual%20Progress%20Report%202016%20English.pdf. [2]

Ministry of Industry and Handicraft (2016), *Cambodia Industrial Development Policy 2015-2025*, http://www.mih.gov.kh/File/UploadedFiles/12_9_2016_4_29_43.pdf. [1]

Ministry of Industry and Handicraft (2016), *MIH Summarised Report 2016*, http://www.mih.gov.kh/File/UploadedFiles/4_20_2017_3_18_48.pdf. [6]

National Institute of Statistics (2016), *Cambodia Socio-Economic Survey 2015*, http://www.nis.gov.kh/nis/CSES/Final%20Report%20CSES%202015.pdf. [8]

Neb, S. (2017), "One window service offices: Improving government transparency and responsiveness", *Social Science Asia*, Vol. 3/2, pp. 12-24. [18]

Niazi, T. (2011), *Deconcentration and Decentralisation Reforms in Cambodia: Recommendations for an Institutional Framework*, Asian Development Bank, https://www.adb.org/sites/default/files/publication/28879/deconcentration-decentralization-cambodia.pdf. [4]

Phnom Penh Post (2017), *Efforts to Formalise SMEs Fall Short*, http://www.phnompenhpost.com/business/efforts-formalise-smes-fall-short. [5]

Phnom Penh Post (2015), *Paving the Way for New SMEs*, http://ww.phnompenhpost.com/business/paving-way-new-smes. [16]

World Bank (2017), *Trade Development Support Project Completion Report*, World Bank. [14]

World Bank (2016), *World Integrated Trade Solution (WITS): Cambodia Trade Summary 2016 Data*, https://wits.worldbank.org/CountryProfile/en/Country/KHM/Year/LTST/Summary. [7]

Chapter 4. Indonesia

Indonesia has one of the most complex regulatory environments in Association of Southeast Asian Nations (ASEAN) for small and medium-sized enterprises (SMEs), with 22 ministries involved in regulatory policymaking and applying various regulatory policy processes and tools. The government recognises the importance of simplifying and improving administrative processes and regulations. As such, it has mandated regulatory impact analysis to be undertaken for all new regulations as of late 2017, although evaluations for existing regulations continue to be done on an ad hoc basis. Indonesia is advanced among ASEAN countries in using information and communication technologies (ICT) in regulatory delivery. There is an abundance of information made available online, with rules and regulations made available through government platforms alongside dedicated non-governmental fora for seeking expert comment or responding to regulations. The government is streamlining its digital portals for business licensing and investment procedures and is making good progress in developing an integrated portal to help businesses get all the permits and information they need in one platform.

Regulatory context

Since September 2015, the Government of Indonesia (GoI) has introduced 16 economic policy packages aimed at accelerating national strategic sectors and projects, improving the competitiveness of Indonesian businesses, attracting investments, and streamlining regulations. These efforts are part of a wider National Strategy for Regulatory Reform 2015-19 spearheaded by President Joko Widodo.

Box 4.1. Economic policy packages in Indonesia

The 16 economic policy packages implemented in Indonesia since September 2015 include:

1. Improving the competitiveness of national industries.
2. Easing permit requirements and simplifying export proceeds requirements.
3. Facilitating financial services, export financing and reducing burden for businesses.
4. Improving social safety net and social welfare.
5. Improving industry and investment climate via tax incentives; deregulating Islamic banking.
6. Stimulating economic activities in border areas; facilitating the developing of strategic commodities.
7. Incentivising economic activities in labour-intensive industries by accelerating land certification processes for individuals.
8. Resolving land acquisition disputes; increasing domestic oil production; encouraging local content and aviation industry.
9. Increasing electricity generation; stabilising meat prices; improving urban-rural logistics.
10. Revising negative investment list; improving protection for SMEs.
11. Supporting SMEs and industries via business facilitation.
12. Improving Indonesia's Ease of Doing Business (EoDB) ranking.
13. Reducing bureaucracy to support construction of low-income housing.
14. Developing an E-commerce Roadmap for providing facilities and incentives to e-commerce and creative industries.
15. Improving the competitiveness of the national logistics system and accelerate business development.
16. Accelerating the Doing Business Policy, particularly in the area of streamlining licensing and regulation.

To date, the first 15 economic packages have deregulated 222 regulations from 167 ministries and agencies, as well as 52 Presidential regulations. The 16th economic package has not yet been evaluated as of January 2018.

Source: BKPM (2018), *Investment Policy Updates: Presidential Regulation No. 91/2017 on Acceleration of Doing Business*, http://www.pma-japan.or.id/bundles/bsibkpm/download/BKPM%20Presentation%20-%20PR%2091-2017_3.pdf.

The most recent 16th economic policy package, launched in August 2017, targeted regulatory reform of business licensing and permitting processes. Enacted as a Presidential Regulation No. 91/2017, the 16th package will be implemented in 2 phases that aim to: 1) establish a special task force to streamline/expedite business licensing and a One-stop Integrated Service Programme (*Pelayanan Terpadu Satu Pintu*, PTSP) for Special Economic Areas, Free Trade Zones, Industrial Areas and Tourism Areas; 2) reform the present business licensing system by clarifying/simplifying licensing regulations and implementing an Integrated Single Submission System across licensing services.

The GoI has announced a goal to improve the country's Ease of Doing Business (EoDB) ranking to 40 by 2017. It first set its EoDB baselines and targets according to various EoDB indicators in a ministerial regulation in 2015 (Table 4.1) (Ministry of Administrative and Bureaucratic Reform, 2015[1]), and has made a number of refinements on the targets for various aspects of the EoDB index, including numbers of days to complete specific business processes. For 2018, Indonesia is ranked at 72nd place in the EoDB index (World Bank, 2018[2]).

Table 4.1. Targets for Ease of Doing Business (EoDB) in Indonesia

Policy targets	Indicators		Baseline	Target 2014
Clean, transparent, and no corruption of bureaucracy	Corruption perception index		34	50
	Finance auditor opinion (unqualified %)	National	76	100
		Local	35	60
Enhance the quality of public service	Public service integrity	National	7.22	8.0
		Local	..	8.0
	EoDB rank		114	75
Enhance the capacity and accountability of bureaucracy performance	Government effectiveness index		..	0.5
	Accountability of public institutions	National	98.76	100
		Provincial	87.88	80
		Regional	44.90	60

.. : Missing value or not available
Source: Ministry of Administrative and Bureaucratic Reform (2015), *Roadmap of Bureaucratic Reform 2015-2020, Regulation No.11/2015*, Jakarta.

BAPPENAS, the Ministry of National Development Planning, has also published specific targets to improve the competitiveness of SMEs and progress towards their achievement in an evaluation of the National Medium-Term Development Plan (BAPPENAS, 2015[3]). This evaluation assesses SME performance according to various economic and labour-related indicators, including investment rate, employment, contributions to exports, proportion of SMEs that have access to financing and apply product standards, etc. (BAPPENAS, 2015, p. 45[3]).

According to the Co-ordinating Ministry for Economic Affairs (CMEA), the biggest challenge for SMEs is not regulatory burden but rather that SMEs are generally insufficiently equipped with the capacity to develop or sustain business; some 80% of SMEs cannot overcome the "valley of death" between operationalising a company and generating revenue. SMEs lack capacity to prepare long or even medium-term business plans and prioritise surviving before growing. Most training programmes provided by the government are not well-adapted to the needs of SMEs. Without a good business plan, SMEs may face even more difficulty in obtaining loans from banks.

Regulatory governance

Institutional and regulatory setup

Table 4.2. Institutional and regulatory setup in Indonesia

	Government
State structure	Presidential Representative Democratic Republic
Head of state	**President**
Executive	The executive power in Indonesia is vested in the **President** and the **Government of Indonesia (GoI)**. The President serves as the Head of Government and is responsible for appointing the cabinet, and additionally holds power to decide on domestic governance and foreign affairs. • **Cabinet of the Republic of Indonesia** is responsible for carrying out government policy and is accountable to the President and the Legislature. Members of the Cabinet are appointed by the President, who can also reshuffle or dismiss them at will. • There are four **Co-ordinating Ministries** that serve as the central oversight ministry responsible for co-ordinating, synchronising and monitoring the performance and functions of various technical ministries under four areas: 1) Politics, Law and Defence; 2) Maritime; 3) Economic Affairs; 4) Human Development and Culture. • **Line Ministries** are responsible for initiating and drafting law and regulation proposals. They also oversee the implementation of regulations in their fields of competence. • **Ministry of Home Affairs** is responsible for co-ordinating local and central authorities on regulatory development and implementation. • **Ministry of Law and Human Rights** coordinates the lawmaking process.
Legislative	**Bicameral legislature** The legislative branch of Indonesia is the **People's Consultative Assembly** (*Majelis Permusyawaratan Rakyat*, MPR), which comprises the House of Representatives (Dewan Perwakilan Rakyat, DPR) and the Regional Representative Council (*Dewan Perwakilan Daerah*, DPD). The constitutional power in Indonesia is vested in the People's Consultative Assembly.
Legal system	• The highest judiciary power in Indonesia is vested in the **Supreme Court**. The Supreme Court is the final court of appeal for criminal and civic disputes, as well as court disputes. The Chief Justice presides over the Supreme Court. • **Constitutional Court of Indonesia** rules over disputes relating to the Constitution, along with matters relating to elections and political parties. • **Public courts** are Indonesia's court of first instance at the district (city and regency) level and high courts at the provincial or appellate levels. Criminal and civic disputes that are not resolved in public courts can be appealed at the Supreme Court. • **Administrative Courts** rule over disputes relating to state officials of bodies at the central as well as regional levels. These courts were established in 1986 to ensure that citizens would not be treated arbitrarily or unfairly by government officials or agencies. The tax court is a specialised court inside the Administrative Court system. • Indonesia's judiciary system also includes **religious courts** and **military courts** for resolving private affairs of Muslim citizens and criminal or civic disputes involving military personnel respectively.
Administrative-territorial structure	34 provinces which are further subdivided into regencies, districts, sub-districts and villages. Sub-districts and villages handle only administrative duties.
Ministry or agency responsible for SMEs or SME-related issues	**Ministry of Co-operatives and SMEs**
Other support structures within government on regulatory policy	• **National Standardisation Agency of Indonesia** (*Badan Nasional Standardisasi*, or BSN) is the national standardisation agency. • **Financial Services Authority (OJK)** is the regulator and supervisor for Indonesia's entire financial services industry. It is an autonomous government agency that has the mandate, functions, duties, and powers to regulate, supervise, inspect and investigate all financial service activities in Indonesia (Act No.21/2011 on the regulation and supervision of financial services). • **Indonesia National Agency of Drug and Food Control** is a government agency responsible for regulating, supervising and evaluating drugs, vaccines, pharmaceuticals, food products, food safety and cosmetics (Presidential Decree No.102/2001).

The GoI has also set up task forces to monitor the implementation of the 16 economic policy packages. Task force members come from the private sector, public sector, academia and think tanks. The responsibilities of the task forces are as follows:

- Accelerating regulatory settlement.
- Identifying obstacles, problems, and cases.
- Evaluating implementation and impact analyses of policy packages.
- Publishing, disseminating and socialising policy packages.

Task forces have also been set up to improve the service, facilitation, simplification and development of online systems to accelerate the process for obtaining business licenses according to Presidential Regulation 91/2017. These task forces operate at the national, ministerial/agency, provincial, county/city levels.

Indonesia's legislative process

Figure 4.1. Legislative process in Indonesia

Note: Approved bills are submitted by House leaders to the President for signature. If the President does not pass the bill after 15 working days, House leaders may request an explanation from the President. If bills are not signed after 30 working days, they automatically become laws.
Source: Republic of Indonesia (2011), *Law 12/2011 on Establishment of Laws and Regulations*, Jakarta.

Draft regulations may be initiated or proposed by any line ministry, according to the lawmaking process accorded by Law 12/2011 on the Establishment of Laws and Regulations. Line ministries are also responsible for overseeing the implementation of regulations in the field of competence.

According to the lawmaking process of Indonesia, a draft regulation must be accompanied by an explanatory description and/or academic research paper (Republic of Indonesia, 2011[4]). The research paper should include an introduction (background, problem identification, objectives and methods), theoretical studies and empirical practices, evaluation and analysis of regulations, the range, the direction of the regulation, sociological and juridical aspects, the scope of material content of local laws and regulations, and the conclusions and suggestions. Once these have been prepared, the Ministry of Law and Human Rights proceeds with the preparation of the Bill. Draft bills can be presented to the House by the House itself, the President or the Regional Representative Council (DPD).

Regulatory policies are drafted according to the principles and objectives of Law 12/2011 on Establishment of Laws and Regulations (Box 4.2).

Box 4.2. Main principles and objectives of regulatory policies in Indonesia

Law No.12/2011 stipulates regulatory policymaking in Indonesia and describes:

- Principles and objectives of the regulatory system.
- Process of regulatory formation.
- National planning for legislative and regulatory frameworks.
- Requirements for mandatory impact assessments.*
- Harmonisation of regulations at national and sub-national levels.

The **main principles** (Article 5 of Law 12/2011) are as follows:

- Clarity of purpose.
- The appropriate institutional or forming authority.
- Suitability between type, hierarchy, and content material.
- Can be implemented.
- Usability and effectiveness.
- Clarity of formulation.
- Openness.

The **main objectives** (Annex I of Law 12/2011) are as follows:

- Identifying and providing solutions to issues faced by citizens, the nation and state.
- Formulating the legal issues faced as a premise to the draft regulation.
- Considering the philosophical, sociological, and juridical aspects of the draft regulation.
- Formulating the objectives of the draft regulations, including its scope, range and direction.

* Law 12/2011 is an amendment of Law No. 10/2004. The mandatory impact assessment in this Law refers to the compulsory academic paper/analysis that must accompany each draft bill or regulation.

Source: Republic of Indonesia (2011), *Law 12/2011 on Establishment of Laws and Regulations*, Jakarta.

The Ministry of Law and Human Rights is in charge of co-ordinating the lawmaking process, as well as carrying out regulatory reform activities and ensuring the quality of legislation, legal services and law enforcement. The Ministry of Law and Human Rights also delivers regular training on Regulatory Impact Assessments (RIA Law No. 12), cost-benefit analysis (in partnership with the academe) and provides advice and support to governments on SME issues and smart regulation. The Ministry of Law and Human Rights often serves as an oversight body that analyses regulations.

The Ministry of Home Affairs is responsible for co-ordinating local and central authorities on regulatory development and implementation.

Laws and regulations relevant for SMEs

Business regulatory policies are generally the same for enterprises of all sizes. Where SME-specific regulatory policies exist, it is usually to give additional government support or incentives to smaller businesses. According to the Co-ordinating Ministry for Economic Affairs (CMEA), the main difference between general business regulatory policy and SME regulatory policy is that the government intervenes more for SMEs to give preferential treatment or support, such as access to dedicated channels of finance.

There is a dedicated SME ministry called the Ministry of Co-operatives and SMEs, which serves as the focal point for SME and entrepreneurship development. It offers support and advisory services to SMEs in the areas of government policy, regulations, business development, financing, insurance and partnerships. According to Presidential Regulation No. 9, the Ministry of Co-operatives and SMEs is responsible for "assisting the President in formulating policies and co-ordinating policies in the field of co-operatives and small and medium businesses" (APEC, 2018$_{[5]}$).

According to Law 20/2008 on Micro, Small, Medium and Large Businesses referenced by the Ministry of Co-operatives and SMEs, MSMEs (micro, small, and medium enterprises) are defined according to Table 4.3.

Table 4.3. SME definition in Indonesia based on Law 20/2008

Criteria	Based on Law 20/2008		Measurement of statistical agencies
	Turnover (IDR)	Assets (IDR)	Workforce
Micro	Max 300 million	Max 50 million land and building excluded	1-5 people
Small	300 million – max 2.5 billion	50 million – max 500 million	5-19 people
Medium	2.5 billion – max 50 billion	500 million – max 10 billion	20-99 people

Sources: Provided to the OECD by the Ministry of Co-operatives and SMEs, 2017; Ediningsih, N. (2012), *Women Empowerment in Cooperative and Entrepreneurship Indonesia*, http://www.ica-ap.coop/AboutUs/women-empowerment-cooperative-and-entrepreneurship-indonesia.

However, there are 22 ministries involved in developing and/or implementing regulations relevant to SMEs. Ministries may define or interpret SME-related regulation and regulatory policies differently, depending on their respective needs. For example, some ministries need only to identify SMEs according to the size of their workforce for tallying purposes. Other ministries, such as the Ministry of Finance, may require more detailed data on company turnover or assets for taxation purposes and track data accordingly.

For example, another generally accepted definition of SME (or UKM, *Usaha Kecil dan Menengah*) is set out in the Small Enterprise Act 9/1995 (*Undang Undang Republik Indonesia Nomor 9 Tahun 1995 Tentang Usaha Kecil*) whereby an SME in any sector is defined as:

- A business that owns net assets worth IDR 200 million or less. However, these assets shall not include land or buildings.[1]
- Annual Sales of IDR 1 billion (net) or less.[2]
- Owned by a citizen of Indonesia.
- An independent economic entity, which is not a subsidiary or branch of a large or medium enterprise and is not directly or indirectly controlled (including where the operator is dispatched from a large or medium enterprise) by a large or medium enterprise.
- The business is managed by an individual, an unincorporated entity, or a co-operative organisation.

As SMEs are subject to general business regulations as well as to sectoral regulations, SMEs may have as much as or more engagement with technical ministries compared with the Ministry of Co-operatives and SMEs. The Ministry of Co-operatives does offer needed support to SMEs as well as SME policy planning, but its small staff and financial capacity pall in comparison with the much larger Ministry of Trade and Ministry of Commerce, etc. Table 4.4 presents an overview of all the different ministries and agencies that are involved in SME policy or regulation.

Table 4.4. Ministries and agencies involved in SME policy and/or regulation

	Ministry/agency	Role(s)
1	Ministry of Co-operatives and SMEs	Focal point of SMEs and entrepreneurship development in Indonesia
2	Ministry of National Development Planning (BAPPENAS)	Strategy planning and development of SME and Entrepreneurship
3	Co-ordinating Ministry of Economic Affairs (CMEA)	SME and entrepreneurship strategy co-ordinator
4	Central Bank of Indonesia (BI)	Macro-financial policy maker
5	Financial Services Authority (OJK)	Providing alternative financial access and programme for SME
6	Statistic Indonesia (BPS)	Centre of SME and entrepreneurship data
7	Ministry of Trade (MoT)	Policy and programme related to market access and promotion for SME and entrepreneurs
8	Ministry of Industry (MoI)	Policy and programme related to market access and promotion for SME and entrepreneurs
9	Ministry of Finance (MoF)	Fiscal policy and financial access for SME and entrepreneurs
10	Ministry of Manpower (MoM)	Policy and programme related to employment, and programme to improve SME productivity
11	Ministry of Research, Technology, and Higher Education (MoRTHE)	Policy and programme related to entrepreneurship, and SME business incubator and technology
12	Ministry of Education and Culture (MoEC)	Entrepreneurship education for elementary and secondary school
13	Ministry of Youth and Sports (MoYS)	Policy and programme for special target (youth) SME and entrepreneurs
14	Ministry of Communication and Informatics (MoCI)	Policy and programme for promoting SME digitalisation
15	Ministry of Social Affairs (MoSA)	Policy and programme for special target (disabilities) SME and entrepreneurs
16	Ministry of Female Empowerment and Child Protection (MoFECP)	Policy and programme for special target (women) SME and entrepreneurs
17	Creative Economy Agency (BEKRAF)	Policy and programme of creative SME and entrepreneurs
18	Ministry of Environment and Forestry (MoEF)	*Program dan kebijakan UKM dan Kewirausahaan* - Social Forestry Programme
19	Ministry of Home Affairs (MoHA)	Main co-ordinator of policy implementation among local government on SME and entrepreneurship
20	Agency for the Assessment and Application of Technology (BPPT)	Promote technology development for the benefits of SME and entrepreneurs
21	Public Procurement (LKPP)	Policy related to involvement of SME in public procurement
22	Indonesia Stock Exchange (IDX)	Programme and policy related to capital market targeted for SME
23	Investment Coordinating Board (BKPM)	Policy and programme related to investment for SME
24	Indonesia Eximbank (LPEI)	Policy and programme to facilitate financial support for SME export
25	Credit Guarantee Indonesia (Jamkrindo)	Programme and policy of SME ratings and related with SME credit guarantee
26	Commission for the Supervision of Business Competition (KPPU)	Monitor and supervise business competition among SMEs
27	Indonesian Chamber of Commerce and Industry (KADIN)	SME representatives
28	Local government	Manage and implement the policy of the SME and entrepreneurship

Source: Provided to the OECD by the Ministry of Co-operatives and SMEs, 2017.

Highlights of regulatory opportunities and challenges to support SMEs

Regulatory clarity

The multitude of agencies involved in SME-related policies and regulations can and does result in confusion about their implementation and oversight. Given that all ministries are at the same level in the government hierarchy, none can claim to have final authority on how to define or implement SMEs regulations or regulatory policies. When disputes arise, it is up to the concerned ministers to discuss and agree amongst themselves how to go forward, and consensus is not always reached.

It is unclear which ministry is in charge of supervising compliance with SME regulatory policies. It appears that there is no clear authority for the oversight of regulatory compliance. There also do not appear to be penalties or sanctions imposed on ministries that fail to comply with or implement regulatory policies, as there is no clear authority to enforce compliance or deliver sanctions.

Nevertheless, the National Development Planning Ministry (BAPPENAS) has recently been assigned a new role to integrate programmes that fall under the priorities of the President. Government Regulation 7/2017 requires programmes under the Annual Government Work Plan (RKP) down to the Ministry/Agency Work Plan (RKL) to have an integrated system of planning. BAPPENAS collaborates with the Ministry of Finance and the Ministry of Administrative Bureaucratic Reform on integrated data planning, budgeting, and performance indicators. A Ministerial Regulation 9/2017 then followed to instruct on the Procedures for Formulating and Reviewing the Work Plan of Ministries and Agencies (Article 29, paragraph 1). Ministries are currently using an information system called KRISNA to collect the information required to synchronise the planning and budgeting process, including inputs into the relevant regulatory frameworks (see section on regulatory quality management).

Regulatory delivery

Preparations for the planning and budgeting of national development programmes are transitioning from a function-based budgeting approach to a programme-based "Money Follow Program" approach. According to Article 3 of Government Regulation 17/2017 on the Synchronisation of the National Development Planning and Budgeting Process, programme-specific performance-based budgeting will be applied to budgeting, regulatory, and general service and investment frameworks.

Presidential Regulation 98/2014 has a section on licensing for micro, small, and medium enterprises (MSMEs) which delegate authority to districts and villages to implement regulatory support for MSMEs and shall be accounted for on the national and regional budgets. The regulation is intended to provide legal certainty as a way to empower MSMEs in setting up business, by defining the scope of responsibilities, provisions, and charges that could be applied or waived for MSMEs and by whom. The regulation also outlines the reporting hierarchy for administrators from the village level up to the minister level.

Regulatory compliance

According to ministries interviewed for this study, a significant challenge faced by regulating authorities is that SMEs may not know much about regulations from the first instance. There is often a lack of awareness about the existing of regulations, or the whys and how of compliance. For example, according to the Ministry of Co-operatives and SMEs, some SMEs may prefer to sell to larger enterprises within Indonesia in believing that the procedures to export products out of the country are more complex, when this may not necessarily be the reality. Officials from other ministries have also suggested that too many officers may be involved in the export process, adding complication through multiple layers of compliance and fees.

Many SMEs also do not see the value of registering their business and prefer to stay in the informal economy. More specifically, SMEs do not necessarily see differences in the incentives that they can gain from registering. The lack of registration impedes ministries and business associations from effectively matching SMEs to programmes (be it financing programmes, matching programmes with large enterprises, tax incentives, subsidies, etc.). Some policymakers interviewed by the OECD have pointed out that some SMEs are sceptical of government reach and believe that business registration is intended to extract benefits and taxes from SMEs, rather than for recording information to make better policies to support SME growth.

Even where SMEs are aware of regulations, compliance can be weak. SMEs are expected to comply with a large number of licences, permit, inspection requirements, often from multiple ministries. Confusion over or complexity (or perceived complexity) of regulatory processes contributes to weak or non-compliance.

Moreover, while there may be fines in regulations, in practice there are rarely sanctions imposed on SMEs. According to BAPPENAS, they do not levy sanctions or fines for failure to implement regulations. They simply advise, review and administer budgets to line ministries.

The CMEA tends to allow small companies to operate as they wish without imposing too many regulations or penalties for regulations, as long as they are not interfering negatively with the local economy.[3] It is only when companies grow to a medium size that they face more regulatory checkboxes to meet and thereby regulatory barriers. For comparison, the key challenge noted by the Ministry of Trade for large enterprises is access to a more educated labour force. By and large, the large companies usually always comply with regulations as they don't want to take the sanctions and risks associated with non-compliance.

Compliance with standards

The National Standardisation Agency of Indonesia (*Badan Nasional Standardisasi*, BSN) is a non-ministerial government institution that is accountable to the President. The BSN is responsible for developing and promoting national standards. It also represents Indonesia in the International Organisation for Standardisation (ISO).

Meeting labelling requirements/sanitary and phytosanitary standards (SPS) is an issue, as identified by the Co-ordinating Ministry for Economic Affairs (CMEA). There is a range of guidelines and requirements that exist regionally and internationally that increase the burden of compliance for SMEs.

There are no current plans or programmes to harmonise or streamline sanitary and phytosanitary requirements (i.e. requirements certification, licensing/product certification, labelling requirements, inspections and testing, etc.) at the national or regional levels.

Enforcement and inspection

Different line ministries and levels of government conduct their own enforcement and inspection of regulatory delivery and compliance. National and sub-national governments work together to co-ordinate the implementation of SME policies.

The CMEA serves as the central oversight ministry responsible for co-ordinating, synchronising and monitoring the performance and functions of various technical ministries that play a role in economic issues. The CMEA is also responsible for maintaining policy harmonisation and programmes to achieve its objectives. It may conduct local visits to ensure that policies are implemented well. The CMEA conducts inspections twice a year to check compliance with regulations in special economic zones, where budget avails.

According to the office responsible for licences in the Ministry of Trade, companies are expected to send a report every semester with information on their licence number, name of business and number of company registration. They are required to register on an online portal, which is now implemented in around 60 districts. In the case of non-compliance, the Ministry of Trade would send a letter of notification to the offending business. Otherwise, the Ministry of Home Affairs is the one that can impose penalties.

For the Ministry of Trade, they check if the Ministerial Decree is implemented by sending officers to check if regulations have been complied with in the 514 districts that it covers, although the number of districts visited in a given year depends on the budget. According to an interview with the Ministry of Trade, on average, they conduct some 30 inspections per year.

There is an effort in place to evaluate the performance of inspection authorities. At the end of each year, the government has to submit two reports: the first about the activities in sectoral departments; the second about the local government. Then, a department responsible for monitoring public service should measure the public satisfaction index.

Administrative simplification

Administrative simplification is one of the key tenets of the 16 Economic Policy Packages issued by the President to date. According to a monitoring report from the Office of the Presidential Staff (KSP), of the 8 811 regulations affected by the policy packages, 1 133 are related to licensing and investments. Details of achievements from the policy packages up to December 2016 are as follows: based on the report up to December 2016 through the Monitoring System at the Office of the Presidential Staff (KSP), out of 8 811 regulations, 1 133 of these regulations were on licensing and investment. Achievements of the policy packages up to the end of 2016 include 324 revoked regulations and 75 revised regulations.

Since 2016, the government has been working on implementing a One-stop Integrated Service (PTSP) which provides a single portal via which businesses can submit and obtain multiple licences at once (Box 4.3). For businesses operating outside of special designated areas (special economic areas, free trade zones, tourism and industrial areas), the PTSP helps to expedite the licensing process through its data sharing system, which can then be synchronised between institutions. The government will also implement an Integrated Single Submission Licensing System (ISSS), where submitted data will eventually be integrated with various services in Indonesia ranging from citizen to business registration, to taxes and import-export. A pilot of the ISSS is planned for January 2018. The ISSS and PTSP will be located in the same building.

Box 4.3. Regulatory simplification for licensing and investment in Indonesia

Following from President Joko Widodo's instruction to central and local governments to undertake progressive regulatory cuts in December 2015, the National Development Planning Agency, Indonesia (BAPPENAS) issued a letter to all ministries, agencies and local governments that outlined a framework for implementing regulatory simplification in the field of licensing and investment. Subsequently, the 2016 programme for regulatory simplification in licensing and investment called for 20 ministries and agencies to support the establishment of a One-Stop Service Centre (PTSP) at the Investment Coordinating Board (BKPM) (Republic of Indonesia, 2015[7]):

- Investment Coordinating Board (BKPM)
- Food and Drug Supervisory Agency (BPOM)
- National Standardisation Agency of Indonesia (BSN)
- Ministry of Agrarian and Spatial Planning
- Ministry of State Owned Enterprises
- Ministry of Energy and Mineral Resources
- Ministry of Law and Human Rights
- Ministry of Maritime Affairs and Fisheries
- Ministry of Health
- Ministry of Manpower and Transmigration
- Ministry of Finance
- Ministry of Communication and Informatics
- Ministry of Environment and Forestry
- Ministry of Tourism
- Ministry of Public Work
- Ministry of Education and Culture
- Ministry of Trade
- Ministry of Transportation
- Ministry of Industry
- Ministry of Agriculture.

Source: Republic of Indonesia (2015), *Presidential Instruction 4/2015 Concerning the Implementation of One-Stop Service Centre (PTSP)*, Jakarta.

As of 2018, integrated business licensing and permitting services are in the process of being unified in an online single submission (OSS) system at Indonesia's Investment Coordinating Board (BKPM) following Presidential Instruction 91/2017. BAPPENAS is supporting the CMEA to implement the OSS (BKPM, 2018[8]).

Prior to the OSS, Indonesia has already introduced one-stop shops across the country to consolidate the delivery of government services to support business start-ups, including information about regulations and their requirements, licensing and permit issuance. Notable examples are Jakarta and Surabaya.

Regulatory quality management

BAPPENAS takes a leading role in regulatory quality management at the national level. BAPPENAS exercises regulatory supervision via defining the national programme and budget planning, which includes setting goals, directions and prioritisation for national development policies and programmes. The Minister of BAPPENAS and the Minister of Finance jointly review the budget framework for all ministries. This involves reviewing the implementation, performance, and budget expenditure for programmes undertaken in the previous year, which then helps to inform budget allocations for the present year and forecast for the next year (Republic of Indonesia, 2017[9]).

According to Law No. 23/2014 on the Local Government, there are two tiers of assessments of regulatory quality. The first is in the province for district-level regulation, and the second in the Ministry of Home Affairs for provincial-level regulation. It is unclear to what extent these regulatory quality assessments are carried out, as there is no tracked data. Furthermore, the Ministry of Home Affairs does not have the mandate to repeal regulations that are found to be of low quality.

The government plans to help synchronise and simplify business licensing for MSMEs, for example by amending the delegation of authority in Presidential Decree 98/2014 (CMEA, 2016[10]).

New Presidential Decrees do not automatically override existing regulations, which means that they may also risk adding administrative burden if older or outdated regulations are not repealed.

BAPPENAS is currently collaborating with Pelita Harapan University to conduct research on the quality of regulations related to SMEs. The research will conduct a cost-benefit analysis (CBA) of the qualitative and quantitative aspects of some 60 regulations related to SMEs that have been issued by various ministries. The objective of the work is to identify overlapping regulations and provide policy recommendations to the CMEA.

Following from Ministerial Regulation 9/2017 on the Procedures for Formulating and Reviewing the Work Plan of Ministries and Agencies, the introduction of the KRISNA integrated information system aims to incorporate submissions to support efficient and suitable regulatory development. Proposed regulatory frameworks for the work plans – which would be input into KRISNA – must meet various criteria according to legal need, urgency and benefit to society (including support to development targets), and burden (including a CBA). The submitted information will help inform the upstream regulatory development process and serve as a basis for regulatory impact analysis/assessment (RIA) that can be incorporated into planning documents.

Regulatory impact assessment

Presidential Instruction (InPres) 7/2017, effective as of 1 November 2017, requires ministers, high-ranking officials and heads of agencies to:

- Report any new regulations they want to issue to the relevant co-ordinator's office and/or President.
- Undertake regulatory impact analysis (including risk analysis) and conduct public consultations for new regulations.

A manual or guidance is available for governments to use when developing RIA for major regulations. When developing RIA, regulators are required to identify the costs and benefits of a new regulation. These are often conducted by ministries, with the assistance of academic institutions. Instead of a standard RIA form, ministries or regulators present this cost and benefit analysis via an academic paper.

A more recent Cabinet Secretary Regulation 1/2018 highlights the importance for ministries to implement RIA – both *ex ante* and *ex post* – during the development of regulations.

E-government

Information and communication technology (ICT) is widely used across the Indonesian government. Most if not all ministries and agencies have their own websites offering information including services, media updates, online rules and regulations, and contact forms. A number of ministries also provide comprehensive databases on legislation and regulations online (Box 4.4). However, there is currently no single website that provides businesses with consolidated information on regulatory policies and procedures. As such, database users can spend significant amounts of time searching for regulatory information across government websites, which may not necessarily be aligned with one another.

Box 4.4. National regulatory databases in Indonesia

Several institutions manage national regulation databases as stipulated by law:

1. The Ministry of Law and Human Rights, represented by the General Directorate of Legislation and Regulation, was mandated in Ministry Regulation of Law and Human Rights No. 1/2007 to publish and disseminate information about legislation. It has responsibilities to update regulation that are stipulated by the President (Law, Government Regulation and Presidential Regulations).
2. The Ministry of State Secretariat and Cabinet secretary have the same role as the General Directorate of Legislation and Regulation, according to Presidential Regulation No. 1/2007.
3. The National Legal Development Board was mandated by Presidential Regulation No. 33/2012 to develop the National Legal Information Documentation Network system. This system comprises members from various institutions, including law department or units dealing with legal documentation in state institutions, central and local government, law libraries in both private and public universities. Board members are responsible for developing and managing the law information system. The system provides regulations as well as their accompanying academic papers.

Regulations at the national level are updated regularly by the institutions above. Regulations at the local level are not always updated (Ministry of Law and Human Rights, 2018[11]; Ministry of State Secretariat and Cabinet, 2018[12]).

Sources: Ministry of Law and Human Rights (2018), *Peraturan Database*, http://ditjenpp.kemenkumham.go.id; Republic of Indonesia (2018), *Database of Laws and Regulations*, http://peraturan.go.id; Ministry of State Secretariat and Cabinet (2018), *Peraturan*, http://setkab.go.id/category/peraturan/.

Indonesia has completed successful pilot and parallel tests of its National Single Window (NSW). As of April 2017, its protocol and legal framework have been ratified by most ASEAN member states, and its Operation and Certification Procedure for the e-ATIGA Form D Certificate of Origin has been endorsed (UNESCAP, 2017[13]). The Indonesia NSW will soon extend to other documents including SPS and certificates of health. The proposed Indonesian NSW will integrate It will also provide comprehensive information on taxes, trade quotas, rates, rules of origin, product standards, statistic and trade activities between Indonesia and other countries.

There is currently no single website that provides SMEs with updated information on regulatory procedures. Multiple government websites offer information on various topics (export, licensing, permit procedures) but may not necessarily be aligned with each other. The government is currently working to synchronise the different investment regulations and online systems that vary from ministry to ministry. Indonesia plans to launch an online single submission (OSS) system which will include comprehensive information on investments, licences, facilities and complaints. A number of ministries are already integrating their systems into OSS Indonesia, which will begin operation in April 2018 (Jakarta Post, 2018[14]).

Stakeholder engagement

According to the lawmaking process of Indonesia, a legislative session is often organised for consultation. This session includes an inter-ministerial committee, experts and stakeholders, and aims to provide stakeholders with a platform to discuss the draft regulation and its accompanying academic paper. A public hearing is also arranged (according to the national legislation programme or *prolegnas*) before the enactment of a regulation in order to obtain input from the community/public on the draft regulation.

Several online databases for public consultations have been introduced in Indonesia, to allow individuals to provide comments or complaints on draft or existing regulations. Examples include:

- Partisipasi Publiik (Ministry of Law and Human Rights)
- Legal Smart Channel
- Konsultasi Hukum Online
- Hukum Online.

Hukum Online, which has grown extensively over time, uploads draft regulations on line and features legal experts who are part of the community and who provide comments and suggestions (BPHN, 2018[15]).

Appeals

If disputes between national and sub-national governments or between ministries arise over a regulation or regulatory policy relating to an economic issue, the CMEA will co-ordinate with the relevant parties to discuss whether to revise or abolish the regulation or regulatory policy.

Disputes or conflicts over an SME regulation may be taken to the Constitutional (for national regulations) or Supreme Court (for local regulations). Articles or regulations deemed burdensome may be challenged in either court. The courts would examine the problem as well as the regulation. The courts may invite an expert to give suggestions. Judgments are published on the court websites.

Judicial review could be triggered by SMEs that disagree with regulations or regulatory decisions.

Recommendations

- **Clarify the roles and responsibilities of ministries involved with SME regulatory policies,** including setting out a clear co-ordination pathway for decision-making. This includes the Co-ordinating Ministry for Economic Affairs, BAPPENAS, the Ministry of Co-operatives and SMEs but also the other 20-plus ministries and agencies that are also involved in SME policymaking.
- **Harmonise the definition of SMEs across ministries** to reduce confusion or inconsistent applications of regulatory policies to SMEs by different ministries.
- **Develop a framework for dealing with regulatory non-compliance, which should be consistently applied.** This could be a risk-based system.
- **Continue consolidating the numerous databases and platforms that house business and investment regulations and processes across different ministries.**
- **Systematically assess the impact of regulations,** which could be risk-based and proportional, and document this information in a centralised portal that could be shared with other ministries.

Notes

[1] According to the Small Enterprise Act 9/1995, this criterion may change according to economic conditions in Indonesia.

[2] Ibid.

[3] Interview with OECD.

References

APEC (2018), *Ministry of Co-operatives and SMEs*, http://www.we-apec.com/directory/ministry-cooperatives-and-smes. [5]

BAPPENAS (2015), *Evaluation of the RPJMN 2015-2019*, https://www.bappenas.go.id/files/publikasi_utama/Evaluasi%20Paruh%20Waktu%20RPJMN%202015-2019.pdf. [3]

BKPM (2018), *Investment Policy Updates: Presidential Regulation No. 91/2017 on Acceleration of Doing Business*, http://www.pma-japan.or.id/bundles/bsibkpm/download/BKPM%20Presentation%20-%20PR%2091-2017_3.pdf. [8]

BPHN (2018), *Kemeterian Hukum dan Ham Republik Indonesia*, http://bphn.go.id/openpartisipasi/index. [15]

CMEA (2016), *Siaran Pers - Kebijakan UMKM Harus Menyeluruh dan Terarah*, https://ekon.go.id/press/view/siaran-pers-kebijakan-umkm.2087.html. [10]

Ediningsih, N. (2012), *Women Empowerment in Cooperative and Entrepreneurship Indonesia*, http://www.ica-ap.coop/AboutUs/women-empowerment-cooperative-and-entrepreneurship-indonesia. [6]

Jakarta Post (2018), *Indonesia to Have World's Best OSS System*, http://www.thejakartapost.com/news/2018/03/09/indonesia-to-have-worlds-best-oss-system-govt.html. [14]

Ministry of Administrative and Bureaucratic Reform (2015), *Roadmap of Bureaucractic Reform 2015-2020, Regulation No. 11/2015*, Jakarta. [1]

Ministry of Law and Human Rights (2018), *Peraturan Database*, http://ditjenpp.kemenkumham.go.id. [11]

Ministry of State Secretariat and Cabinet (2018), *Peraturan*, http://setkab.go.id/category/peraturan. [12]

Republic of Indonesia (2018), *Database of Laws and Regulations*, http://peraturan.go.id. [16]

Republic of Indonesia (2017), *Presidential Regulation No.17/2017*, Jakarta. [9]

Republic of Indonesia (2015), *Presidential Instruction 4/2015 Concerning the Implementation of One-Stop Service Centre (PTSP).* [7]

Republic of Indonesia (2011), *Law 12/2011 on Establishment of Laws and Regulations.* [4]

UNESCAP (2017), *Indonesia National Single Window*, http://www.unescap.org/sites/default/files/26%20Apr%202017%20-%20Indonesia%20Experience.pdf. [13]

World Bank (2018), *Ease of Doing Business Rankings*, http://www.doingbusiness.org/rankings. [2]

Chapter 5. Lao PDR

Regulatory reform in Lao PDR in recent years has been accelerated by the country's accession to the World Trade Organization in 2013 and by ongoing regulatory developments in the Association of Southeast Asian Nations (ASEAN) Economic Community. Lao PDR has already adopted a number of good regulatory practices, including mandatory regulatory impact assessments and stakeholder engagement in the development of new regulations. The government also recognises the importance of reviewing existing regulations on a regular basis, as stipulated in its regulatory impact assessment (RIA) guidelines. In order to align Lao's regulatory processes with regional single market objectives and to facilitate greater Lao participation in global value chains, a significant amount of new regulations is expected to be developed in the coming years. This offers opportunities for Lao PDR to introduce regulatory policies and processes that complement or comply with regional and international standards.

Regulatory context

Small and medium-sized enterprise (SME) development is a national priority in Lao PDR. Several government plans and strategies explicitly address the need to support the growth of SMEs (Box 5.1), with support from the highest political level. The Prime Minister personally attends the full biannual meetings of the Lao Business Forum and has made SMEs and access to finance a strong focus for Lao PDR's ASEAN Chairmanship in 2016.

Box 5.1. National plans emphasising SME development in Lao PDR

The **8th Five-Year Plan for National Socio-Economic Development (2016-20)** marks the promotion of SMEs as a key output, with activities to (UNDP, 2016[1]):

- Create production chains between large enterprises and SMEs.
- Improve taxation procedures for SMEs, including developing detailed guidelines on lump-sum tax payments and a simple accounting system.
- Improve and utilise the SME promotion fund.
- Provide business development support to SMEs.

10 Year Development Strategy to 2025

There have also been three SME Development Plans in Lao PDR, each setting out policy priorities for a five-year period. The first development plan focused on setting up an enabling environment for businesses to grow in both the domestic and international market through regulatory and administrative reforms and encouraging entrepreneurial attitudes and characteristics within the society. The second development plan focused on building on the achievements and progress from the last development plan while rolling out new services to provide support to a growing SME base. This includes enhancing business linkages between large enterprises and SMEs and upgrading the quality, standards and level of productivity among SMEs.

- The current and third SME Development Plan (2016-20) aims to:
- Promote productivity, technology and innovation.
- Enhance access to finance.
- Enhance access to business development service (BDS).
- Enhance SME accession to expanding domestic and international market.
- Create and develop entrepreneurs.
- Create an enabling environment for the establishment and operation of SME business.
- Policy on customs-taxation and finance.

Source: UNDP (2016), *The 8th Five-Year National Socio-Economic Development Plan 2016-2020*, www.la.undp.org/content/lao_pdr/en/home/library/poverty/the-8th-five-year-national-socio-economic-development-plan--2016.html.

Lao PDR has been described as a "deal-based" rather than a "rules-based" economy. For example, it is common for fees to be negotiated between businesses or between businesses and the relevant ministry. A number of well-drafted laws and regulations exist, including in the English language, although their delivery and oversight are less consistent. Regulatory reform is underway, however, and the government recognises the need to establish clearer, more robust regulatory frameworks, as well as improve their enforcement.

The ASEAN Economic Community (AEC) Blueprint is shaping the direction of Lao policy and regulatory development, which aims towards regional convergence. Lao progress in regulatory development has also been accelerated by its accession to the World Trade Organization (WTO). The next WTO review for Lao PDR will be in 2019. A large inflow of new regulations will be a significant challenge for businesses – and SMEs in particular. Enforcement will also be a major challenge for the state.

The government is currently working with many development partners to implement SME regulatory support programmes. Key players include the World Bank, Asian Development Bank (ADB) and the ASEAN Secretariat.

Regulatory governance

Institutional and regulatory setup

Table 5.1. Institutional and regulatory setup in Lao PDR

	Government
State structure	Single Party Socialist Republic
Head of sate	**President**
Executive	The executive power in Lao PDR is vested in the **President**. The President appoints the Prime Minister and the Council of Ministers, with approval from the National Assembly. • The Government is headed by the **Prime Minister**. It is responsible for implementing the Constitution as well as laws and resolutions of the National Assembly, Presidential edicts and decrees. It can submit draft laws to the National Assembly, draft Presidential Edicts to the National Assembly Standing Committee, and draft Presidential Decrees to the President. It may also issue decrees and resolutions on state administration and management in various governance areas including defence, security, foreign affairs, natural resources, science and technology. The government may propose to the National Assembly the creation of abolishment of ministries and ministry-equivalent organisations as well as definitions the boundaries of provinces and cities and may suspend or cancel decisions or instructions of ministry or ministry-equivalent organisations if they contradict other laws and legislation. (Article 70, 2015 Constitution of Lao PDR). • **Line Ministries** are responsible for initiating and drafting law and regulation proposals. They also oversee the implementation of regulations in their fields of competence. • **Ministry of Justice (MOJ)** is in responsible for quality control of all laws and regulations. A Centre for Regulatory Impact Assessment is established within the MOJ.
Legislative	**Unicameral legislature** The legislative power in Lao PDR is vested in the **National Assembly**, which is responsible for making decisions on national affairs, national plans and strategies, adopting or amending constitutions and laws (including cancelling legislation), and monitoring their implementation. It may also elect or remove the President, Vice President, and members of its Standing Committee.
Legal system	• The **Supreme Court** is the highest judiciary power. It presides over the decisions of the peoples' courts and military courts. • Three levels of **People's Courts** exist below the Supreme Court; 1) area or district courts of first instance; 2) provincial or city courts of first instance; 3) regional appellate courts in the north, middle and south of Lao PDR for decisions adjudicated by provincial or city courts. Regional courts can also issue orders, judgments and final decisions to law enforcement authorities for implementation.

	• **Central Military Tribunal** adjudicates criminal cases relating to military matters or occurring within military compounds. • **Labour chamber** rules over disputes arising from labour contracts, occupational health and safety, and salary and wage claims. • **Commercial chamber** rules over disputes arising from commercial contracts, payment instruments, intellectual property, bankruptcy and liquidations, partnerships, loan and financing, insurance, and international trade.
Administrative-territorial structure	17 provinces and one prefecture
Ministry or agency responsible for SMEs or SME-related issues	**Department for Small and Medium Enterprise Promotion (DOSMEP)** under the Ministry of Industry and Commerce
Other support structures within government on regulatory policy	• **Investment Promotion and Management Committee** is a cross-cutting committee headed by the Deputy Prime Minister with representatives from ten ministries that approve and oversee all investment in controlled business sectors and areas. • **Department of Standardization and Metrology (DOSM)** is the national standardisation agency, and also represents Lao PDR in the International Standards Organization (ISO). • **National Chamber of Commerce and Industry (LNCCI)** is a private sector body representing private sector interests, but with clear government involvement. LNCCI is regularly consulted by government on draft regulations. An SME Service Centre exists in the LNCCI. • **Lao National Business Committee** issues Certificates of Origin (C/O) for some trade agreements that are not issued by the Ministry of Industry and Commerce.

Lao PDR's legislative process

Figure 5.1. Overview of the legislative process in Lao PDR

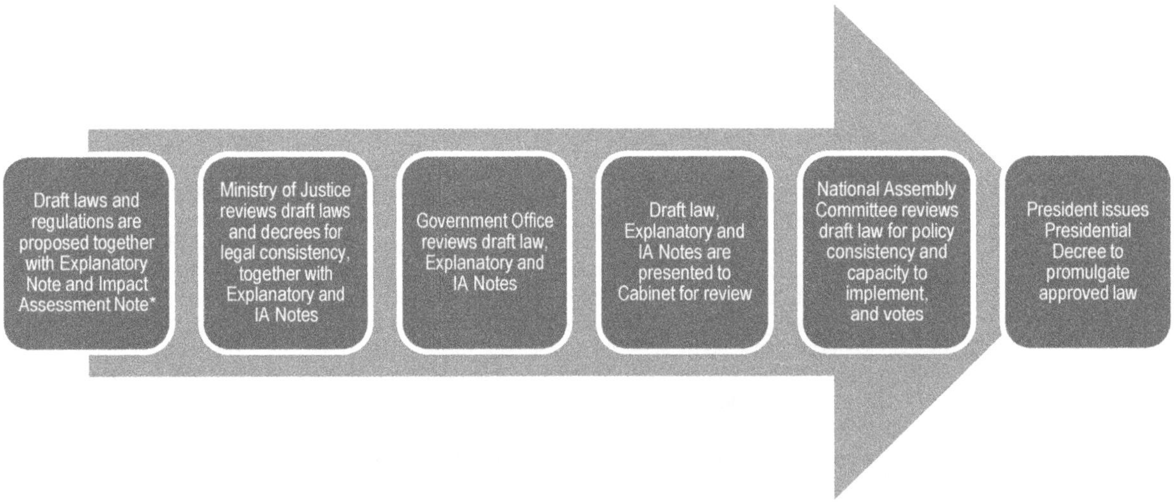

Note: Draft laws may be proposed by the following: President; National Assembly Standing Committee; Government; Office of the Supreme Public Prosecutor, People's Supreme Court, State Audit Organisation; Lao Front for National Construction and other major central agencies (Article 59, 2015 Constitution of the Lao PDR). Decisions of the Prime Minister or Minister have the same steps of impact assessment and consultation. Some but not all Prime Minister decisions go on to Cabinet.

Line ministries are responsible for initiating law and regulation proposals, drafting them and having the laws, regulations processed through the lawmaking process required by the Law on Making Legislation 2012 (Box 5.2).

Box 5.2. Law on making legislation in Lao PDR, 2012

Brief extract of roles and responsibilities (Article 28):

The authority in charge of law making – the relevant ministry – shall (Government of Lao PDR, 2012[2]):

- develop a lawmaking and amendment plan, with budget
- set up a legal unit (responsible to the ministry)
- appoint a law drafting committee, chaired by a Vice-Minister or Deputy Head of Authority
- provide policy guidelines to the law drafting committee
- propose the draft law and unsolved issues to the government
- propose to the Prime Minister to appoint a draft law defending committee to present to the National Assembly
- assess the implementation of laws in their area of responsibility
- collect and analyse information
- conduct public consultation, direct consultation with concerned sectors and parties and ask for comments from domestic and foreign experts
- prepare explanatory note (background and problem, objectives, rationale and needs, explanation of important articles, resources, mechanisms and implementing authority, expected outcomes) and impact assessment.

The Ministry of Justice shall:

- conduct comprehensive review and research of draft law, particularly legal structure
- send comments back to drafting authority (ministry)
- invite the drafting committee and relevant sectors to review and edit to ensure consensus before submission to the government.*

Cabinet consideration:

- representatives of the National Assembly committees and other relevant parties may attend the meeting considering the draft law
- focuses on issues raised by the government office.

* The Drafting Authority retains responsibility of the proposed law; however, in practice, it tends to adopt the opinion of the Ministry of Justice.

Source: Government of Lao PDR (2012), *Law on Making Legislation (Unofficial translation)*, https://ial-online.org/wp-content/uploads/2018/05/Laos-Making-Legislation-Law.pdf.

Regulatory process for business-related laws

In the case of business-related laws, the main responsible ministries are the Ministry of Industry and Commerce and the Ministry of Planning and Investment.

An Investment and Promotion Management Committee established under the Amended Investment Promotion Law approves and overseas investments in controlled business sectors, concessionary businesses and special economic zones (SEZs). This committee is headed by the Deputy Prime Minister and features representatives from ten ministries.

Laws and regulations relevant for SMEs

Regulatory policies for businesses in Lao PDR are generally the same for all enterprises regardless of their size. Almost all businesses in Lao PDR are SMEs; out of some 80 000 companies in Lao PDR, more than 97% are SMEs. SMEs accounted for roughly 82% of employment in Lao PDR in 2013 (GIZ, 2014[3]).

There is, however, a dedicated Law No. 11/NA on the Promotion of SMEs which sets out a number of SME promotion activities aimed at creating an enabling environment for SMEs, including building on and improving existing regulations to be more transparent and improving the efficiency of government administrative services (Government of Lao PDR, 2011[4]). There is also specific mention of enhancing co-operation between SME and large enterprises as well as foreign investment enterprises by enacting the relevant legislation and measures.

SMEs are categorised into production, trade and service sectors in order to recognise the different assets and turnover scales in the respective sectors (Table 5.2). There is no standard difference for the regulation of SMEs in different sectors. However, there is a difference in taxation threshold and procedure according to SME size.

Table 5.2. Definition of SMEs in Lao PDR

	Employees	Assets (LAK)	Annual turnover (LAK)
Micro-enterprise			
Micro-enterprise - production	1-5	< 100 million	<400 million
Micro-enterprise - trade	1-5	<150 million	<400 million
Micro-enterprise - services	1-5	<200 million	<400 million
Small enterprise			
Small enterprise - production	6-50	up to 1 billion	up to 2 billion
Small enterprise - trade	6-50	1 billion	3 billion
Small enterprise - services	6-50	1.5 billion	1.5 billion
Medium enterprise			
Medium enterprise - production	51-99	up to 4 billion	up to 4 billion
Medium enterprise - trade	51-99	4 billion	6 billion
Medium enterprise - services	51-99	6 billion	4 billion

Source: Phaophongsavath, P. (2017), "Decree on Classifying SME categories", Small and Medium Enterprises Development in Laos, PowerPoint presentation, https://toi.boi.go.th/information/download/472.

The Investment Promotion Law (amended in 2017) provides tax incentives to businesses of all sizes investing in "promoted sectors" depending on where the investment is located. Agriculture, industry, handicrafts and services are designated as promoted sectors.

Highlights of regulatory opportunities and challenges to support SMEs

Regulatory clarity

A dedicated SME Promotion Strategy includes indicators and targets for specific policy areas (Table 5.3) (OECD, forthcoming[5]). However, the procedures to achieve them are not clear.

Table 5.3. Policies and targets in the promotion of SMEs (Prime Minister's Decree 42)

No.	List of seven policies	Indicators
1	Promote productivity, technology and innovation	The average annual productivity must increase from USD 9 000/person to USD 12 000/person.
2	Enhance access to finance	The percentage of SMEs access to finance increase from 20% in 2016 to 30% in 2020.
3	Enhance access to business development service (BDS)	Increasing the ratio of SMEs who have received business development service from experts increase from 4.28% in 2013 to 30% in 2020.
4	Enhance SME accession to expanding domestic and international markets	The value of SMEs export increase from 12.91% of total export value in 2016 to 20% by 2020.
5	Create and develop entrepreneurs	The business population increase from 2% in 2013 to 4% in 2020. The employment from SMEs sector increase from 82.18% in 2013 to 85% in 2020.
6	Create an enabling environment for the establishment and operation of SME businesses	The time required to start a business (days) have to decrease from 67 days in 2016 to 25 days by 2020. The cost of starting a business decrease from 4.6% of per capita gross domestic product (GDP) in 2016 to 4% by 2020.
7	Policy on customs-taxation and finance	The percentage of SMEs who have a profit increase from 41% in 2013 to 60% by 2020. The number of SMEs using computers for business management increase from 6.2% in 2013 to 15% by 2020.

Source: OECD (forthcoming), *ASEAN SME Policy Index 2018: Boosting Competitiveness and Inclusive Growth in ASEAN*, OECD Publishing, Paris.

SMEs are expected to comply with a number of licences, permit, and inspection requirements. Confusion over or complexity (or perceived complexity) of regulatory processes contributes to weak or non-compliance.

Regulatory delivery

Regulatory compliance

Compliance with regulations is generally weak. According to the Ministry of Agriculture and Forestry, the dissemination of policies, laws and regulations has not been widely spread to local and production areas, resulting in poor implementation and compliance (Ministry of Agriculture and Fisheries, 2016[6]). Even where SMEs are aware of regulations, compliance usually remains low. Some fines exist for regulatory non-compliance although, in practice, sanctions are rarely imposed on SMEs.

There is no policy on inspection authorities, although every ministry section (including the Department for Small and Medium Sized Enterprise Promotion, or DOSMEP) has an internal inspection department whose function is to check internal procedures and activities.

Compliance with product or service standards

The Department of Standardization and Metrology (DOSM) established under the Ministry of Science and Technology (Ministerial Decree No. 826/MST, 21 December 2011) is the national standardisation agency. It supports the development of national standards, accreditation, conformity assessments and other related activities. DOSM is the representative agency of Lao PDR in the International Standards Organization (ISO).

There are currently no mandatory national standards in Lao PDR. There are however 250 voluntary Lao national standards for various products, issued by various ministries. These voluntary standards may be applied according to the Law on Standardization and the PM Decree to Implement the Law on Standardization (Government of Lao PDR, 2014[7]). For meeting standards in other countries, third-party certification from Thailand is sometimes used, where applicable.

Meeting sanitary and phytosanitary (SPS) requirements of other countries is a challenge. For example, ASEAN SPS requirements are not harmonised, which adds to the difficulty of knowing the rules for each trading partner. There is a specific objective in the 8th Five-Year National Socio-Economic Development Plan to "formulate and improve legislation on sanitation and phytosanitation as a commitment and action toward international treaties" (Ministry of Planning and Investment, 2016[8]). Developing an SPS system and production standard system in Lao PDR is also a "first priority activity" for the Ministry of Agriculture and Fisheries (2016[6]).

There is an intention to harmonise regulatory and procedural frameworks for trade and investment with ASEAN through a programme called the Regional Economic Integration of Laos into ASEAN, Trade and Entrepreneurship Development (RELATED). The RELATED programme is intended to support the government in managing the process of regional economic integration, translate ASEAN agreements into Lao legislation and align their implementation. The overall objective of the RELATED programme is to help Lao enterprises improve their competitiveness as well as access to markets in the broader ASEAN Economic Community (AEC) (GIZ, 2018[9]).

Administrative simplification

The principle of regulatory simplification is endorsed in the 8th NSEDP and the SME development plans. However, there is no explicit policy for regulatory simplification in Lao PDR, although specific areas such as business registration and customs clearance are subject to review and may have dedicated programmes for this purpose.

There is an ongoing review of business licensing promoted by the Department for SME Promotion (DOSMEP) and supported by the World Bank. The review is supporting the Ministry of Industry and Commerce in: 1) reviewing and reforming of the business registration process; 2) preparing an inventory of all business licences and permits; 3) assessing and reforming of a subset of the processes with the highest administrative burden using the Standard Cost Model methodology. The final outcome will be a clear and business-friendly inventory of all licences and a streamlined business registration process.

The Department of Enterprise Registration and Management is currently consulting with the Department of Tax and the Office of Public Security on reducing business registration procedures.

The "one-stop shop" idea is known and is used in SEZs. It is called the "Small Administrative-Wider Society Office" (Box 5.3). "One-stop" customs inspections are also being piloted in Lao PDR. So far there has been a pilot joint clearance with Savannakhet–Mukdahan in 2013, a single window one-stop clearance inspection node between Dansawan Savannakhet (Laos), Lao Bao and Quan Tri (Viet Nam) and a Thailand-Laos-Viet Nam transitional Customs Transit System (CTS), which will eventually be replaced by ASEAN system.

Box 5.3. One-stop service in Lao PDR's special economic zones

The Small Administrative-Wider Society Office (One-Stop Service) is the service centre used in Lao PDR's special economic zones (SEZs). It provides a wide range of services including receiving documents or proposals from investors, supporting the documentation process, approving and returning the document to entrepreneurs. Types of documents supported by the office include (Ministry of Planning and Investment, 2018[11]):

- Land title deed.
- Enterprise registration certificate.
- Import-export (raw materials, machinery, construction materials, goods, etc.) permission.
- Licence on labour import (identity card and labour card).
- Tax and customs collection (salary and VAT).
- Licence on the construction of office buildings, service centres, supermarkets and factory.
- Environmental licence.

Source: Ministry of Planning and Investment (2018), *Special Economic Zone*, www.investlaos.gov.la/index.php/start-up/special-economic-zone.

Regulatory quality management

Regulatory impact assessment

RIA is governed by the Law on Making Legislation (No. 19/NA 12/7/2012) and the Decision on the Impact Assessment of Draft Legislation (No. 517/MOJ 7/7/2014). The Law (Article 29) requires analysis, public consultation, explanatory note and impact assessment of regulatory and budgetary impacts to accompany draft legislation. This information should be reported in an Impact Assessment Note (IA Note). All draft laws that go to the National Legislative Assembly require an IA Note to be completed.

In 2011, an Inter-Ministry RIA Task Force was established to guide the introduction of RIA into the pilot ministries and design the system. Subsequently, a Centre for RIA was established within the Ministry of Justice (MOJ) in 2014. The role of the centre is to advocate for, support and quality control the RIA system, which is not specific to SMEs. The Centre sits alongside the MOJ's other responsibility to review the legal quality of draft laws and regulations. The centre also has a responsibility to inform and train line ministries as well as the public on RIA. In 2016, the centre issued a set of guidelines for ministries in conducting *ex ante* assessments.

RIA is done for all draft laws, including:

- Draft Laws.
- Draft Presidential Ordinances.
- Draft Government Decrees, except decrees to implement Resolutions of the National Assembly, of the Standing Committee of the National Assembly, the national socio-economic development plan and decrees on establishment and activities of a ministry or a government organisation.
- Draft Decisions of the Prime Minister, Ministers, Head of Government Authorities, provincial governors or Vientiane.

RIA does *not* cover: district or village regulation, resolutions, or other government decrees (e.g. to implement the resolution of the National Assembly, socio-economic development plans or strategic plans).

A light form of RIA is currently used and assessed impacts must be projected for the next five years. To date, over 600 training and awareness fora have been conducted on RIA but there remains limited compliance among ministries.

Ex post *evaluation*

There is no routine evaluation or survey to assess SME regulations or regulatory policies for their efficiency in meeting their goals. However, the new Impact Assessment (IA) Note includes a section on 'post-implementation review' which outlines timelines, responsible parties, and particular areas for review. These guidelines should be periodically reviewed for relevance and effectiveness over time.

E-government

Many laws and regulations are available on the Lao Trade Portal, which serves as a single point access to information about trade regulations. Some drafts of regulations and standards are also published online at the Lao Trade Portal for consultation, although this practice is not yet widespread.

As of 2015, the Ministry of Justice has also launched a one-stop website that provides a range of legal information for legal practitioners as well as the general public (UNDP, 2015[12]). Information is provided on legal aid, laws, international treaties to which Lao PDR is party and judiciary processes.

The Laos National Single Window (NSW) Steering Committee has completed a legal gap analysis, national operating agreement, as well as supplementary agreements and joint ventures between 2011 and 2013. The NSW was due for completion by the end 2016 but remains in progress as of the end of 2017.

Various e-government projects including e-treasury, e-procurement, e-post, e-tax, e-inventory and control have been prepared and are at various stages of progress (Inthara, 2016[13]; Luanglath, 2010[14]). Lao is in the process of linking customs with the Automated System for Customs Data (ASYCUDA).

Stakeholder engagement

For all new draft regulations, there is a requirement that stakeholders should be consulted at least twice. Law on Making Legislation 2012 contains many articles about consultation. The Decision on Impact Assessment underlines the importance of consultation and makes the specific minimum requirement of a 60-day consultation period for the draft Impact Assessment Note with draft legislation and draft explanatory note. The Impact Assessment Note also includes a section on comments received, which can potentially explain why inputs have been taken into account or rejected. However, there is no existing guideline to inform ministries of the process they need to undertake this. There is limited but increasing compliance with this requirement. The Impact Assessment Note is not currently published with the final promulgated legislation.

The Lao National Chamber of Commerce and Industry (LNCCI) is a private sector body representing private sector interests, but with clear government involvement. The LNCCI has a particular interest to represent SMEs. The LNCCI is regularly consulted on draft regulations and receive support from professional legal advisory firms to comment on them. They may also funnel draft legislation to other Chambers for comment. The DOSMEP is collaborating to support the SME Service Centre within the LNCCI. The centre is expected to play a role in regulatory consultation. The LNCCI hopes to use their new SME Centre as a forum for SME consultation. The LNCCI is headquartered in Vientiane but has plans to establish an office in each region soon.

The public may also call hotlines to the Prime Minister's Office and some ministries, such as the Ministry of Finance to express concerns (Laotian Times, 2017[15]).

Appeals

Regulatory appeal options are very limited for SMEs in Lao PDR. For example, there is no mechanism for a domestic investor to appeal a decision by the Ministry of Planning and Investment. Administrative decisions cannot be challenged before a court. As a result, local SMEs are highly unlikely to challenge regulatory decisions. In practice, regulatory disputes are rather more frequently settled by negotiation or submission. An example of an explicit arrangement for an appeal is set out in the Decision of Food Inspection No. 297 (Ministry of Public Health, 2012[16]).

Box 5.4. Appeal process in the decision on food inspection No. 297/MOH 24/02/2012

Article 35 on Appeals:

Where a person or legal entity is aggrieved by a decision of an inspector, he or she has the right to file an administrative appeal to the director of the Food and Drug Department (FDD), stating the grounds for the claim. The director shall submit his or her decision regarding the claim within 30 days of receipt of the appeal. Where the person is still not satisfied, he or she may make an administrative appeal to the minister within 45 days of receipt of the Director General's submission. The minister shall render his or her decision within 60 days or receipt of the appeal.

Where the person is still not satisfied, he or she has the right to take the action to court in accordance with relevant Lao PDR legislations (Ministry of Public Health, 2012[16]).

Source: Ministry of Public Health (2012), *Decision on Food Inspection No. 297/MOH*, http://extwprlegs1.fao.org/docs/pdf/lao141174.pdf.

The Law on Judgment Enforcement provides for the execution of final, legally effective and proper court instructions, orders, decisions at first instance, decisions on appeal, decisions on cassation, and other juridical acts. The law gives the executive branch, through the MOJ, strong powers to issue orders to enforce court judgments, including the seizure of assets. Judgment enforcement officers may issue orders to confiscate, seize or move property, subject to notice to the asset owner or debtor. Before being sold at auction to pay off the debt, the assets must be evaluated by an evaluation committee and the evaluation result published. Fines and other measures are applicable to persons or entities that do not comply with enforceable court judgments.

SME linkage policies

The Law on the Promotion of SMEs encourages co-operation between SMEs and large size enterprises and foreign investment enterprises. It includes a number of policy objectives and some measures for their achievement as follows:

- Increasing productivity.
- Accessing and expanding markets.
- Business clustering.
- Allocating business location.
- Promoting advanced technology utilisation.
- Using and protecting intellectual property (IP): also facilitating SMEs on registration, managing and protecting IP.
- Providing and accessing information.

The Government of Lao PDR, in collaboration with a third party, provides infrastructure, training and business-matching services for SMEs to connect with foreign investors through the Lao SME programme.

The Amended Investment Promotion Law 2016 has increased government scrutiny of domestic investors conducting business outside the Lao PDR - now subject to approval by the One-Stop Service Office of the Ministry of Planning and Investment (MPI) (Box 5.5).

Special economic zones

Lao has been developing special economic zones (SEZs) since the early 2000s. To date, ten SEZs have been established, of which two are fully operational. The first SEZ, Savan-Seno, successfully attracts investors from many different economic sectors and helps diversifies the Lao's economy, which is otherwise heavily dependent on natural resource extraction. The Lao government is currently preparing an SEZ law that will require SEZs to have their own regulatory framework, according to international practice (OECD, forthcoming[17]).

Responsible business conduct

Lao PDR aims to improve its regulatory framework for responsible business conduct (RBC). The Law on Investment Promotion of Lao PDR includes a detailed section of responsible business obligations (Art. 69) for investors, and also features a section (Art. 70) on environmental obligations. Lao PDR is also considering establishing a focal point for RBC within the government. The inclusion of extensive investor obligations in its Investment Law is an innovative legal practice that aims to strike a better balance between investors' rights and obligations (OECD, forthcoming[17]).

Box 5.5. Criteria for investing outside of Lao PDR

Article 65 (New) conditions for overseas investment

Domestic investors going to invest overseas shall fulfil the following conditions:

- Have investment target overseas.
- Have the financial reports for the last two financial years as certified by financial authority or independent audit firm.
- Have fulfilled financial obligations due to the Government of Lao PDR in compliance with laws.
- Be in compliance with regulations of the Bank of the Lao PDR, other relevant laws and regulations of Lao PDR.

Article 66 (New) rights and obligations of domestic investors investing overseas

Domestic investors investing overseas shall have the following rights:

- Bring money and assets to invest overseas and bring them back to the home country after fulfilling their obligations under the laws and regulations of the host country.
- Bring the profits and other incomes generated by their business operation to the home country.
- Obtain facilitation and incentives as per laws and regulations of Lao PDR.
- Employ Lao labour in their overseas-invested enterprise in compliance with Lao PDR laws and regulations and those of the host country.

Domestic investors investing overseas shall also have the following obligations:

- Comply with laws and regulations of the host country.
- Perform reporting regime on financial aspect and operation to the investment one-stop service office in order to inform the Ministry of Finance and Bank of the Lao PDR.

After the end of their overseas investment, the investor may bring back capital and assets to the home country according to the relevant laws (DFDL, 2017[18]).

Sources: *Lao Legal Update: Lao Government Makes Significant Reforms to Investment Promotion Law*, http://www.dfdl.com/resources/legal-and-tax-updates/lao-legal-update-lao-government-makes-significant-reforms-to-investment-promotion-law/.

Recommendations

- **Clarify the specific processes required to achieve policy targets and develop indicators and measures as appropriate to track their progress**. For example, the SME Promotion Strategy sets out policy priorities and indicators to track their achievement but does not include the procedures that need to be taken.
- **Develop national standards that are aligned with international standards for goods and services.** Given that Lao PDR has not yet developed national standards for its products and services, it is an opportunity to begin introducing standards that can be compliant with regional and international trading partners. Harmonise the definition of SMEs across ministries to reduce confusion or inconsistent applications of regulatory policies to SMEs by different ministries.
- **Develop a framework for dealing with regulatory non-compliance, which should be consistently applied**. For example, through a risk-based system.
- **Develop a guideline for conducting stakeholder consultation** to help ministries fulfil this requirement effectively in the introduction of new draft regulations.
- **Impact Assessment Notes that are required for all new regulations, and which include a section on comments received**, should be published along with the final promulgated legislation.

References

DFDL (2017), *Lao Legal Update: Lao Government Makes Significant Reforms to Investment Promotion Law*, http://www.dfdl.com/resources/legal-and-tax-updates/lao-legal-update-lao-government-makes-significant-reforms-to-investment-promotion-law/. [18]

GIZ (2018), *Regional Economic Integration of Laos into ASEAN, Trade and Entrepreneurship Development (RELATED)*, https://www.giz.de/en/worldwide/17473.html. [9]

GIZ (2014), *SMEs in Laos*, http://www.giz.de/en/downloads/giz2014-en-sme-laos.pdf. [3]

Government of Lao PDR (2014), *Standard Law (Amended) No. 49*, http://www.laotradeportal.gov.la/index.php?r=site/display&id=763. [7]

Government of Lao PDR (2012), *Law on Making Legislation (Unofficial translation)*, https://ial-online.org/wp-content/uploads/2018/05/Laos-Making-Legislation-Law.pdf. [2]

Government of Lao PDR (2011), *Law on the Promotion of Small- and Medium-Sized Enterprises (unofficial translation)*, http://www.laoofficialgazette.gov.la/kcfinder/upload/files/Law%20on%20the%20%20Promotion%20of%20%20Small%20and%20Medium%20Sized%20Enterprises.pdf. [4]

Inthara, K. (2016), *E-Government Status of Laos*, https://www.slideshare.net/laonog/egovernment-status-of-laos. [13]

Laotian Times (2017), *Ministry of Finance Opens Hotline for Public*, https://laotiantimes.com/2017/04/20/ministry-finance-opens-hotline-public/. [15]

Luanglath, C. (2010), *Lao National E-Government Project*, http://unpan1.un.org/intradoc/groups/public/documents/ungc/unpan043423.pdf. [14]

Ministry of Agriculture and Fisheries (2016), *Agriculture Development Strategy to 2025 and Vision to the Year 2030*, http://www.maf.gov.la/wp-content/uploads/2016/01/MDS-2025-and-Vision-to-2030-Eng.pdf. [6]

Ministry of Planning and Investment (2018), *Special Economic Zone*, http://www.investlaos.gov.la/index.php/start-up/special-economic-zone. [11]

Ministry of Planning and Investment (2016), *8th Five-Year National Socio-Economic Development Plan 2016-2020*, http://www.la.undp.org/content/lao_pdr/en/home/library/poverty/the-8th-five-year-national-socio-economic-development-plan--2016.html. [8]

Ministry of Public Health (2012), *Decision on Food Inspection No. 297/MOH*, http://extwprlegs1.fao.org/docs/pdf/lao141174.pdf. [16]

OECD (2017), *OECD Investment Policy Reviews: Lao PDR*, OECD Investment Policy Reviews, OECD Publishing, Paris, http://dx.doi.org/10.1787/9789264276055-en. [10]

OECD (forthcoming), *ASEAN SME Policy Index 2018: Boosting Competitiveness and Inclusive* [5]

Growth in ASEAN, OECD Publishing, Paris.

OECD (forthcoming), *Inclusive Investments in GVCs: Opportunities for ASEAN SMEs*, OECD Publishing, Paris. [17]

Phaophongsavath, P. (2017), "Decree on classifying SME categories, PowerPoint presentation", *Small and Medium Enterprises Development in Laos*, https://toi.boi.go.th/information/download/472. [19]

UNDP (2016), *The 8th Five Year National Socio-Economic Development Plan 2016-2020*, http://www.la.undp.org/content/lao_pdr/en/home/library/poverty/the-8th-five-year-national-socio-economic-development-plan--2016.html. [1]

UNDP (2015), *Ministry of Justice Goes Digital and Strives for More Inclusive Participation in Law-making*, http://www.la.undp.org/content/lao_pdr/en/home/presscenter/pressreleases/2015/12/1/ministry-of-justice-goes-digital-and-strives-for-more-inclusive-.html. [12]

Chapter 6. Malaysia

Malaysia has been using good regulatory practice (GRP) tools to enhance productivity and competitiveness. Since 2007, the government has undertaken a number of initiatives through the Modernising Business Regulation (MBR) programme to reduce regulatory burden and facilitate business processes in the country. The government continues to innovate by proactively identifying regulations that affect businesses, including through regular regulatory mapping exercises. E-government activities have also been used to lessen paperwork and ease day-to-day operations of small and medium-sized enterprises (SMEs). More initiatives are being introduced to improve regulatory delivery with a focus on compliance, enforcement and inspection activities. For example, the government has introduced a number of programmes and informational sessions to improve the capacity of businesses - notably SMEs - to comply with new regulations. These initiatives have been introduced with support from academia as well as from industry.

Regulatory context

In 2007, Malaysia launched the Modernising Business Regulation (MBR) programme. The programme envisions enhancing the productivity and competitiveness in the country by modernising the business regulatory structure. This entails the need to progressively improve the quality of new and existing regulations (Figure 6.1).

Figure 6.1. Framework for Modernising Business Regulation in Malaysia

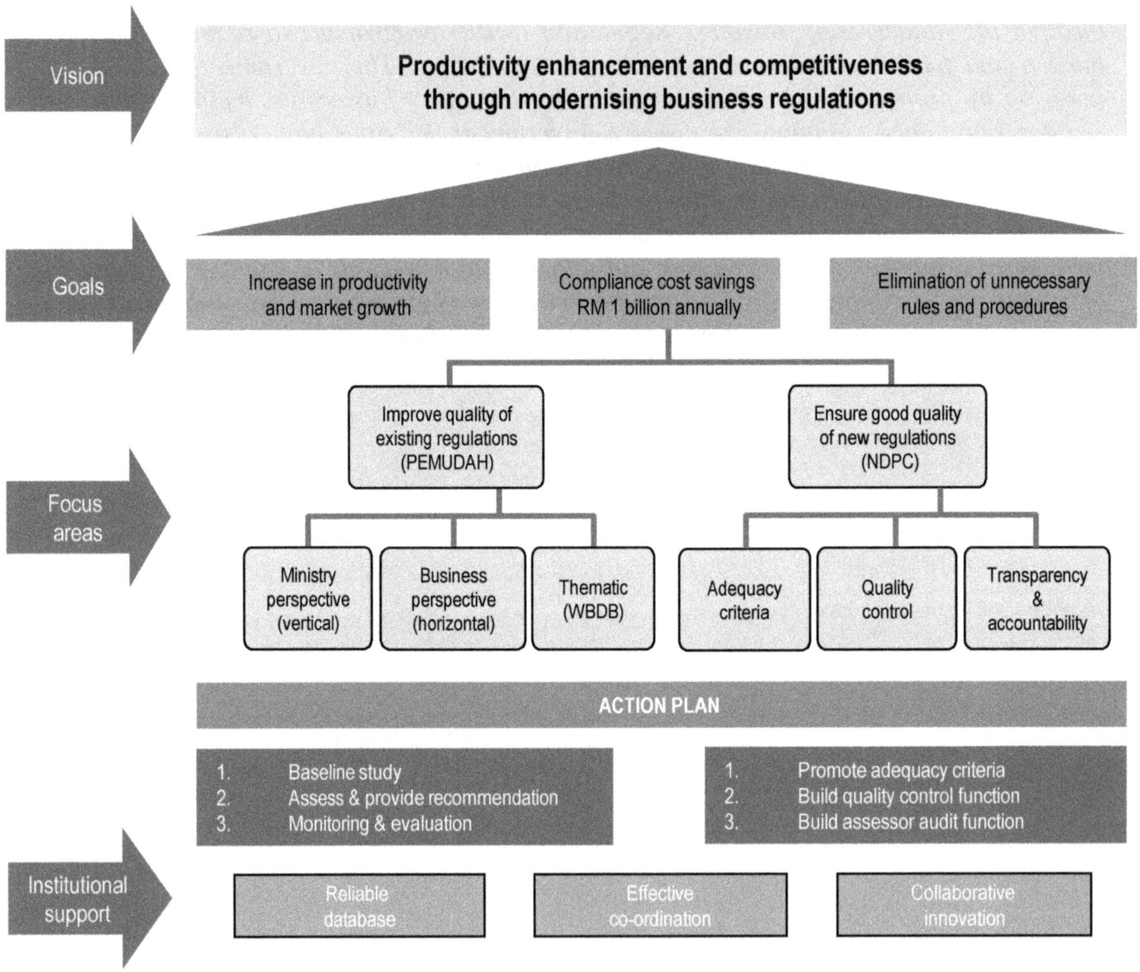

Source: Malaysia Productivity Corporation (2016), *Annual Report on Modernisation of Regulations*, http://www.mpc.gov.my/wp-content/uploads/2016/12/ARMR-2016.pdf.

In the same year, the government established the Special Task Force to Facilitate Business (PEMUDAH), a private-public sector collaboration that is responsible for spearheading work related to public service delivery. The establishment of PEMUDAH and its secretariat, the Malaysia Productivity Corporation (MPC), was motivated by regulatory issues raised in relation to the ease of doing business in Malaysia.

Malaysia envisions becoming a high-income and developed nation by 2020. In line with this vision, Malaysia launched the National Policy for the Development and Implementation of Regulations (NPDIR) in 2013, which aimed to standardise and improve the overall regulatory process and enhance the transparency, accountability, and credibility of regulatory decisions through private-public collaboration and people-centred approach.

Prior to the NPDIR, there has been no policy that sets the direction and principles for the implementation of good regulatory practices. Nonetheless, Malaysia has continuously committed itself to adopting and sharing best practices for implementing good policies in the country.

Malaysia's regulatory reform initiatives are well reflected in the NPDIR. It has provided the government with a structured approach to addressing public policy objectives and promoting good governance in the country. Initial efforts have been focused on reducing inefficiencies and burden in existing regulations faced by both the public and the business sector, notably SMEs. The National Small and Medium Development Act of 2017 has also emphasised the importance of reviewing and simplifying business-related regulations.

SME development landscape

Small and medium-sized enterprises (SMEs) in Malaysia represent 98.5% of the total business establishments in the country. In 2016, SMEs contributed to around 36.6% of the country's gross domestic product (GDP) and 18% of the total exports (OECD, forthcoming[1]). Given its growing importance in the overall economy, the government continues to encourage business formation and the growth of enterprises, notably among potential high-growth and innovative firms. To do this, the country has set important targets for SMEs by 2020 – that is, it aims to increase the contribution of Malaysian SMEs to the overall GDP to 41% and of exports to 23%.

A distinct feature of the Malaysian SME landscape is the focus on *Bumiputera* entrepreneurs, which represent around 50% of the country's SMEs. *Bumiputera* refers to the diverse ethnic or indigenous community in the country, such as the Malays, Orang Aslis and natives from Sabah and Sarawak. A number of programmes and initiatives have been introduced to encourage the growth of SMEs that fall under this category.

Furthermore, Malaysia has emphasised increasing entrepreneurship among women. The country's SME authority, SME Corporation Malaysia (SME Corp.), has introduced a wide range of programmes to strengthen the role of women in the Malaysian economy. This includes a number of training sessions and seminars that are aimed at fostering awareness and receiving feedback and ideas concerning issues that women entrepreneurs face.

Regulatory governance

Institutional and regulatory setup

Table 6.1. Institutional and regulatory setup

	Government
State structure	Federal government
Head of state	**Yang di-Pertuan Agong (YDPA),** an elected monarch that holds extensive power as defined by the constitution. The YDPA oversees the executive with the advice of the cabinet and holds power over the legislative body and can dismiss or dissolve parliament, with the guidance of the Prime Minister.
Executive	**Prime Minister** is appointed by the YDPA and heads the executive body and government. **Cabinet** is also appointed by the YDPA and is collectively responsible for reporting back to parliament.
Legislative	Bicameral • **Lower house** (House of Representatives or *Dewan Rakyat)* with 222 elected members from single-member districts. • **Upper house** (Senate or *Dewan Negara)* with 70 members serving within a three-year term, 26 of which are elected by assemblies and the rest appointed by the YDPA, with the advice of the Prime Minister.
Legal system	Common law and, to a lesser extent, Islamic law Legislative appeals can be done through the **Magistrate Court, Sessions Court, the High Court, the Court of Appeals, and the Federal Court**.
Administrative-territorial structure	13 states All states adopt a Westminster Parliamentary system with a unicameral state legislative assembly. There are nine monarchical states (Johor, Kelantan, Negeri, Pahang, Perak, Perlis, Selangor, Sembilan, and Terengganu), seven of which are headed by sultans who are eligible for the position of YDPA. The rest of the states (Malacca, Penang, Sabah, and Sarawak) are headed by governors.
Ministry or agency responsible for SMEs or SME-related issues	**SME Corporation**, a body under the Ministry of International Trade and Industry, responsible for formulating, co-ordinating, and overseeing policies and strategies on SMEs.
Regulatory oversight body or bodies	• **Special Task Force to Facilitate Business (***Pasukan Petugas Khas Pemudahcara Pernuagaan,* PEMUDAH*)* oversees the service delivery of policies related to investment or starting a business. Representatives of PEMUDAH include individuals from both the public and private sectors. • **National Development Planning Committee (NPDC**) is responsible for overseeing and assessing the overall implementation of the National Policy for the Development and Implementation of Regulations (NPDIR) and also examines all regulatory impact statements (RIS) of regulations to check for quality and appropriateness. • **Malaysia Productivity Corporation (MPC),** a body under the Ministry of International Trade and Industry, is responsible for delivering high impact services with regard to productivity enhancement, innovation and global competitiveness. MPC also helps implement the NPDIR and assists the NPDC in developing and reviewing regulatory impact assessments (RIA) and RIS, developing programmes and guidelines, and conducting related reviews and capacity building programmes.
Other support structures within government on regulatory policy	• **Companies Commission of Malaysia** is responsible for all business registration services in the country. • **National Institute of Public Administration (INTAN)** supports MPC in providing capacity building training for RIA and RIS. • **Attorney General's Chamber** provides legal advice to the cabinet or minister.

Regulatory process

There are a number of legislative and regulatory instruments that affect businesses and these are formulated at the parliament, state level, or concurrently between the parliament and the state.

At the parliamentary level, a bill can be introduced by either house. Once this has been reviewed and agreed within the responsible house, it would then need to pass it to the other house for review and approval. The contents of the bill would need to undergo a number of readings and discussion among the members. Finally, the bill is passed on to the *Yang di-Pertuan Agong* (YDPA) for assent.

At the state level, ministries or regulators can formulate their own policies. Together with the proposal, the responsible ministry would need to provide a regulatory impact assessment (RIA), consult with the public, and prepare the regulatory impact statement (RIS). Ministries can also draft their RIA concurrently when drafting laws. The RIA and RIS are then reviewed by the Malaysia Productivity Corporation (MPC) and the National Development and Planning Committee (NPDC). If the quality of the RIS is deemed unsatisfactory, the issues would need to be addressed by the responsible ministry and then reviewed once again by MPC and the NPDC before it is passed on the cabinet of ministers for approval and then to parliament for it to be passed as an Act (OECD, 2015[2]).

Figure 6.2. Regulatory-making process in Malaysia

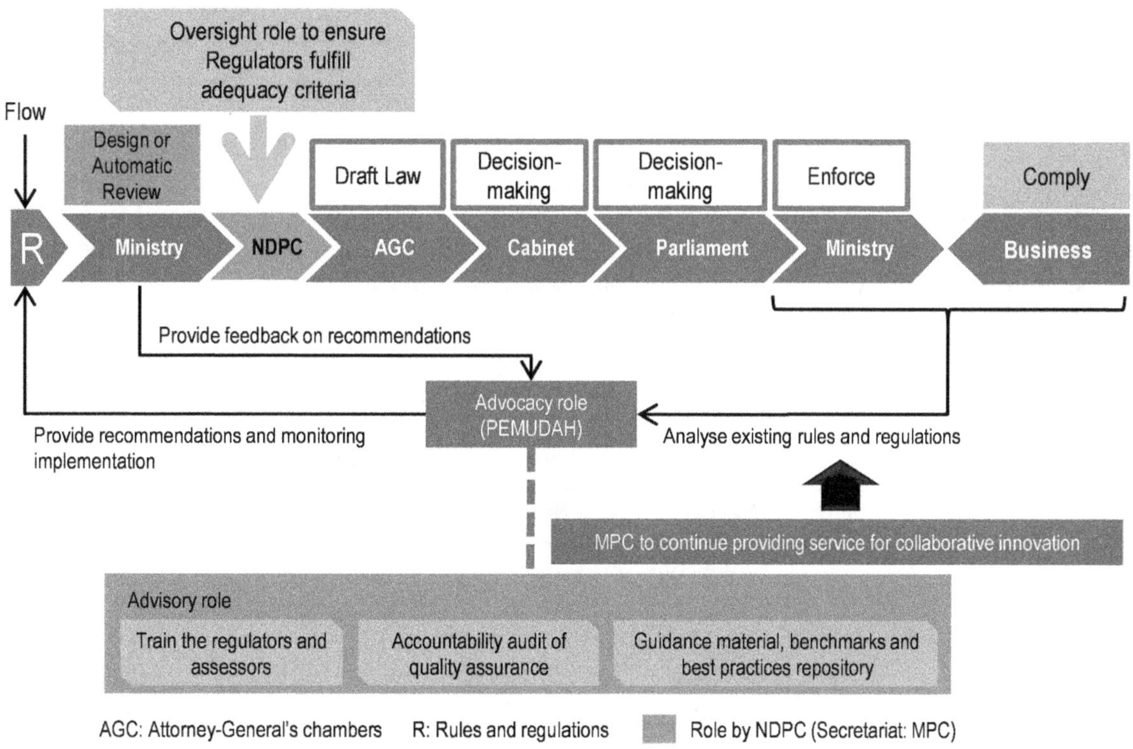

Source: Malaysia Productivity Corporation (2016), *Annual Report on Modernisation of Regulations*, http://www.mpc.gov.my/wp-content/uploads/2016/12/ARMR-2016.pdf.

Business laws and regulations

There is no separate regulatory policy directed to SMEs. SMEs in Malaysia are therefore subject to all business regulations unless otherwise specified (World Bank, 2017[3]). Nonetheless, in 2017, the government passed a National SME Bill to help better facilitate the oversight of SME policies and programmes. The Bill aimed to complete the realisation of the SME Master Plan (2012-20) launched by the government in July 2012. The SME Master Plan intended to create a conducive ecosystem to accelerate the growth of SMEs towards achieving a high-income economy. The plan covered all sectors, regions, and strategic areas, complementing the existing national economic strategies and outlining 32 measures and 6 high impact programmes that would help achieve the 4 strategic goals of the SME Master Plan.

Table 6.2. Business-related laws and regulations in Malaysia

Type	Description
Banking and credit laws	Islamic Banking Act 1983 Banking and Financial Institutions Act 1989 Central Bank of Malaysia Act 1958
Commercial and company laws	Companies Act 1965 (revised 1973, amended 2007) Companies Regulations 2017; Companies Act 2016
Labour laws	Employment Act 1955; Code of Conduct for Industrial Harmony and Areas for Co-operation and Agreed Industrial Relations Practices
Customs law	Customs Act

Source: World Bank (2017), *Law Library*, http://www.doingbusiness.org/law-library/ (accessed on 8 March 2018).

Since 2005, ministries, agencies and institutions involved in SME development programmes have adopted a single SME definition. As a result of a growing SME sector and new developments in the economy, a new SME definition has been endorsed and simplified in 2013 (SME Corporation Malaysia, 2013[4]). SMEs can be qualified by either its number of employees **or** sales turnover:

Table 6.3. SME definition in Malaysia

Type	Micro		Small		Medium	
	No. of employees	Sales turnover (MYR)	No. of employees	Sales turnover (MYR)	No. of employees	Sales turnover (MYR)
Manufacturing	< 5	< 300 000	5 to < 75	300 000 to < 15 million	75 to ≤ 200	15 million to ≤ 50 million
Services and other sectors	< 5	< 300 000	5 to < 30	300 000 to < 3 million	30 to ≤ 75	3 million to ≤ 20 million

Source: Information provided by SME Corporation Malaysia, 2018.

Business registration

The Companies Commission of Malaysia (*Surahanjaya Syarikat Malaysia*, SSM) is responsible for all business registration in the country. There are three forms of business entities in Malaysia: sole proprietor (enterprise or trading co), partnership, or private limited company. For the latter, the enterprise would need to specify in its articles of association the type of company (limited or unlimited). In order to register a business, the company would need to prepare the needed information and supporting documents and visit the nearest SSM office. The certificate can often be obtained within one hour after payment. Upon registration and incorporation, the enterprise or company would need to obtain the needed licences and permits before it is allowed to operate (Suruhanjaya Syarikat Malaysia, 2018[5]).

Table 6.4. Registration requirements in Malaysia

	Sole proprietorship	Partnership	Company
Description	One-person business	Business owned by at least 2 and not more than 20 partners	Limited by shares
Registration requirements	• At least 18 years • Malaysian citizen or permanent resident • Company name and business activity • Photocopy of identity card • Supporting proof and documents		• Minimum of two subscribers • Minimum of two directors (has not been bankrupt, convicted, or imprisoned for prescribed offences) • Licensed or accredited company secretary • Company name and business activity • Incorporation documents (memorandum and articles of association specifying whether limited or unlimited and other supporting proof)
Setup fee	MYR 30 (when using personal name) MYR 60 (when using trade name) + MYR 5 for each branch + MYR 10.60 business information print-out	MYR 60 (when using trade name) + MYR 5 for each branch + MYR 10.60 business information print-out	Fees between MYR 1 000-70 000 depending on authorised share capital + MYR 30 for name registration
Continuity of the business entity	Renewal for a period of 1 year and not more than 5 years (with fee)		Perpetual succession unless wound up
Closure of business	Cessation Bankruptcy Death of owner Court order	Winding up or striking off	Closure of business

Source: Suruhanjaya Syarikat Malaysia (2018), *Registration*, www.ssm.com.my/en/services_registration (accessed on 8 March 2018).

Highlights of regulatory opportunities and challenges to support SMEs

Administrative simplification

Since 2007, PEMUDAH has been working with the Malaysia Productivity Cooperation (MPC) to address regulatory issues concerning the ease of doing business. In the 10th Malaysia Plan (2010-2015), MPC was granted the mandate to improve the government's regulatory management system, which led MPC to undertake a review to assess, repeal or modify unnecessary rules and compliance costs that negatively impact businesses or the economy.

This regulatory review was carried out as part of Malaysia's Modernising Business Regulation (MBR) programme, which included the following key initiatives implemented by the Malaysia Productivity Corporation (Malaysia Productivity Corporation, 2016, p. 10[6]):

- Reducing Unnecessary Regulatory Burden (RURB).
- Facilitating initiatives in Ease of Doing Business.
- Conducting comprehensive scanning of business licensing.
- Promoting Business Enabling Framework for 18 services subsectors.
- Developing policy and guidelines for ensuring the quality of new regulations such as the National Policy on the Development and Implementation of Regulations.

A Guideline on Reducing Regulatory Burden was established to help guide policymakers in identifying and analysing areas for burden reduction. Initial activities under the programme have been focused on increasing efficiency within the government by simplifying the administrative requirements related to the issuance of permits and licences.

Box 6.1. Identifying regulatory burden in Malaysia

In Malaysia, regulatory burdens are considered as regulations or processes that can adversely impact businesses such as those that require a change in behaviour or practices. Some of the costs faced by businesses usually fall into four categories:

1. Administrative and operational requirements, e.g. reporting, record keeping, legal advice, training.
2. Requirements on production and supply, e.g. prescriptions on production, labelling requirements, occupational registration requirements.
3. Requirements on the characteristics of the product or supply, e.g. providing airbags for all motor vehicles and requiring specific topics for teachers or trainers to focus on.
4. Prohibitions that lead to loss of production and marketing opportunities, e.g. where certain products are banned or strictly regulated.

Source: Malaysia Productivity Corporation (2015), *Reducing Unnecessary Regulatory Burdens (RURB) – Malaysia Productivity Corporation (MPC)*, http://www.mpc.gov.my/reducing-unnecessary-regulatory-burdens-rurb-2/.

Subsequently, PEMUDAH expanded the Modernising Business Licensing (MBL) programme, which involved reforming a number of business licensing process across the government – from ministries to agencies and from the national to the federal level (Malaysia Productivity Corporation, 2016[6]). As a result of the MBL review carried out between 2011 and 2014, 767 business licences were re-engineered, 454 converted into composite licences and 29 were abolished (Malaysia Productivity Corporation, 2016, p. 10[6]). Consequently, the government was able to save up around MYR 729 million (approximately USD 185 000 000) (Jayasiri, 2016[7]; Malaysia Productivity Corporation, 2016[6]). A similar exercise was also carried out at the local level across the 13 Malaysian states. 2 659 licences were reviewed and were then reduced to 1 915 with an estimated cost savings of MYR 1.7 billion.

Additionally, a Business Licensing Electronic Support System (BLESS, www.bless.gov.my) was launched to serve as an online one-stop shop for business licensing in the country (Box 6.2).

Box 6.2. Improving business licensing in Malaysia

The Malaysian government launched the Business Licensing Electronic Support System (BLESS, www.bless.gov.my) as part of the Modernising Business Regulation Programme. The system served as an online one-stop shop for business licensing in the country and aimed to make license issuance more efficient by automating the process. The online tracking and monitoring function of the system allowed for faster, more transparent and more predictable business licensing processes.

The system currently provides the following features: multiple licensing application; simultaneous processing and updating by respective agencies; composite and standard forms; online submission, approval and notification; online query; online tracking and monitoring; electronic payment; feedback mechanism; and bilingual access. As of December 2017, services linked to the application of 214 licences from 75 federal agencies are available in the system. More licences from other agencies are being integrated into the system. Each licence included in the system will have their own set of conditions and requirements based on current policies set by licensing agencies. To facilitate this, the website provides businesses with a checklist and a set of guidelines as they submit their application.

Sources: Jayasiri (2016), Good Regulatory Practice (GRP) in Malaysia, Presentation, https://www.capam.org/files/2016BiennialPresentations/ExperiencesOnGRPImplementation-J_Jayasiri.pdf; Malaysia Productivity Corporation (2016), *Annual Report on Modernisation of Regulations*, http://www.mpc.gov.my/wp-content/uploads/2016/12/ARMR-2016.pdf.

The MBL programme was followed by a Reducing Unnecessary Regulatory Burden (RURB) initiative in 2014 and 2015. Through this initiative, 23 regulatory burden reduction activities were carried out between 2014 and 2015 for specific industries such as construction, healthcare, logistics, and oil and gas and other issues related to the movement of goods and registration requirements. These activities were considered to generate around MYR 2.5 billion in savings (Malaysia Productivity Corporation, 2016[6]).

Table 6.5. Summary of administrative simplification activities and cost savings

Initiative or programme	Year	Objective	Result	Potential cost savings (MYR)
Modernising Business Licensing – national	2011-14	Review 767 licences	29 licences abolished Reduced to 454 licences	729 million
Modernising Business Licensing – state	2011-14	Review 2 659 licences	Reduced to 1 915 licences	1.7 billion
Reducing Unnecessary Regulatory Burden	2014-15	Implement 23 regulatory burden reduction activities	Provided recommendations	2.5 billion

Source: Malaysia Productivity Corporation (2016), *Annual Report on Modernisation of Regulations*, http://www.mpc.gov.my/wp-content/uploads/2016/12/ARMR-2016.pdf.

Apart from the government-wide administrative simplification programmes, the government has also targeted efforts in18 services subsectors to identify bottlenecks and facilitate business-related processes. For example, Box 6.3 shows how burden reduction was carried out for licensing in private hospitals. The exercise involved simplifying regulations and the regulatory process by ensuring coherence across multiple agencies involved.

Box 6.3. Case study: Reducing Unnecessary Regulatory Burden on private hospitals

Background

A number of members from the Association of Private Hospitals of Malaysia (APHM) highlighted that the process of renewing their hospitals' operating licensing was tedious and time consuming. This appeared to be the most burdensome aspect of private hospital regulation, which is contributed by various factors which include the requirement for documentation during the submission of a renewal application.

The business found that applying for operating licence renewals requires a lot of documentation that contribute to **heavy burdens in paperwork and administrative overheads** for private hospitals. For example, if the hospital has 500 personnel, at least 500 interactions (with regulators) are required to prepare the documentation for licensing personnel, all documents are to be submitted in 3 sets and Annual Practising Certificate (APCs) are to be validated. The renewal fee and the cost of processing amounts to more than MYR 10 000 and it takes approximately 9 months to obtain the approval.

Issues to be addressed

The tedious process of operating licence renewal application and the heavy paperwork (documentation requirements) is burdensome to businesses.

Recommendation

The use of information technology (e.g. online licence renewal application for private hospitals' or clinics) and a move from "evidence-based" to "information-based" procedure (removing duplication of requirements by different regulators within the Ministry of Health) in the process of renewal licence application.

Source: Malaysia Productivity Corporation (2016), *Annual Report on Modernisation of Regulations*, http://www.mpc.gov.my/wp-content/uploads/2016/12/ARMR-2016.pdf.

E-government

As Malaysia continues to adapt and implement good regulatory practices, new tools and platforms are needed to support this. The Digital Malaysia programme headed by the Multimedia Development Corporation (MDEC) under the Ministry of Communications and Multimedia (MCMC) aims to create a more connected economy. This includes facilitating processes for SMEs, continuously reviewing the quality of regulations and streamlining processes to enable the use of these tools.

The SME Hub, formerly known as One Referral Centre, is a platform operated by SME Corp. Malaysia and serves as a one-stop shop for SMEs to access information on various business aspects (start-up, access to finance, industry development and market access, etc.) both on line and off line. At present, the SME Hub is rolled out in almost all states and an SME Hub-on-wheels have also been developed as a way to further reach out to SMEs in the rural areas. Other information available in the Hub includes programmes from partner organisations and government agencies such as *Suruhanjaya Syarikat Malaysia* (SSM), *Majlis Amanah Rakyat* (People's Trust Council, MARA), the Central Bank of Malaysia and Telekom Malaysia, among others.

Malaysia has been progressively searching for new ways to encourage SMEs to adopt and use new technologies, as a way to help SMEs connect better with their clients and increase their potential of increasing their client base.

Box 6.4. Adopting e-payment for SMEs in Malaysia

As a way to encourage SMEs to adopt hassle-free and secure payment systems, the government had introduced an e-payment system.

However, in order to be part of the scheme, the business must ensure that they are recognised as legal entities under the Business Act 1956 or Company Act 1965 and fulfil the criteria of an SME. In order to benefit from this system, interested businesses must enable their e-payment service through a Third Party Acquirer: www.mangepay.com or www.revenue.com.my.

Source: Information provided by the Government of Malaysia, 2017.

Regulatory quality management

Regulatory impact assessment

According to the 10th Malaysia Plan (2011-15), the Malaysia Productivity Corporation (MPC) is responsible for undertaking research in productivity and the impact of regulations on SMEs. There is no distinct regulatory process for SME regulations. All regulations need to undertake a regulatory impact assessment (RIA) and are required to systematically identify and assess the cost and benefits underlying these regulatory objectives. This also applies to feasible alternatives, including non-regulatory options, as a way to ensure that all possible options are systematically reviewed and chosen.

In 2011, the government had developed a roadmap for the implementation of GRP within the next five years. The initial phases of the roadmap focused on engaging and consulting with stakeholders in the government and private sector on the proposed plan and implementation activities. Following the responses, three pilot projects were carried out as a way to assess possible implementation issues in 2012. These tests, therefore, led to the introduction of the National Policy for the Development and Implementation of Regulations (NPDIR) in 2013.

Figure 6.3. Roadmap to GRP implementation

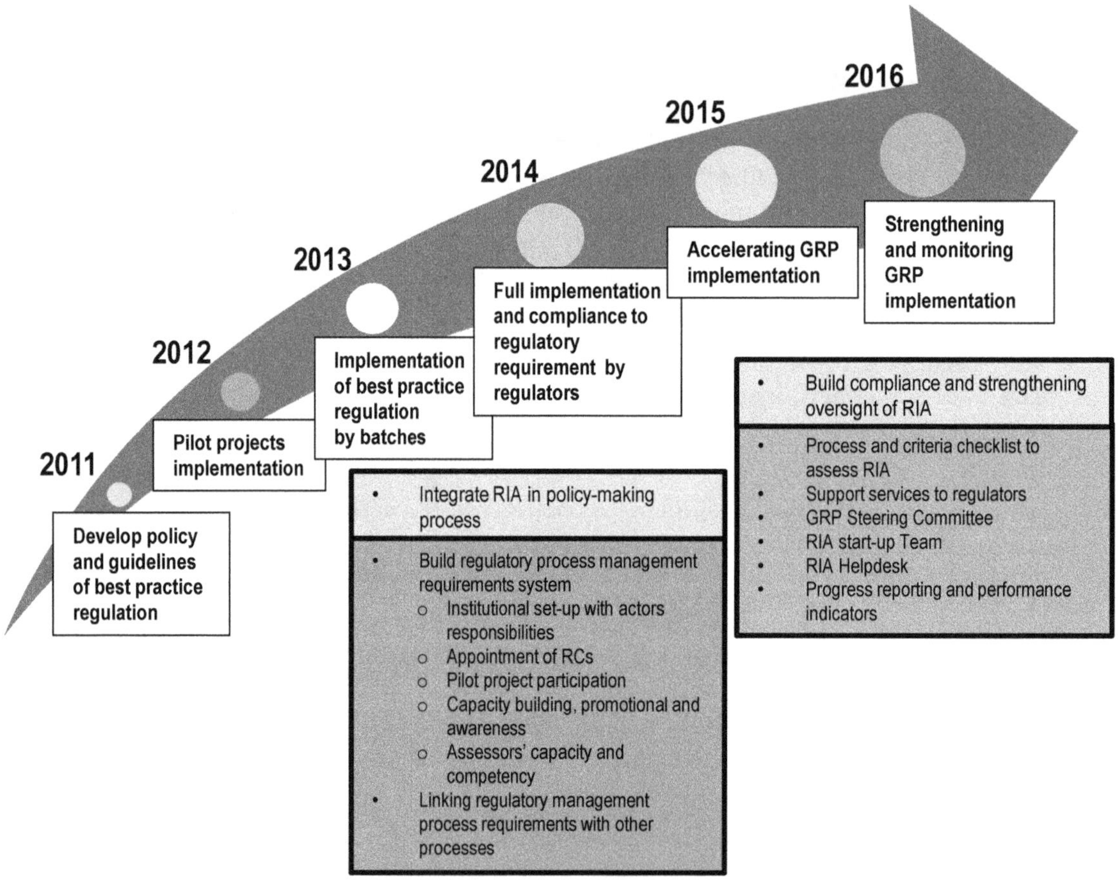

Source: Malaysia Productivity Corporation (2016), *Annual Report on Modernisation of Regulations*, http://www.mpc.gov.my/wp-content/uploads/2016/12/ARMR-2016.pdf.

The NPDIR paved the way towards the introduction of the concept of good regulatory practices, notably regulatory impact analysis (RIA). RIA was introduced as an important step in the decision- and regulatory-making process and serves as a way to further enhance transparency and guarantee the quality and credibility of new regulations, including regulatory proposals that concern small and medium-sized enterprises (SMEs). The following years then focused on training and outreach as a way to accelerate GRP implementation and disseminate its use and importance among regulators and stakeholders. Events focused on best practice sharing are also organised on a regular basis by the MPC to help strengthen and monitor its implementation.

Following the introduction and pilot of RIA, the number of regulatory notifications forms (RNFs) received by MPC increased from 41 in 2014 to 54 in 2015. The number of completed regulatory proposals (regulatory impact statement or RIS) also increased from five to seven in the respective years. Around 50% of RNFs received that year focused on health and safety and 20% on domestic and consumer affairs. Since then, the number of RIA done for regulatory proposals has continued to increase and its quality improving over time.

Box 6.5. Considering small businesses in the development of new regulations

The Best Practice Regulation Handbook mentions that regulations may have a disproportionate impact on small business. This entails that small firms would need to allocate a greater proportion of their resources to meet regulatory requirements. Therefore, it is necessary to ensure that decision-makers are aware of the various impacts on small businesses. For example, any new regulation introduced should consider the degree of impact on individual small businesses, the number for small businesses affected and whether the overall impact on small business is proportionate to the impact on other businesses or groups. This is given particular attention to compliance cost impact on small businesses and the ability or inability of these businesses to absorb such costs.

Source: Malaysia Productivity Corporation (2013), *Best Practice Regulation Handbook*, http://www.mpc.gov.my/wp-content/uploads/2017/04/Best-Practice-Handbook-2013.pdf.

Several documents have been developed to support policymakers and regulators to implement the NPDIR, namely: the Guideline on Reducing Unnecessary Burden, the Best Practice Regulation Handbook, a Quick Reference Best Practice Regulation Handbook, and the Guideline on Public Consultation Procedures (Malaysia Productivity Corporation, 2013[8]).

RIA is exempted in cases where the impact of the proposed regulation is minor and does not significantly change existing regulatory arrangements. In this situation, the regulator may implement the regulation after the approval of the decision maker, in accordance with the law, and MPC is informed when the regulation has been issued (Malaysia Productivity Corporation, 2016[6]).

Ex post *evaluation*

The NPDIR specifies that all requirements on regulatory process management would apply to all concerned regulators. Since 2015, the government continues to focus on reviewing regulations according to specific sectors and topics as a way to make them more targeted. To date, the government has reviewed regulations and processes that are linked to logistics, medical professional, construction, professional services in the building industry, warehousing services and processed food products (Malaysia Productivity Corporation, 2015[9]).

Plans for regulatory review are prepared by regulators on an annual basis. The regulators subsequently notify the MPC with this information in January of each year, which are compiled in an annual regulatory report to inform the government and the public of proposed regulatory actions for the year. This also provides the possibility for stakeholders to be familiar with upcoming activities and contribute to the process.

Regulatory delivery

Regulatory compliance

Compliance with standards

Non-tariff barriers (NTBs), particularly linked to specific standards, impede the growth of Malaysian SMEs into the global value chains (GVCs). Oftentimes, this is linked to the lack of capacity from SMEs to be able to cope with emerging standards and labelling requirements that need to be met from trading or potential trading partners. Non-recognition of certain standards, labelling requirements, as well as importing requirements can create significant burden among SMEs that are willing to grow and export abroad

The initiatives in reviewing NTBs are carried out at the federal level. This allows the government to identify areas in which regulation can be improved, consolidated or simplified to reduce unnecessary burdens related to these issues. Analysis is not conducted on the non-tariff measures (NTMs) per se, but rather on the regulatory process and the procedural requirements associated with the NTBs, which cut across various agencies and ministries, including regulatory and enforcement practices that might impede the productivity in trade-related businesses.

In parallel, a number of capacity building workshops and programmes are organised by SME Corp. Malaysia as well as relevant ministries and agencies as a way to strengthen the capacity and capability of SMEs (SME Corporation Malaysia, 2018[10]).

Ministries have introduced ways to standardise the branding, packaging, and labelling of a product. For example, the Ministry of Agriculture and Agro-based Industry (MOA) through the Muda Agricultural Development Authority (MADA) supports agricultural entrepreneurs to upgrade the branding and packaging of agricultural products.

Stakeholder engagement

In October 2014, the government released a set of guidelines on public consultation procedures. The guideline ensures that the following principles are met: 1) transparency with accessibility; 2) accountability; 3) commitment; 4) inclusiveness that is equitable; 5) timely and informative; and 6) integrity with respect.

Figure 6.4. Public consultation process in Malaysia

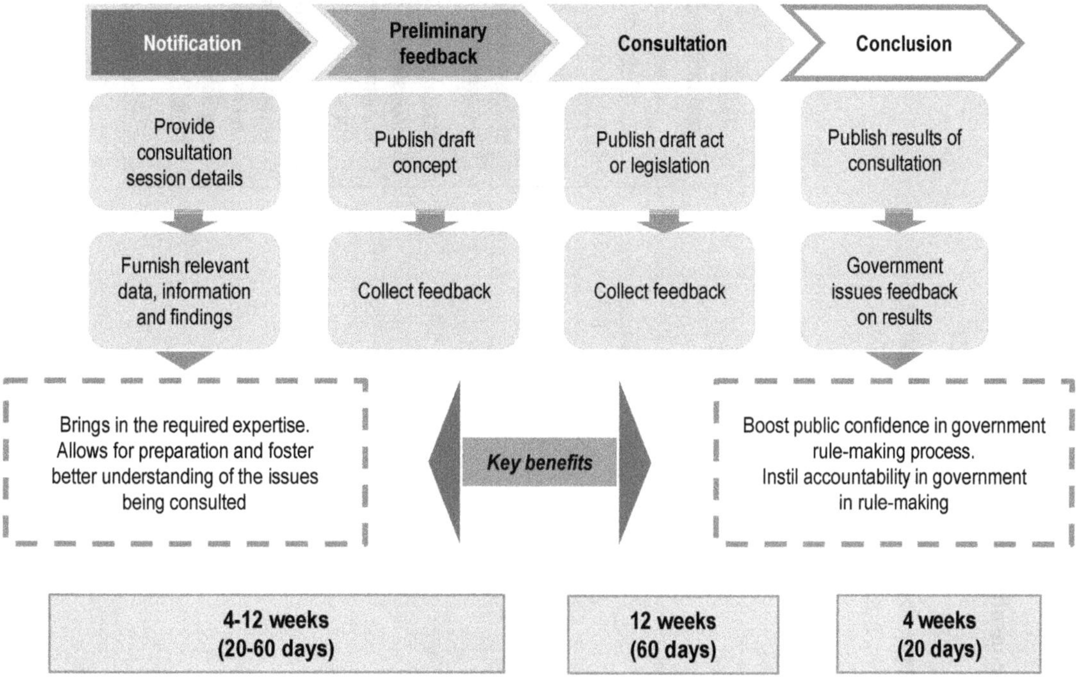

Source: Malaysia Productivity Corporation (2016), *Annual Report on Modernisation of Regulations*, http://www.mpc.gov.my/wp-content/uploads/2016/12/ARMR-2016.pdf.

The Government of Malaysia strives to create an inclusive public consultation for citizens and businesses. Concerned stakeholders are involved throughout the regulatory process – from notification to the finalisation of the draft regulation.

PEMUDAH, the Special Task Force to Facilitate Business, serves as an important agency that drives the implementation of good regulatory practices and helps strengthen discussion with the public sector. In addition to taking an active role in the regulatory-making process, PEMUDAH also holds monthly meetings with the public to discuss initiatives to enhance the country's business environment. To do this, the government has established a number of focus groups and working groups to devote their attention to specific issues of interest. Furthermore, PEMUDAH also welcomes complaints and suggestions through their web portal from the public, to consider in their annual work programme (Malaysia Productivity Corporation, 2016[6]).

The government is currently in the process of developing a unified online public consultation platform to strengthen the implementation of good regulatory practices in the country. The aim of the website is to create an even more inclusive regulatory process by developing an accountable and transparent system.

Figure 6.5. Framework for establishing a unified public consultation mechanism in Malaysia

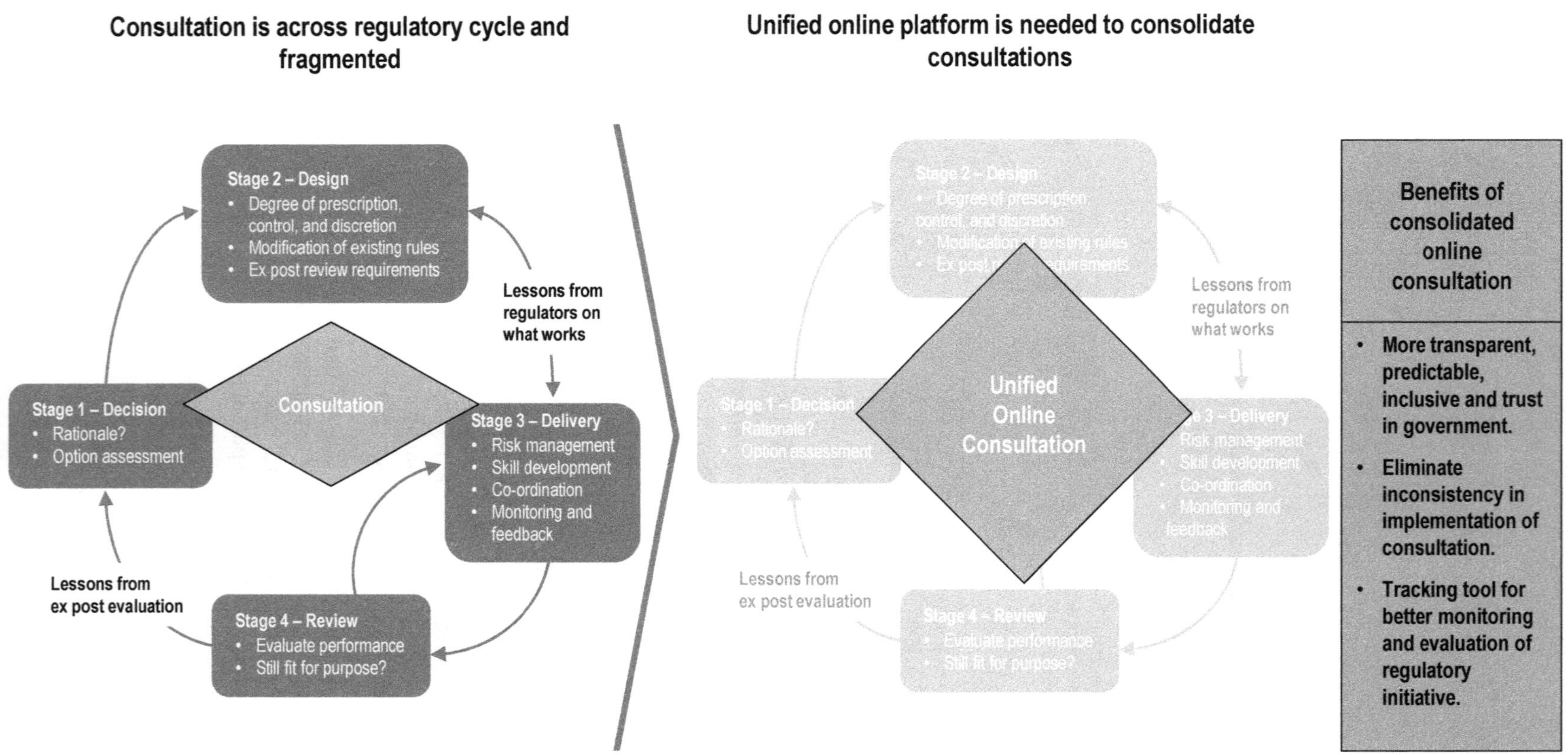

Source: Figure provided by Malaysia Productivity Corporation, 2018.

SME linkage policies

Information and networking

To support potential exporters, businesses can access the Beginner's Guide to Exporting, published by the Malaysia External Trade Development Corporation (MATRADE, 2016[11]). The guide is regulatory update by MATRADE and provides businesses or corporations with the needed information when deciding to export products, including the various legal requirements and international requirements and standards needed to succeed.

Table 6.6. Capacity building programmes in Malaysia

Programme	Description
Business Accelerator Programme (BAP)	An integrated assistance programme to enhance capabilities of small and medium-sized enterprises (SMEs) through business advisory and financial support. The programme supports a wide range of capacity building initiatives to assist SMEs to grow their businesses locally and abroad. Two types of financing available under the Business Accelerator Programme (BAP) are Matching Assistance and Soft Loan.
SME University Internship Programme	This programme helps link SMEs to universities as a way to create and strengthen synergies between SMEs and universities. The programme aims to assist SMEs in improving their business performance and enhance productivity while also providing a platform for students to have exposure in a business environment and acquire the skills to create and manage their own enterprises.
SME@University Programme	This programme helps develop capacity among SME CEOs by providing them with the possibility to have a more structured learning environment in the SME University of Japan.
SME Mentoring Programme	Together with Nestlé Malaysia and Halal Industry Development Corporation, a two-day mentoring programme is offered to SMEs in the Halal Food and Beverage industry as a way to enhance their knowledge and improve their performance internationally. This includes a set of knowledge enrichment activities as well as a focus on design and management aspects such as product optimisation, food regulations, labelling requirements, and other operational activities.

Source: SME Corporation Malaysia (n.d.), *Our Programmes*, www.smecorp.gov.my/index.php/en/ (accessed on 21 January 2018).

The Business Linkage (BLing) Programme of SME Corp. Malaysia aims to identify synergies and linkages with SMEs and large companies, multinational corporations or government-linked corporations to support vertical growth of enterprises in the country. These networking opportunities are carried out through business matching sessions or annual flagship events. In 2016, around 443 SMEs have been involved in the programme and have generated around MYR 714.7 million in potential sales.

Special economic zones

Malaysia has two special economic zones (SEZ). The first economic zone is the East Coast Economic Region, which was inaugurated in 2009. This SEZ aims to stimulate entrepreneurship and growth in specific industries and regions, notably in the oil and gas sector. In 2017, Malaysia launched the world's first Digital Free Trade Zone (DFTZ), which is aimed to be completed in 2020. Once completed, the 409-hectare DFTZ will host a large air cargo, aerospace and aviation, digital and internet-related, and logistics industry.

Labour mobility

Foreign workers are permitted to work in specific sectors in the country, namely: manufacturing, construction, plantation, agriculture and services. These must also come from only a selected list of countries, as stated in the Immigration Act and the Ministry of Home Affairs' Immigration Department (Ministry of Home Affairs, 2018[12]).

Customs

Launched in 2009, Malaysia's National Single Window for Trade Facilitation system aims to reduce the time and costs of doing business and increasing efficiency in export-import, facilitating the electronic exchange of trade-related information or data and improving service delivery with regard to product clearance, among others.

Box 6.6. Features of Malaysia's National Single Window (NSW)

Malaysia's National Single Window features five elements for its first implementation (Ministry of International Trade and Industry, 2017[13]). These include:

- **E-Declare**, which allows electronic declaration of all customs forms.
- **E-Permit**, which allows fast, automatic issuance of permits from permit-issuing agencies.
- **Electronics Fund Transfer (EFT)** as a way to facilitate payment of customs fees.
- **E-Preferential Certificate of Origin**, which provides users with the possibility to access and download their application for a certificate of origin.
- **E-manifest,** which allows users to submit manifests on line.

Source: Ministry of International Trade and Industry (2017), *National Single Window*, www.miti.gov.my/index.php/pages/view/1149/ (accessed on 21 January 2018).

Recommendations

- **Continue to strengthen the use of RIA** by exploring other approaches to further improve the analysis regulations.
- **Strengthen *ex post* evaluation activities as a way to considerably improve the stock of regulation and to ensure its relevance in the long run**. Consider other forms of review *ex post* reviews, including post-implementation review and sunset reviews, among others.
- **Adopt a whole-of-government approach to regulatory policy,** by linking the different efforts in improving RIA, *ex post* evaluation and stakeholder engagement.
- **Review the NPDIR based on experience and implementation to date**. This exercise will be useful in highlighting the efforts and achievements based on its implementation, as well as evaluate its feasibility and relevance in the long run.
- **Streamline and strengthen governance among industry leaders across the different priority sectors that support SME growth**. Empower the actors across sectors to identify issues of concern with regard to reducing regulatory burden and encourage continuous dialogue in the long run.

References

Jayasiri, J. (2016), *Good Regulatory Practice (GRP) in Malaysia*, https://www.capam.org/files/2016BiennialPresentations/ExperiencesOnGRPImplementation-J_Jayasiri.pdf. [7]

Malaysia Productivity Corporation (2016), *Annual Report on Modernisation of Regulations*, Malaysia Productivity Corporation, http://www.mpc.gov.my/wp-content/uploads/2016/12/ARMR-2016.pdf. [6]

Malaysia Productivity Corporation (2015), *Reducing Unnecessary Regulatory Burdens (RURB) – Malaysia Productivity Corporation (MPC)*, Malaysia Productivity Corporation, http://www.mpc.gov.my/reducing-unnecessary-regulatory-burdens-rurb-2/. [9]

Malaysia Productivity Corporation (2013), *Best Practice Regulation Handbook*, Malaysia Productivity Corporation, http://www.mpc.gov.my/wp-content/uploads/2017/04/Best-Practice-Handbook-2013.pdf. [8]

MATRADE (2016), *Beginner's Guide to Exporting - MATRADE*, MATRADE, http://www.matrade.gov.my/en/malaysian-exporters/going-global/beginner-s-guide-to-exporting. [11]

Ministry of Home Affairs (2018), *Foreign Workers*, http://www.imi.gov.my/index.php/en/main-services/foreign-workers.html. [12]

Ministry of International Trade and Industry (2017), *National Single Window*, Ministry of International Trade and Industry, http://www.miti.gov.my/index.php/pages/view/1149/ (accessed on 21 January 2018). [13]

OECD (2015), *Implementing Good Regulatory Practice in Malaysia*, OECD Publishing, Paris, http://dx.doi.org/10.1787/9789264230620-en. [2]

OECD (forthcoming), *ASEAN SME Policy Index 2018: Boosting Competitiveness and Inclusive Growth in ASEAN*, OECD Publishing, Paris. [1]

SME Corporation Malaysia (2018), *Our Programmes*, http://www.smecorp.gov.my/index.php/en/ (accessed on 21 January 2018). [10]

SME Corporation Malaysia (2013), *Guideline for New SME definition*, http://www.smecorp.gov.my/images/pdf/Guideline_for_New_SME_Definition_7Jan2014.pdf. [4]

Suruhanjaya Syarikat Malaysia (2018), *Registration*, http://www.ssm.com.my/en/services_registration (accessed on 08 March 2018). [5]

World Bank (2017), *Law Library*, http://www.doingbusiness.org/law-library/ (accessed on 8 March 2018). [3]

Chapter 7. Myanmar

The regulatory environment for Myanmar is relatively less burdensome compared to its Association of Southeast Asian Nations (ASEAN) neighbours, in part due to fewer laws and regulations in place overall. Yet a rapid enactment of new laws in the past decade risks creating an increasingly fragmented regulatory environment if ministries do not make concerted efforts to assess regulatory needs and impacts together. The government has nevertheless developed a clear and formal policy to support small- and medium-sized enterprise (SME) development, which has been accompanied by an SME law to support its implementation. National standards for products and services have not yet been developed in Myanmar, so businesses deciding to export must comply with foreign standards negotiated on a case-by-case basis. This risks limiting the scale of trade opportunities for SMEs by imposing excessive administrative and financial burdens on SMEs striving to meet multiple standards for different buyers.

Regulatory context

The lifting of international sanctions in 2012 saw Myanmar open up its economy to the world with the introduction of the Foreign Investment Law, which set out the rules and regulations applicable to foreign investors separately from those applicable to local investors, which otherwise followed the Citizens Investment Law of 1994.

In 2016, the Foreign Investment Law and the Citizens Investment Law were replaced by a single Myanmar Investments Law, effectively streamlining investment legislation for both domestic and foreign businesses as well as opening up a number of previously-restricted sectors to foreign investment. It also aimed to increase investment protection and channel investments into diverse economic sectors beyond natural resources and telecommunications, which had been the primary recipients of foreign direct investment (FDI) to date. The new Investment Law also established the Myanmar Investment Commission, which was assigned to process and approve investments.

Myanmar's efforts to transition to an open, market-based economy with supporting reforms have been successful in improving the country's investment climate and attracting a large wave of FDI in a relatively short period of time. Between 2013 and 2016, approved FDI in Myanmar increased markedly from USD 1.4 billion to USD 9.48 billion (DICA, 2017[1]).

Around 69% of FDI in Myanmar goes to a limited number of sectors that are dominated by a handful of large national or multinational enterprises (MNEs) – namely, oil and gas (31%), electricity (24%), transport and telecommunication (14%) (DICA, 2018[2]). Domestic investments are target primarily to real estate development (26%), transport and communication (16%) and other (16%) (DICA, 2018[3]).

Yet the vast majority of businesses in Myanmar are small and medium-sized enterprises (SMEs) operating in sectors *outside* the aforementioned sectors. SMEs account for 99% of all businesses and 70% of total employment in Myanmar and the bulk of them are concentrated in the food and beverage industry (67%), followed some ways behind by construction (8%) and garments (4%) (Sanyal and Eisinger, 2016[4]).

All in all, this means that there is relatively little FDI going towards SMEs in general, and even less towards diversifying SMEs. On the positive side, this also means that there is a significant opportunity for SMEs in Myanmar to grow in just about any sector.

The government has recognised SMEs as the main engine for job creation and economic prosperity for the broader population, and has introduced a dedicated SME Development Policy in 2015 (hereafter the "SME Policy") to support the "creation of regionally innovative and competitive SMEs across all sectors that enhance income generation and contribute to the social-economic development mission" of Myanmar (Government of Myanmar, 2015, p. 2[5]).

For the first time, the SME Policy underscored the importance of SMEs in the country and laid out a number of important supporting policies including increased access to government funding support, training and capacity building, and some tax-related exemptions. The SME Policy also set out the government's commitment to helping SMEs improve trade and export and to reduce the administrative burden for SMEs.

The SME development agenda is supported by a broader 12-point economic policy issued in July 2016, which gears towards transitioning Myanmar to a market-oriented economy in all sectors. Point 11 further emphasises the government's commitment to supporting

SMEs by improving the ease of doing business, increasing access to financial services, and developing a higher skilled labour force (Myanmar Times, 2016[6]).

Overall, the regulatory context for Myanmar has been changing rapidly. Between 2011 and 2016, 232 pieces of legislation were passed, 105 (45%) of which were amendments or re-amendments and 17 repeals of previous laws (Egreteau, 2017[7]). The influx of new laws or amendments and the speed with which they have been introduced have prompted concerns about regulatory overlap or inconsistency, not to mention added considerable complexity to Myanmar's regulatory framework as well as its processes. The government is aware that, if these processes are not sufficiently co-ordinated or streamlined, they may risk creating regulatory bottlenecks for attracting or approving investments, advancing project developments, and ultimately impact the achievement of policy goals.

Regulatory governance

Business laws and regulations in Myanmar

In Myanmar, all business-related laws, notifications, regulations and directives apply to enterprises of all sizes, including SMEs. As SMEs account almost all domestic private sector businesses in Myanmar, it can be said that the general business regulatory framework is *de facto* sufficient for capturing local SMEs. Business-related laws which have been enacted by the State Law and Order Restoration Council and are still in place include:

- Union Tax Law (2017)
- Specific Goods Tax Law (2016) (amended 26 July 2017)
- Income Tax Law (1974) (amended 31 August 2016)
- Private Industrial Enterprise Law (1990)
- Commercial Tax Law (1990) (amended 2015)
- Myanmar Investments Law (2016)
- Myanmar Companies Law (enacted December 2017).

A draft SME law is also being prepared by the Department of SMEs as of November 2017. The draft law focuses on the following four areas: production set up; service; trading; and other. It is intended to support the implementation of the SME Policy.

In the meanwhile, in order for an SME to qualify for the benefits and exemptions outlined in the SME Policy, it must fall under the definitions of small- and medium-sized enterprises listed in Table 7.1 and not be a public company or subsidiary of a public company.

Micro-enterprises are defined separately by the Promotion of Cottage Industries Law 1991 and overseen by a different ministry – the Ministry for Agriculture, Fisheries and Livelihood – which has maintained its historical mandate to develop cottage industries.

In December 2017, a new Myanmar Companies Law (hereafter Companies Law) was enacted to comply with the Investment Law passed in October the previous year. The Companies Law combined and updated elements from the Myanmar Companies Act (1914) and the Special Companies Act (1950) to reduce restrictions on setting up companies, facilitate online business registration, and develop Myanmar's capital market. The Companies Law aimed to attract more foreign investment, which the government considers one of the best development channels for the country and includes provisions such as allowing foreigners to legally own unmovable properties including condominium apartments for the first time. The Companies Law was developed with technical assistance from the Asian Development Bank.

Table 7.1. Definition of MSMEs in Myanmar

Category	Micro	Small	Medium
Power (horse power) used	Between 0.25 and 5	3 to 25	26 to 50
Number of workers	Up to 9*	up to 30*	51 to 100
Capital investment (Kyat)		Up to 1 million	Between 1 and 5 million
Production value per year		Up to 2.5 million	Between 2.5 to 10 million
Annual revenue		Up to 50 million*	

* The Companies Law of 2017 also updated certain definitions of small companies. Micro-enterprises are defined differently by the Cottage Industries Law (amended 2011).
MSME: micro, small, and medium enterprise.
Note: SMEs in the industry sector are defined by the Private Industry Enterprises Law of 1999.
Source: Provided to the OECD by the Ministry of Industry, 2017.

The Companies Law 2017 also updated the definition of small companies as a (non-public) company which employs less than 30 workers *and* has an annual revenue of less than MMK 50 million in the previous financial year (DICA, 2017[8]). However, it is unclear whether pre-existing definitions of SMEs under other categories have been overwritten by this Companies Law.

Micro, small, and medium enterprises (MSMEs) must register with the government to be eligible for SME development schemes. SMEs may register with the government via three different channels: 1) the Department of SMEs under the Ministry of Industry; 2) the City Development Committees; 3) Directorate of Investment and Company Administration (DICA) under the Ministry of Planning and Finance. Micro-enterprises may register with the Ministry of Agriculture, Livestock and Fisheries.

The various definitions and registration channels for SMEs have led to governance challenges in data collection, monitoring and evaluation. Presently, SME data collection duties in Myanmar are dispersed among the following agencies: Directorate of Industrial Supervision and Inspection (DISI); SME Development Centre (SDC); city and township development committees; and the Central Statistical Organisation (CSO) – some or all of which may compile statistics using different definitions of SMEs.

Data on MSMEs in Myanmar is generally limited, in part because MSMEs do not always register with the government. The current data on SMEs is tracked by the Ministry of Industry and only focuses on the industry sector. There is no official data collected on the service sector. There is a draft regulation on collecting SME data, although progress is unclear.

As a result of poor registration rates, few MSMEs are captured by tax collection. The Ministry of Agriculture, Livestock and Fisheries acknowledges that micro-enterprises are generally too small to pay tax. The Ministry of Industry, which registers SMEs, likewise notes that many SMEs do not register or do not want to register, and the ministry has limited capacity to enforce registration. Many MSMEs in Myanmar operate informally, particularly if they prefer to keep operations at a local scale.

There is no policy document on regulating the informal economy or government initiative to improve data collection on the informal economy.

Institutional and regulatory setup

Table 7.2. Institutional and regulatory setup in Myanmar

	Government
State structure	Parliamentary Republic
Head of state	**President**
Executive	The executive power of the Union of Myanmar is vested in the President. Within the executive branch, several institutions intervene at different stages of the regulatory cycle: • **Office of the President** supports the President in the exercise of his functions, and monitors and periodically evaluates public policies, with the aim of contributing to decision-making by the Executive. The President may make changes or additions to ministries as necessary and is responsible for appointing ministers and the Attorney General, with the approval of the *Pyidaungsu Hluttaw* (Assembly of the Union). • The **Presidential College** elects the President. It comprises three groups: the two houses of the *Pyidaungsu Hluttaw* and the third from *Hluttaw* representatives of the Defence Services as nominated by the Commander-in-Chief. • The **Vice President** ranks directly after the President and serves the functions of the deputy head of state. There are two Vice Presidents in Myanmar, who each serve five-year terms. • **State Council** was created in April 2016 to work across all areas of government and serve as the link between the executive and legislative branches, comparable to the Prime Minister's Office in other countries. • **National Defence and Security Council (NDSC)** comprises 11 individuals, six of whom – including the Commander-in-Chief - are appointed directly from the Defence Services. The NDSC has a prominent role in executive decision-making relating to foreign and military affairs in Myanmar. • **Financial Commission** consists of seven groups of individuals, including the President as the Chairman. It submits the Union budget to the *Pyidaungsu Hluttaw* and advises the executive on financial affairs. • **Line Ministries** are responsible for putting forth national public policies in their area of competence. There are currently 23 ministries in Myanmar. Since November 2017, a new **Ministry of the Office of the Union Government** is responsible for co-ordinating all agencies and ministries under the office of the President. Its tasks include performing administrative, planning and finance matters. It is also responsible for the submission of bills to the *Pyidaungsu Hluttaw*. • **Ministry for International Co-operation**, also established in November 2017, is responsible for managing international co-operation in political and economic issues. This new ministry takes over some of the international co-operation duties previously tasked to the Ministry of Foreign Affairs and the Ministry of Planning and Finance.
Legislative	• **Assembly of the Union (*Pyidaungsu Hluttaw*; officially the Republic of the Union of Myanmar)** is the national bicameral legislature of Myanmar. The *Pyidaungsu Hluttaw* passes, amends or appeals the majority of the laws in Myanmar. Each member serves for a term of five years, after which they are replaced via by-elections by the Union Election Commission. Between 2011 and 2016, the Union Parliament rarely initiated the policymaking process; rather, most of the 232 laws enacted by the legislature were prepared by the executive branch or a non-legislative union-level body like the Union Election Commission or the Office of the Attorney General. (Egreteau, 2017[7]). • **House of Nationalities (*Amyotha Hluttaw*)** is the upper house of the *Pyidaungsu Hluttaw*, founded in January 2011. It comprises 224 members, 168 of whom are directly elected with equal representation (12 representatives) from each state or region, and the remaining 56 representatives appointed by the Myanmar Armed Forces. • **House of Representatives (*Pyithu Hluttaw*)** is the lower house of the *Pyidaungsu Hluttaw*. It comprises 440 members, 330 of whom are directly elected and the remainder appointed from the army by the Commander-in-Chief of the Defence Services. • Each state or region also has its own ***Hluttaw*** or unicameral legislative assembly. Lawmaking powers of the state or region *Hluttaw* are limited to localised issues such as land revenue, municipal taxes, land and property leasing, or off-grid power generation within the region or state. Laws passed by the *Hluttaw* may be overwritten by laws passed by the *Pyidaungsu Hluttaw*. Compared to the *Pyidaungsu Hluttaw*, the region/state *Hluttaws* have passed very few laws.

Legal system	The federal judiciary power is vested in the **Supreme Court**. A Judiciary review or Constitutional Tribunal may be triggered only by ministers and other executive representatives of the union, states, regions and self-administrative areas to determine whether the measures taken by ministers and executive representatives are in conformity with the Constitution.
Administrative-territorial structure	14 state and regions
Ministry or agency responsible for SMEs or SME-related issues	**Department for SMEs**, Directorate of Industrial Supervision and Inspection (DISI), Ministry of Industry. The Ministry of Industry also runs the **SME Development Centre**.
Other support structures within government on regulatory policy	**Directorate of Investment and Company Administration (DICA)** is responsible for business registration, investment application processing and approval, data monitoring on businesses including SMEs.

According to Myanmar's 2008 Constitution, the executive branch and the Union President has a leading role in law making. Most draft laws between 2011 and 2016 originated in the executive branch, before being discussed in the Union legislature (Egreteau, 2017[7]).

Regulatory process for SMEs

Established in 2012, the Department for SMEs in the Ministry of Industry is responsible for developing the country's SME Policy as well as the new SME Law. It also oversees an affiliated SME Development Centre in Yangon. The Department of SMEs has a budget approved by the State Council to carry out its activities. The Department of SMEs is based in Nay Pyi Taw, where it co-ordinates with more than 50 regional offices across the country. SMEs may register with various branches of the Department of SMEs located throughout the country, after which they can benefit from a number of support services provided by the department, including access to government loans, training and capacity building. The cost of registering a business with the Department of SMEs is MMK 30 000 as of September 2017.

SMEs in Nay Pyi Taw, Yangon or Mandalay may also obtain licences to operate from the appropriate City Development Committee (CDC). In Yangon and Mandalay, a simple licence issued by the CDC suffices to enable an SME to operate within the city. The functions and duties of the CDCs may differ from each other according to their founding legislation and differ yet again from the functions and duties of state or regional governments. The Yangon CDC offers an online service for business registration and other information (Yangon City Development Committee, 2018[9]).

The third option for business registration is with the Directorate of Investment and Company Administration (DICA) under the Ministry of Planning and Finance, which is the statutory authority for investment promotion, streamlining business regulation and investment procedures. It is responsible for registering and monitoring local and foreign businesses under the Myanmar Companies Act 1914. The cost of registering a private business at DICA is much higher (MMK 500 000) compared to registering with the CDC or the Department of SMEs. However, it is obligatory to register with DICA if a company, joint venture, association or non-profit wishes to export, and of the three business registration channels, only DICA is authorised to incorporate businesses and to provide tax incentives such as the three-, five- and seven-year tax exemptions according to the Myanmar Investments Law 2016 and the Myanmar Companies Law 2017.

Figure 7.1. Registration process for SMEs in Myanmar

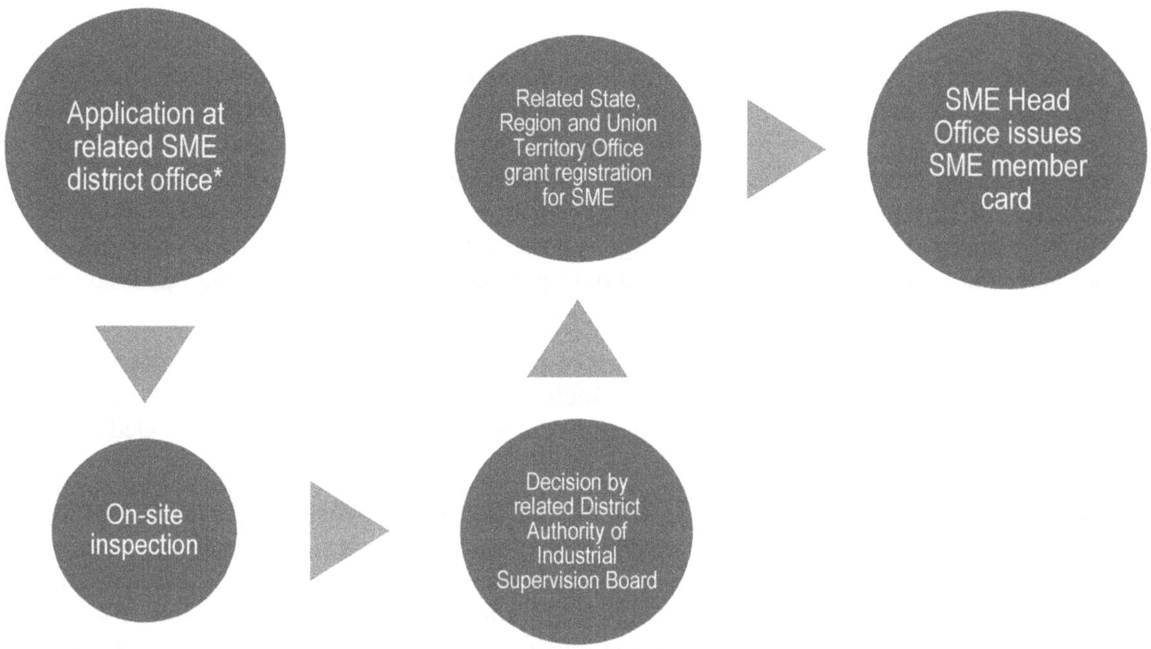

*The initial application should include the following: Form (A) SME registration application form; Form (B) SME member application form; Form (C) SME member renewal/extension application form.
Source: Myanmar SME Development Department, Ministry of Industry, 2017.

There is a plan to establish an SME Agency which, if established, may take over the SME Development Centre.

Micro-enterprises are regulated by the Department of Cottage Industries within the Ministry of Agriculture, Fisheries and Livestock. Previously, the department had been under the Ministry of Co-operatives and Cottages, but the latter has been absorbed into the Ministry of Agriculture, Fisheries and Livestock. This causes some confusion as not all micro-enterprises as in the agricultural sector, and presently micro-enterprises are regulated separately from SMEs, which fall under the mandate of the Ministry of Industry.

Director Generals have authority to implement the basic principles of relevant laws, to consult and carry out tax relief measures in consultation with the Ministry of Planning and Finance, to organise sale of local products at foreign trade exhibitions, to negotiate to obtain local and foreign loans and grants, to carry out public consultation or media promotion of companies, call for accounts or inspection of any company under its jurisdiction (whether registered or not) in the relevant law, revoke or cancel the registration of entrepreneurs that have not abided by the orders or directives under the relevant law, issue orders and directives related to the category of businesses under its jurisdiction, delegating duties and powers to any officer in the department or to any working body.

Ministers are responsible for presenting draft laws in the executive branch. Ministers also have authority to grant, suspend or cancel business registration, formulate programmes or bodies to promote, assist or supervise businesses, and take the final decision in the case that an entrepreneur appeals against the decision of a DG.

Highlights of regulatory opportunities and challenges to support SMEs

Regulatory clarity

The SME Policy of 2015 articulated the importance of SME growth and diversification, establishing a clear purpose and political commitment to increase support to SMEs. The policy outlined a number of regulatory improvement goals including reducing difficulties and constraints faced by business start-ups, encouraging the free flow of capital, building capacity for entrepreneurship, enhancing information networks and flow, and facilitating business operation. The policy also recognised the importance of developing value-added products for export and trading with regional partners, as well as converging Myanmar social and economic standards with ASEAN development.

An accompanying SME Law (development in progress) will support the implementation of the SME Policy. Proposed provisions included in the SME Law include a reduced corporate tax rate for SMEs and other incentives, which have not yet been revealed as of the end of 2017.

Government support for SMEs is further emphasised in the Myanmar Investment Law 2016, which stipulates that "the Government may undertake subsidies, funding, capacity building and training to Myanmar citizen investors and citizen-owned small and medium-sized enterprises. The Government may also allow exemptions and reliefs for the locations where Myanmar citizen-owned businesses are operated or other economic activities" (Pyidaungsu Hluttaw, 2016[10]).

Regulatory quality management

Compliance with business registration

One of the biggest regulatory challenges for policymakers is that MSMEs may lack understanding of formal business practices, or even prefer to operate informally in order to avoid administrative burden and taxation. This extends into regulatory challenges for authorities when MSMEs are unwilling to engage in the first stage of the regulatory process: registering their businesses. The government has introduced various policies and programmes to encourage SMEs to register including capacity building, access to loans, lower tax rates, tax holidays and business matching. While both the Cottage Industries Law and draft SME Law indicate financial penalties for failure to register, these penalties are rarely enforced in practice.

The government has taken some initiative to streamline registration procedures. For example, DICA offers a one-stop service for registration and is also in the process of establishing an online registration portal. DICA also serves as the Secretariat for the Myanmar Investment Commission (MIC), which is responsible for processing and approving investment applications. DICA receives online investment applications on MIC's behalf.

Compliance with product or service standards

There is no national standards body in Myanmar and, at present, product standards are agreed upon between seller and buyer on a deal-by-deal basis. This results in a reliance on the importer to designate the desired standards and may burden local producers to comply with multiple standards for the same product.

More efforts to align national to international standards are in progress. For example, Myanmar's hotel star rating system is matched to international norms. A memorandum of understanding (MOU) has also been signed between the Myanmar Department of Research and Innovation and SPRING Singapore to share expertise in the accreditation of conformity assessment bodies based on international standards and requirements (DICA, 2017[11]).

Compliance with intellectual property laws

There is no statutory law specifically dedicated to intellectual property (IP) protection in Myanmar, which may result in higher risk or perceived risk for businesses intending to set up in Myanmar or work with local companies. Some forms of IP protection are offered for certain patents and designs but these are considered outdated and offer limited protection for intellectual property (WIPO, 2016[12]).[1]

Enforcement and inspection

In the context of investments, an Investment Monitoring Division (IMD) overseen by DICA is responsible for inspection and oversight functions relating to permits, endorsements, import licences for raw materials and machinery, tax incentives and payments, business visas, land rights authorisations and business monitoring. The IMD can recommend to the Commission Office an administrative penalty be imposed on an Investor under Section 85 of the Law.

Regulating the informal economy

Most micro-enterprises and many SMEs do not register their businesses, preferring to operate in the informal economy. Similarly, much of the labour force in MSMEs is informal and difficult to track. There are no policies, regulations or sanctions pertaining to informal labour.

Administrative simplification

In November 2015, the government adopted priorities to improve the efficiency of the Myanmar administration and the ease of doing business across all sectors. One of the first major reforms implemented by the government was a reduction in the number of ministries in the Union Government from 36 to 21. Notably, the six ministries that comprised the previous President's office were merged into one.

In the years following, many regulatory reforms have aimed at creating incentives for both local and foreign investors and reducing barriers to business operations, for example by introducing multiple exchange rates, reducing import restrictions and export tax, and liberalising import/export procedures.

The Union Government is establishing one-stop shops around the country as part of its ongoing public sector reforms. Myanmar has set up more than 70 one-stop shops across the country to deliver transparent and efficient government administrative services to citizens. These one-stop shops include counters from various government agencies delivering public services ranging from electricity, internal revenue, public health, social welfare, police, immigration, complaints and queries (UNDP, 2018[13]).

Customs facilitation

The Customs Department has an explicit policy to simplify or remove outdated regulations, in line with international best practice and standards.[2] Some examples of customs-related regulatory simplification achieved to date include:

- Reduction of a number of unnecessary requirements for trade and customs procedures, including the use of the e-customs system (Myanmar Automated Cargo Clearance System, MACCS) for import and export of goods since 2017.
- Removal of double taxation on firms by calculating commercial tax before adding customs duty.
- Removal of requirement for exporters to produce a bank certificate as proof that they have been paid for goods before exportation is permitted.

The Customs Department also has a plan to develop an umbrella of various trade facilitation measures in line with the ASEAN Economic Co-operation (AEC) Master Plan including customs valuation, post-clearance audits, and an authorised economic operator. Procedures for customs valuations, post-clearance audits, advance ruling of classification (i.e. H.S. code) and valuation have been issued and applied in 2017. Procedures for an authorised economic operator have also been submitted to the Union Minister for approval. Public awareness campaigns are underway.

E-government

Myanmar's Customs Department has been developing its e-Customs system since 2013, with support from the Government of Japan. The system includes the MACCS and the Myanmar Customs Intelligence System (MCIS). As of November 2017, MACCS is operational in Yangon and will be extended to the Myawadi border areas in June 2018. A large number of government departments are already participating in MACCS, including the Trade Department, Myanmar Port Authority, Food and Drug Administration, Plant and Animal Quarantines, Fisheries department, Myanmar Economic Bank and various other imports, exporters and customs brokers.[3] The MACCS and MCIS form the basis for Myanmar's National Single Window.

The Ministry of Communications is in the process of building up Myanmar's e-Government with support from the Government of Korea. The Ministry of Commerce has already started to use some e-Government systems, for example in customs. The Ministry of Labour, Immigration and Population has also implemented an e-visa system for both tourist and business travellers since 2016.

Stakeholder engagement

Since 2012, there is a legal requirement to conduct Public-Private Consultations. Ministries are free to conduct these consultations as they see fit, as there is currently no existing guideline on how this should be carried out. Nonetheless, these consultations are often carried out on an ad hoc basis with concerned associations, companies, chambers, and other representatives from the private sector. Prior notification is provided to these stakeholders before the consultation. During these consultations, the private sector provides comments to specific draft SME regulations, which are then considered in the final draft.

Consultations are recorded by the respective ministry; however, these are not made public.

Regulatory assessments

The government has started to explore regulatory impact assessments (RIA) on a pilot basis and has provided some training on its applications with the support of international partners. The government occasionally conducts a review of existing legislation with the goal of identifying those that are obsolete. A Legislative Review Committee meets every week to review legislation under the Union Legislative List. It may prepare a report on resolving or simplifying legislation, which is presented to the Attorney General's Office.

Currently, there are no *ex ante* or *ex post* regulatory impact assessments in place in Myanmar's regulatory process.

Appeals

An appeals process is in place, although seldom triggered by businesses in practice. If there is a dispute or conflict over a regulation, "any person conducting a private industrial enterprise or any entrepreneur who is dissatisfied with an order or decision of the DG (of the Directorate of Regional Industrial Co-ordination and Industrial Inspection) may file an appeal to the minister within 30 days of the receipt of such order or decision" and the minister makes the final decision (Private Industrial Enterprise Law 1990). Enforcement decisions relating to customs laws (such as the Sea Customs Act) may be appealed at the administrative level at the Revenue Tribunal Office in Nay Pyi Taw.

SME linkage policies

Myanmar relies heavily on foreign donor support to develop the necessary framework for integrating SMEs into global value chains (GVCs). Efforts to date are primarily confined to special economic zones.

Special economic zones

Myanmar has been developing special economic zones (SEZs) to attract foreign investment. It currently has three SEZs in Dawei, Kyaukphyu and Thilawa,. All three SEZs are located along the western coast of Myanmar and are intended to serve as windows for international export for goods from China, Japan, Thailand and other border trading partners, as well as products from Myanmar itself. More SEZs and industrial zones are in the government planning pipeline. There is no preferential treatment for SMEs in SEZs; SMEs can join SEZs as long as they follow SEZ laws and regulations.

The first SEZ in Thilawa was developed in co-operation with the Government of Japan. It began operations in late 2015 with a legal framework - including preferential laws and regulations – developed by the Japan International Co-operation Agency (JICA). Japanese businesses account for more than half the companies active in the SEZ. The other companies come from China, Thailand, the United States and other countries. Sectors represented in the SEZ include garment and toy manufacturing, steel products, radiators, aluminium cans, packaging and waste management.

Myanmar also has nine industrial zones. The industrial zones are inland and primarily target local manufacturers serving the domestic market (OECD, 2014[14]).

Table 7.3. Good practices in SEZ policies in Myanmar

Foreign/local ownership	No limitations/Equal treatment
Catering to domestic market	• Liberalised • Criteria-based • Subject to regular, non-zone, import regulations
Purchases from domestic market	• Companies eligible for exporter benefits since these should be treated as exports from domestic markets
Eligibility for benefits	• No minimum export requirements • Foreign and domestic companies • Private zone developers • Manufacturers and service providers
Labour policies	• Full consistency with international norms, including International Labour Organization (ILO) labour standards and OECD *Guidelines for Multinational Enterprises*
Private zone development	• Competition with government-managed zones on a level playing field • Developers eligible for full benefits • Criteria are clearly defined in legislation

Source: OECD (2014), *OECD Investment Policy Reviews: Myanmar 2014*, http://dx.doi.org/10.1787/9789264206441-en.

The fiscal incentives for companies operating in Myanmar's SEZs are more generous under the Special Economic Zone Law 2011 compared to the general Foreign Investment Law. For example, all businesses - large or small - in the SEZ may benefit from a tax exemption for three consecutive years starting from the year of operation, plus a further tax holiday or relief for companies that are considered beneficial to the state. The benefits may include:

- Exemption or relief from income tax on profit which is reinvested within one year.
- Relief from income tax up to 50% on the profit from exports.
- Right to deduct research and development expenditure.
- Exemption or relief from customs duty and other taxes on.
- Imported machinery and equipment for use during the construction period.
- Imported raw materials for the first three years of commercial production following the completion of construction.

Responsible business conduct

Responsible Business Conduct (RBC) has been referenced in a number of legal documents in Myanmar. In the 2016 Investment Law, Myanmar included an explicit reference to responsible investment as a top objective. RBC is likewise included in the assessment criteria (Rule 64.d and 64.g) in the 2017 implementing rules for the Investment Law. The Myanmar Investment Commission (MIC), which is tasked with developing responsible and accountable businesses, may consider whether the investors or their associates have contravened the law, including in other jurisdictions on issues relating to the environment, labour, tax, corruption and human rights (Rule 66). A set of accompanying rules also asked investors to report on any applicable environmental, social, economic and land-use impacts from their businesses and how they will carry out their investments in a sustainable way (OECD, forthcoming[15]).

Recommendations

- **A formal arrangement to consolidate inputs from different ministries before new legislation is put in place could help reduce occurrences and risks of overlapping or contradictory regulations.** At present, there remains limited consultation between ministries and no formalised arrangement to consult between ministries in the creation of new legislation.
- **Systematically review and evaluate present regulations to ensure that they are necessary**, and if so, that they meet their intended objectives efficiently and effectively. There is currently no mandatory *ex ante* or *ex post* impact assessments to assess regulatory needs ahead of introducing new legislation, nor are existing legislation regularly reviewed for their performance. The Government of Myanmar does not measure individual or aggregate regulatory burdens as an explicit objective to lessen administrative costs for citizens or businesses.
- **Establish a centralised administrative business registry where information can be shared and accessed by all relevant government agencies**. This would simplify the registration process as well as reduce administrative and cost burdens for government and SMEs alike. A centralised business registry would also allow the government to conduct centralised data collection about SMEs, which would improve access to better quality SME statistics for data and policy analyses going forward.
- **Share findings from stakeholder consultations between ministries in a designated portal,** which could further disseminate stakeholder feedback for better and more co-ordinated policymaking and policy delivery.
- **Develop a clear policy to align and adapt national product and services standards with regional (ASEAN) or international product or service standards.**

Notes

[1] Limited forms of intellectual property protection are provided for in the following laws: Registration Act (1908); Penal Code (1860); Merchandise Marks Act (1889); Sea Customs Act (1878); Specific Relief Act (1877); Patents and Design (Emergency Provisions) Act (1946); Private Industry Enterprise Law (1990); Science and Technology Development Law (1994); Electronic Transactions Law (2004).

[2] The Sea Customs Act (1878) and Land Customs Act (1924) have been amended in March 2015 in line with international practices, such as the Revised Kyoto Convention.

[3] ASEAN Single Window (2018), *Myanmar General Information,* http://asw.asean.org/nsw/myanmar/myanmar-general-information (accessed on 21 August 2018).

References

ASEAN Single Window (2018), *Myanmar General Information*, http://asw.asean.org/nsw/myanmar/myanmar-general-information (accessed on 21 August 2018). [16]

DICA (2018), *Foreign Investment of Existing Enterprises as of 28/2/2018 by Sector*, http://www.dica.gov.mm/sites/dica.gov.mm/files/document-files/fdi_sector_6.pdf. [2]

DICA (2018), *Myanmar Citizen Investment of Existing Enterprises as of 28/2/2018 by Sector*, http://www.dica.gov.mm/sites/dica.gov.mm/files/document-files/mcil_4.pdf. [3]

DICA (2017), *Draft Myanmar Companies Bill*, http://www.dica.gov.mm/sites/dica.gov.mm/files/document-files/mcl_english_version_june_2017_abc_comments_clean.pdf. [8]

DICA (2017), *Myanmar and Singapore Reaffirm Bilateral Ties at 6th Singapore-Myanmar Joint Ministerial Working Committee Meeting*, http://www.dica.gov.mm/en/news/myanmar-and-singapore-reaffirm-bilateral-ties-6th-singapore-myanmar-joint-ministerial-working. [11]

DICA (2017), *Yearly Approved Amount of Foreign Investment by Country*, http://www.dica.gov.mm/sites/dica.gov.mm/files/document-files/yearly_by_country.pdf. [1]

Egreteau, R. (2017), *Parliamentary Development in Myanmar: An Overview of the Union Parliament*, https://asiafoundation.org/wp-content/uploads/2017/05/Parliamentary-Development-in-Myanmar.pdf. [7]

Government of Myanmar (2015), *Small and Medium Enterprise Development Policy*, http://www.industry.gov.mm/en/download/file/fid/338. [5]

Myanmar Times (2016), *Government Reveals 12-point Economic Policy*, http://www.mmtimes.com/business/21664-nld-12-point-economic-policy-announcement.html. [6]

OECD (2014), *OECD Investment Policy Reviews: Myanmar 2014*, OECD Publishing, Paris, http://dx.doi.org/10.1787/9789264206441-en. [14]

OECD (forthcoming), *Inclusive Investments in GVCs: Opportunities for ASEAN SMEs*, OECD Publishing, Paris. [15]

Pyidaungsu Hluttaw (2016), *Myanmar Investments Law No. 40/2016*, http://www.dica.gov.mm/sites/dica.gov.mm/files/document-files/myanmar_investment_law_official_translation_3-1-2017.pdf. [10]

Sanyal, S. and F. Eisinger (2016), *Enabling SME Access to Finance for Sustainable Consumption and Production in Asia*, http://www.switch-asia.eu/fileadmin/user_upload/Publications/2016/Green_Finance_Study_-_2016_-_Myanmar.pdf. [4]

UNDP (2018), *One Stop Shops across Myanmar*, http://www.mm.undp.org/content/myanmar/en/home/ourwork/povertyreduction/successstories/O [13] ne_Stop_Shops_in_Myanmar_A_Step_Towards_Bringing_Service_Closer_to_Peoples.html.

WIPO (2016), *Development of Intellectual Property System in Myanmar*, http://www.wipo.int/edocs/mdocs/aspac/en/wipo_tm_tyo_2_16/wipo_tm_tyo_2_16_3_4.pdf. [12]

Yangon City Development Committee (2018), *Online Business License*, https://app.ycdc.gov.mm/business_license/index.php (accessed on 10 August 2018). [9]

Chapter 8. Philippines

*The Philippines is improving its regulatory framework to improve the country's business climate. Many activities conducted by the National Competitive Council have focused on reducing administrative burden and cutting red tape for businesses. Government agencies across the country are also making meaningful steps to improve databases and information systems to provide practical and timely information to its citizens. For example, the government has automised a number of its services through the use of one-stop shops or "*negosyo*" (business) centres to simplify the business registration process. The government also offers programmes to increase small and medium-sized enterprises' (SMEs) capacity to adhere to design and labelling requirements, including information and mentoring sessions organised specifically for SMEs.*

Regulatory context

In 2007, the government passed Republic Act No. 9485 or the Anti-Red-Tape Act (ARTA), which focused on improving the efficiency of public delivery by reducing red tape and preventing graft and corruption in the country. The law called for the need to re-engineer the different systems and procedures within offices and agencies that offer frontline services (Government of the Philippines, 2007[1]). The Senate Bill 1311/House Bill 6579 passed in 2017 proposes amendments to the ARTA to further promote transparency in the government, notably in relation to business registrations by mandating cities and municipalities to follow a set of standards in processing business permits and licences. The amendment requires government agencies and local governments to, among others, undertake regulatory impact assessment (RIA) to ensure that regulations do not add undue regulatory burden and costs. The amendments also include the creation of an Anti-Red Tape Authority as the policy-making body on business registration and regulatory management.

In 2014, Republic Act (RA) 10644 or the *Go Negosyo* Act was enacted into law by former President Benigno Simeon C. Aquino III. The act was aimed at improving the ease of doing business in the country and at facilitating the access of micro, small, and medium enterprises (MSMEs) to the different government services through the establishment of *Go Negosyo* centres or one-stop shops. Through this act, recent regulatory policies for MSMEs have resulted in the push for the computerisation of registration for certain government agencies through the Philippine Business Registry (PBR).

The aforementioned laws help guide the Department of Trade and Industry in developing five-year MSME Development Plans. These Development Plans include various initiatives and programmes to be implemented by various stakeholders and are often focused on: 1) promoting an enabling business environment; 2) enhancing access to finance; 3) enhancing access to markets; and 4) improving productivity and efficiency.

The most recent MSME Development Plan 2017-22 builds on the objectives and achievements of previous plans and focuses on improving the business environment, increasing access to finance and markets, and raising productivity and efficiency (MSMED Council, 2016[2]). However, it also aims to tackle new issues such as security and border protection in light of increasing integration and mobility concerns, as well as disaster risk reduction and effective management in light of precarious financial markets. In addition, it integrates the Philippines long-term vision, also known as *AmBisyon Natin 2040*, which reflects the aspirations that Filipinos want to realise for the country and themselves by 2040.

The MSME Development Plan includes a number of key performance indicators to be achieved by 2022 in terms of employment, registered SMEs and value-added contribution of MSMEs to the economy (Table 8.1).

Table 8.1. Overall key performance indicators for the MSME Development Plan 2017-21

Proposed Indicators	Baseline	Target
Increase in employment of MSME	4.784 million	8.282 million
Percentage increase in number of registered MSMEs (%)	18.74 (896 839)	20
Proportion of small-scale industries (enterprises) in total value added increased (%)	35.7	50-55*

* Following the targets of ASEAN-6, particularly Malaysia and Singapore.
Source: MSMED Council (2016), *Micro, Small and Medium Enterprise Development Plan 2017-2022*, p. 45.

Ease of Doing Business

On 31 October 2017, President Rodrigo Duterte reaffirmed the government's commitment to improving the ease of doing business in the country. To do this, the government seeks to undertake new projects, including new legislation or amendments to improve existing legislation.

Box 8.1. Improving the ease of doing business in the Philippines

The Government of the Philippines plans to undertake a series of reforms and improvements as a way to improve the ease of doing business in the country (Department of Trade and Industry, 2018[3]; National Competitiveness Council, 2017[4]). These include:

Jumpstarting a business

More specifically:

1. *Full operationalisation of the* company registration system in November 2017, an online registration for companies operated by the Securities Commission.
2. Setting up of an enhanced one-stop shop from January 2018 in Quezon City, Metro Manila, which co-locates all concerned units or offices in one facility, including the Business Permits and Licensing Office, the Zoning Office, the Treasurer's Office, and the Bureau of Fire Protection.
3. Institutionalising a single window transaction project through the Bureau of Internal Revenue, where applicants can submit documents and be issued the Certificate of Registration and Authority to Print.

These measures are expected to reduce procedures for starting a business from 16 to 10 days and the processing time from 28 days to 16 days.

Streamlining licences and permits

The government aims to streamline the issuance of business permits and licensing through amendments to the Anti-Red Tape Act (ARTA) and improvements in the issuance of construction permits. In relation to construction permits, some measures taken include: 1) an establishment of a one-stop shop for construction-related permits in the Quezon City, Metro Manila; and 2) making business clearance a post-requirement. These measures are expected to reduce the procedures related to this transaction from 8 to 23 days and the processing time from 122 to 36 days.

Improving systems and databases

Improvements include: 1) the Philippine Business Registry, an online registration system; 2) the Philippines Data Bank, a business database to validate identities and licences; 3) the Credit Information system, an online database for lenders; 4) the Collateral Registry, a database for movable properties and other assets; 5) the eCourts system, an online appeals system and information database on judicial processes; and 6) the National Single Window (NSW), as part of the efforts within the ASEAN region to automate and harmonise import and export application processes.

Sources: Department of Trade and Industry (2018), *Press Statement on Ease of Doing Business Reforms by CEODBG Undersecretary Rowel S. Barba*, https://dti.gov.ph/media/speeches#press-statement-on-ease-of-doing-business-reforms-by-undersecretary-rowel-s-barba-may-2018; National Competitiveness Council (2017), *The Duterte Administration Strengthens its Efforts on Improving Ease of Doing Business in the Philippines*, http://www.competitive.org.ph/stories/1389 (accessed on 22 February 2018).

Several efforts to improve the regulatory process have been carried out by the government to support the growth and development of MSMEs in the country. Good Regulatory Practices were first introduced in the Philippines in 2007 when the ASEAN Consultative Committee for Standards and Quality (ACCSQ) had certified the ASEAN Good Regulatory Practice (ASEAN GRP). Since then, the government has endeavoured to adopt various frameworks and tools to improve the development of regulations, such as the introduction of the quality regulatory management system (QRMS) that includes the use of regulatory impact assessments (RIA).

Regulatory governance

Institutional and regulatory setup

Table 8.2. Institutional and regulatory setup

	Government
State structure	Unitary state
Head of state	**President**, who is elected through a direct vote and serves a single, non-renewable 6-year term
Executive	**Vice President**, also elected by direct vote and serves the same period of tenure as the President, is the second highest official in the executive. The **Cabinet**, led by the Cabinet Secretary, are appointed by the President with the consent of the Commission on Appointments (Republic of the Philippines, 2017[5]).
Legislative	Bicameral The Congress of the Philippines is composed of (Republic of the Philippines, 2017[6]): • **House of Representatives** with 250 elected individuals at the municipal or district level, of which 20% are party-list members. • **Senate** with 24 elected officials (senators) at the national level by qualified voters. Each senator is responsible for specific committees corresponding to specific priority issues.
Legal system	Mixed system (common and civil law) Legislative acts can be appealed via the Supreme Court, Court of Appeals, Court of Tax Appeals, Regional Trial Courts, and Shari'a District Courts. The *Sandiganbayan* is a special court to ensure the highest official conduct among public servants. The Office of the Ombudsman is responsible for investigating and trying government officials on allegedly guilty crimes, notably graft and corruption.
Administrative-territorial structure	Local government unit (LGU) comprises of four elected administrative divisions: 1) autonomous regions; 2) provinces; 3) municipalities or cities; and 4) *barangays*. Each administrative unit holds legislative assemblies that formulate plans and policies through legislative measures and are likewise responsible for reviewing and enacting these legislations.
Ministry or agency responsible for SMEs or SME-related issues	**MSME Development Council** serves as the co-ordinating and oversight body for all agencies involved in SME policy development. The council is represented by 19 officials from both private sector and government. Some regions and provinces also have regional MSME Development Council, which act based on the instructions from the National MSME Development Council. **Bureau of Micro, Small and Medium Enterprises** within the Department of Trade and Industry (DTI), which oversees the operations and development of SMEs in the country.
Oversight body or bodies	• **National Economic and Development Authority (NEDA)** serves as the socio-economic planning body of the country, is responsible for advising high-level policymakers, and serves as a co-ordinating body for the formulation of national and subnational policies.
Other support structures within government on regulatory policy	Two out of the three constitutional commissions: **Civil Service Commission (CSC)** and **Commission on Audit (COA)** • **National Competitiveness Council (NCC)** is a joint private-public council that is aimed at promoting a competitive business environment in the country. • **Philippine Competition Commission (PCC)**, which is an independent and quasi-judicial body mandated to oversee national competition policy and promotes and protects competitive markets. • **Development Academy of the Philippines (DAP)** serves as the training and education arm of the civil service sector.

Sources: OECD compilation; Republic of the Philippines (2017), *The Executive Branch*, www.officialgazette.gov.ph/about/gov/exec (accessed on 5 December 2017); Republic of the Philippines (2017), *The Judicial Branch*, http://www.officialgazette.gov.ph/about/gov/judiciary/ (accessed on 6 December 2017).

Regulatory process

There is no central body in the Philippines that oversees the implementation and review of regulatory policies or, more specifically, SME regulatory policies. Laws and regulations that affect businesses can be passed at different levels of government, from the *barangay* to the central or national level.

In most cases, the formulation of new regulations related to SMEs and its implementation is contingent on the mandates of concerned line agencies. The executive body can produce the following forms of policies or regulations:

Table 8.3. Types of policies and regulations passed at the executive level

Type	Description
Executive orders	General rules or orders based on constitutional or statutory powers
Administrative orders	Relate to a specific governmental operation
Proclamations	Defines a date or status or condition of public interest and holds the same force as executive orders
Memorandum orders	Refer to administrative detail of subordinate interest which is directed towards a specific government body or public official
Memorandum circulars	Relate to internal administration matter or information for which the President would like to call into attention for compliance within departments, bureaus, or offices of the government
General or special orders	Commands of the President within his capacity as commander-in-chief of the Armed Forces of the Philippines

The involvement of the legislative bodies in SME policy is focused on the creation of appropriate laws with line agencies under the executive branch and local government units (LGUs) formulating and implementing their respective business-related regulations. These legislations come in the form of ordinances or resolutions.

- An *ordinance* refers to a local law that regulates specific people or property following prescribed, uniform and permanent rules of conduct.
- A resolution refers to a position or policy of a local administrative unit.

When drafting laws, both the Senate and Congress produce two main documents: 1) resolutions, which are principles or sentiments conveyed by either the Senate or the House of Representatives and are further classified into joint resolutions, concurrent resolutions and simple resolutions; and 2) bills, which are "laws in the making" that would also need to be approved by both houses and Office of the President.

The legislative process in the country starts with a bill that is filed with the secretary of either the lower (House of Representatives) or upper (Senators) house. The bill then undergoes three readings. The first reading involves the identification and description of the bill and its referral to the appropriate committee for consideration. The second reading includes a full reading of the bill and any proposed amendments, which is then followed by a debate among the members of the house. If approved, the bill will proceed to the third reading where it will be submitted for the final vote and conveyed to the other house for approval. The other house will then undergo a similar process.

Figure 8.1. Legislative process in the Philippines

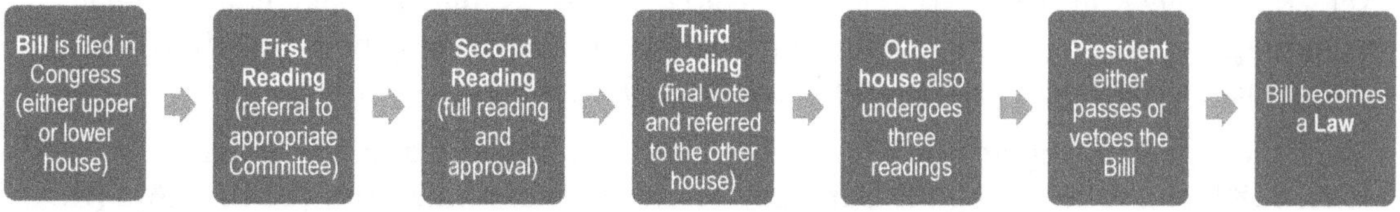

In any case that the other house introduces new amendments which are not in accordance with the house from where it has originated, the amendments would need to be agreed within a Conference of Committees that convenes both houses.

Once the bill has been approved by both houses, it is transmitted to the President for approval. If approved, the bill officially becomes a law. If otherwise, the President can exercise his or her veto power and the Congress may re-pass the bill. The bill would need two-thirds of both houses, voting separately, to approve its enactment of the law.

Business laws and regulations in the Philippines

In general, business regulations are uniformly implemented across all enterprise sizes; however, incentives are often provided to certain MSMEs to encourage, among other objectives, entry into the formal economy or compliance to international standards, as stipulated in the aforementioned laws (World Bank, 2017[7]).

Table 8.4. Business-related laws and regulations in the Philippines

Type	Description
Banking and credit laws	General Banking Law of 2000; Act Providing for the Creation, Organization, and Operation of Rural Banks, and For Other Purposes (R.A. 7353); Revised Non-Stock Savings and Loan Association Act of 1997; Financing Company Act R.A. 8556 of 1998); An Act Providing for the Mortgaging of Personal Property and for the Registration of the Mortgages so executed (Act No. 1508)
Bankruptcy and collateral laws	An Act Providing for the Rehabilitation or Liquidation of Financially Distressed Enterprise and Individuals (R.A. 10142 of 2010); Financial Rehabilitation and Insolvency Act (FRIA) of 2010; Securitization Act of 2004; Rules and Procedure on Corporate Rehabilitation (Supreme Court Administrative Matter No. 00-8-10-C); Securities Regulation Code (R.A. 8799); Presidential Decree No. 1799
Commercial and company laws	Corporation Code of the Philippines
Labour law	Labor Code of the Philippines; Labor Code (Presidential Decree No. 442); Social Security Act of 1997; Wage Rationalization Act
Land and building laws	Securitization Act of 2004; National Building Code of the Philippines; Implementing Rules and Regulations on the National Building Code of the Philippines (Presidential Decree 1096, revised 2005)
Securities laws	Securities Regulation Code (R.A. 8799); Securitization Act of 2004
Tax laws	National Internal Revenue Code of the Philippines
Customs law	Tariff and Customs Code of the Philippines

Source: World Bank (2017), *Law Library*, http://www.doingbusiness.org/law-library/ (accessed on 8 March 2018).

Micro, small, and medium enterprise (MSME) regulatory policy is enshrined in the Magna Carta for MSMEs, which was first passed by the Philippine Congress as Republic Act (R.A.) 6977 in 1991. The Magna Carta serves as the national policy aimed at promoting, supporting and strengthening the growth and development of MSMEs in the Philippines (Department of Trade and Industry, 2017[8]).

Given the rapidly changing business environment, the Magna Carta was amended in 1997 (R.A. 8289) and followed by the Barangay Micro Business Enterprise (BMBE) Act (R.A. 9178), which was passed by the government in 2002. The BMBE Act aimed to encourage the growth of micro-businesses at the barangay level - the smallest administrative unit in the country, comparable to a village or neighbourhood - by providing incentives such as exemptions from tax or minimum wage requirements. Six years later in 2008, the Magna Carta was amended again (R.A. 9501) to modify the definition of SMEs and revise the rules and regulations governing the allocation of credit resources for MSMEs – notably to increase transparency on financial instruments and institutions and to enhance access to credit for MSMEs by mandating financial institutions to allocate a portion of their credit portfolio to MSMEs (Department of Trade and Industry, 2017[8]).

The present definition of MSMEs is based on Section 3 of the Magna Carta and is as follows:

> *"Engaged in any business activity or enterprise engaged in the production, processing or manufacturing of products or commodities, including agro-processing, trading and services whether single proprietorship, co-operative, partnership or corporation".*

These MSMEs are then further sorted into specific categories based on total assets of the enterprise, more particularly:

Table 8.5. MSME categories in the Philippines

	Total Assets (PHP)
Micro	> 3 000 000
Small	3 000 001 – 15 000 000
Medium	15 000 001 – 100 000 000

Source: Information provided by the Department of Trade and Industry Philippines, 2017.

As of 2016, there are 915 726 registered MSMEs in the country. Micro-enterprises make up the bulk with 89.63% of the total enterprises, followed by small enterprises with 9.50% and medium enterprises with 0.43% (Figure 8.2). In addition, MSMEs share a substantial portion of total employment, with around 63% of workers in sectors run by MSMEs. Most MSMEs in the Philippines are concentrated in wholesale and retail trade and repair of motor vehicles and motorcycles (46.93%) followed by accommodation and food services activities (13.07%) and manufacturing (12.64%). MSMEs also contribute to around 25% of the total exports revenue and around 60% of the total exporters are categorised as MSMEs, mainly due to subcontracting arrangements with larger firms or as suppliers for exporting companies (Department of Trade and Industry, 2016[9]).

While large enterprises account for less than 0.43% of total enterprises, they employ the greatest share of workers at 37%. These large enterprises are primarily concentrated in the manufacturing (63%) and the services sector (49%) (Philippine Statistics Authority, 2015[10]).

Figure 8.2. Distribution of enterprises by size (left) and by employment (right)

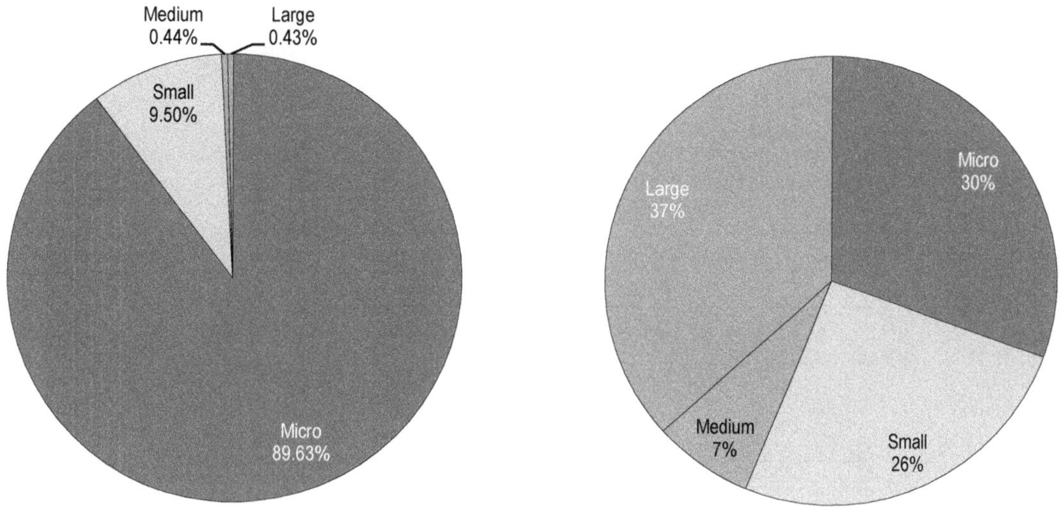

Source: Department of Trade and Industry (2016), *2016 MSME Statistics*, http://www.dti.gov.ph/dti/index.php/2014-04-02-03-40-26/news-room/179-workshop-on-market-access-for-smes-set.

Depending on the type of business, business registration is handled by various government agencies. For sole proprietorships, the most important step is to register the business through the Department of Trade and Industry (DTI). This is done by filling up a form with the unique business name. Business names can be cross-checked via the DTI website. Following this procedure, the enterprise will receive a DTI Certificate of Registration, which must be used to register with the local government units (LGUs) within their respective jurisdiction, e.g. mayor's office and *barangay*. Once this has been completed, a certificate of business registration (from the *barangay*) and a business permit and licence (from the mayor's office) is provided to the proprietor.

Following this step, the business would need to proceed to the closest regional district office (RDO) of the Bureau of Internal Revenue (BIR) for tax purposes. If there are employees working within the enterprise, other additional procedures also include the need to register with the social security service (SSS) and the Philippine Health Insurance Company (PHIC). Recently, the government has made efforts to improve the business registration procedure through the Philippine Business Registry that aims to connect all the different government agencies in one platform (Philippine Business Registry, 2018[11]).

On the other hand, instead of the DTI, the Securities and Exchange Commission (SEC) is responsible for registering partnerships and companies or corporations. The requirements are the same, with the exception of the articles of partnership or incorporation and by-laws. The registration procedure for all types of business can range from a few days to a few months.

Table 8.6. Registration requirements in the Philippines

	Sole proprietorship	Partnership	Corporation
Registration area	• Department of Trade and Industry (DTI) • Local government unit (Mayor's Office or *barangay*) • Bureau of Internal Revenue (with employees: Social Security System, Philippine Health Insurance System; Home Development Mutual Fund)	• Securities and Exchange Commission • Local government unit (Mayor's Office or *barangay*) • Bureau of Internal Revenue (with employees: Social Security System, Philippine Health Insurance System; Home Development Mutual Fund)	
Description	One-person business	A firm or organisation with two or more business partners*	A legal entity with distinct roles from its shareholders and directors**
Registration Requirements (DTI)/ Securities and Exchange Commission (SEC)	Three business names (for proposal) until confirmed on website to receive certificate of registration	• Unique business name • Articles of Incorporation and by-laws	
Registration requirements (*barangay*) and Mayor's Office	• Certificate of registration from DTI • Two valid proof of identification • Proof of address, e.g. contract lease or land title		
Registration requirements (BIR)	• BIR form • Certificate of registration from DTI • *Barangay* clearance • Mayor's Business Permit • Proof of address, e.g. contract lease or land title • Valid identification		
Setup fee	Registration fee varies across different jurisdictions and each step includes a fee. The enterprise must also take into account other related costs (e.g. inspection fees, printing and photocopies of documents)***		
Continuity of the business entity	Yearly renewal		
Closure of business	Termination of renewal	• By partners' cessation or dissolution • Winding up or striking off	

* The definition of partnership under the New Civil Code of the Philippines, Article 1767 is as follows: "By the contract of partnership two or more persons bind themselves to contribute money, property or industry to a common fund, with the intention of dividing the profits among themselves".

** The definition of a corporation under the Corporation Code of the Philippines, Section 2 is as follows: "A corporation is an artificial being created by operation of law, having the right of succession and powers, attribute and properties expressly authorised by law or incident of its existence".

*** Information on registration fees can be found here: www.bnrs.dti.gov.ph/web/guest/faqsfees.

Source: Philippine Business Registry (2018), *Philippine Business Registry*, https://www.business.gov.ph/web/guest/bn-search (accessed on 21 February 2018).

Highlights of regulatory opportunities and challenges to support SMEs

Administrative simplification

The Anti-Red Tape and Competitiveness Bureau of the Department of Trade and Industry (DTI) and the private sector through the National Competitiveness Council (NCC) have been developing a number of tools and mechanisms to improve business-related regulatory reforms, notably those that affect SMEs, by focusing on cutting red tape in the country as mandated in R.A. 9485 or the Anti-Red Tape Act (ARTA) of 2007. A number of its activities have been carried out through Project Repeal (Box 8.2) (National Competitiveness Council Philippines, 2017[12]).

Through Project Repeal, the government also runs a series of workshops on standard cost models, as a way to measure the business compliance cost and to support the development of a tool for regulators to assess administrative burden.

The National Competitiveness Council (NCC) regularly provides capacity building for officers of Business Process Licensing Offices at the subnational level in order to update them with the latest licensing procedures.

Box 8.2. Reducing the burden on businesses in the Philippines

The National Competitiveness Council (NCC), a joint public-private body, leads the regulatory reduction initiatives in the Philippines. Among these initiatives is Project Repeal, a whole-of-government approach to regulatory reform launched in 2016 and is aimed at cutting red tape that affects the ease of doing business and the delivery of social services in the country.

Project Repeal intends to rationalise the current pool of department issuances by weeding out outdated, redundant and burdensome regulations. In doing so, administrative processes are simplified and regulatory burdens to business and the public are reduced.

This long-term strategic policy reform initiative is implemented using a holistic, developmental and phased approach to improve the country's Global Competitiveness Index, especially in the World Bank Doing Business criteria. This government-wide regulatory reform initiative is expected to directly benefit the business sector as cutting the costs of doing business will facilitate the entry and growth of trade and investments, create new businesses, and promote education and innovation in the country.

From an initial 8 agencies, the initiative has expanded to over 86 line and attached agencies. Since its inception, over 4 837 policy issuances have been reviewed.

Source: National Competitiveness Council Philippines (2017), *Project Repeal: The Philippine Anti-Red Tape Challenge*, http://www.competitive.org.ph/node/1361 (accessed on 7 December 2017).

In 2015, the Development Academy of the Philippines (DAP) and the National Economic and Development Authority (NEDA) initiated the Modernising Government Regulations (MGR) Programme which seeks to reduce regulatory burden in the country by 25% by 2020 (Development Academy of the Philippines, 2016[16]) (Box 8.3). Several workshops and training sessions on RIA for government agencies have been rolled out with the view to institutionalise Regulatory Management System (RMS) at the industry level and expand the use of regulatory impact assessments across government agencies and strengthening the national regulatory architecture in the country (Development Academy of the Philippines, 2017[17]).

Box 8.3. Modernising Government Regulations (MGR) programme

The MGR programme is a five-year programme led by the Development Academy of the Philippines (DAP) and the National Economic and Development Authority (NEDA). The programme aims to accelerate the improvements in regulatory quality in the country as a way to promote growth and employment and attract foreign and local investment. Since its implementation in 2014, the Modernising Government Regulations (MGR) programme has organised over five workshops and training sessions on regulatory policy tools and mechanisms with government officials. The programme is gradually expanding its outreach to the different key industries. A number of events have focused on mapping regulatory issues faced across different industries.

Since 2014, six industry dialogues have been organised to gather inputs from business owners on the perceived issues and best practices. Specific activities include: 1) interviewing businesses to gather information on business processes; 2) cross-checking processes with citizens charters of agencies; 3) collecting details on regulations from government agencies; and 4) drawing regulatory maps for the specific industry.

As of 2017, there were 47 agencies that benefited from the RIA training sessions conducted with various government agencies. In 2018, the MGR programme will focus on infrastructure, healthcare and consumer goods. DAP has scheduled four basic regulatory impact assessment (RIA) training sessions this year. In addition, two RIA conventions will be held to gather past RIA training participants. This will be a venue to share agency experiences, best practices and challenges in RIA implementation.

In addition, the government also plans to adopt a single business ID, implement a harmonised Business Regulation Information System (BRIS) and improve the business and licensing process.

Sources: Abad Santos, C. (2017), *Capacity Building on RIA: The Philippines Experience*, Phnom Penh; Development Academy of the Philippines (2016), *Modernizing Government Regulations: Renewed APEC Agenda for Structural Reform (RAASR) 2016-2020*; Development Academy of the Philippines (2017), *Accomplishment Report First Quarter: Modernizing Government Regulations Program.*

One-stop business centres

As a way to further facilitate the business process, the *Go Negosyo* Act was passed into law in 2014. The act mandated the creation of *negosyo* centres to serve as one-stop business assistance centres and to house both government and private sector enablers working together to facilitate business processes in the country (Box 8.4).

The establishment of *negosyo* centres initiated the review of various processes and regulations of different public services offered through these centres. For example, to expedite the process of issuing licences and permits through *negosyo* centres, the Department of Trade and Industry (DTI), Department of the Interior and Local Government (DILG) and Department of Information and Communications Technology (DICT) have issued a Joint Memorandum Circular that aims to revise the standards in processing business permits and licences in all local government units (LGUs).[1] These include using a unified form and adopting a standard process and processing time.

Box 8.4. *Go Negosyo* Centres: A one-stop shop for businesses in the Philippines

In 2014, the Go *Negosyo* Act or Republic Act No. 10644 was signed into law by former President Benigno S. Aquino. The act was aimed at strengthening micro, small and medium enterprises (MSMEs) and promoting inclusive growth in the country. The law called for the establishment of *negosyo* centres to facilitate the delivery of services to MSMEs in each local government unit (LGU). These *negosyo* centres provided services such as business registration, business advisory services, business information and advocacy, and monitoring and evaluation of improvement in business processes.

In addition to these advisory and processing services, entrepreneurs are also able to access a start-up fund from these *negosyo* centres. The start-up fund, also introduced in the Magna Carta for MSMEs, aims to provide financing to MSMEs that are engaged in priority sectors identified in the MSME Development Plan.

As of February 2018, there are currently 789 *negosyo* centres in the Philippines. Of the total, 48% are located in the island of Luzon, 23% in Visayas, and 28% in Mindanao (Department of Trade and Industry, 2014[13]).

Source: Department of Trade and Industry (2014), *Go Negosyo Act*, http://www.dti.gov.ph/programs-projects/negosyo-center/go-negosyo-act.

E-government

In 2012, the government conducted a study to assess the state of e-government in the Philippines. The assessment led to the development of the e-government section in the Philippine Digital Strategy 2011-16 and also informed the development of a digital blueprint for the whole-of-government or the E-Government Master Plan (EGMP). A number of improvements have already been made in relation to the master plan to support the facilitation of certain services, both for the private and public sector.

For example, the Philippine Business Registry system (https://bnrs.dti.gov.ph) allows sole proprietorships to register their businesses with the Department of Trade and Industry on line. Services include name registration, validation of existing tax identification numbers and employment registrations, online payment for application, renewal of application and trademark application. All these are done through web-based DTI tellers.

Regulatory delivery

Enforcement and inspections

Implementation of MSME regulations depends on the mandate and jurisdiction of the line agencies concerned. Some agencies that operate at the national level have provincial or regional counterparts that are also responsible for ensuring the implementation of regulations passed at the national level.

Other than line agencies, local government units are also responsible for ensuring compliance with regulations, including enforcement and inspection activities.

Compliance

Compliance with standards

MSMEs in the Philippines face low compliance with national and international standards, such as quality and environmental standards that hinder their possibility to participate in the global value chains. Oftentimes, this is attributed to the limited technical knowledge and training among potential MSMEs and start-ups.

Marketing and labelling requirements in the Philippines are guided by the Consumer Act of the Philippines (R.A. 7394) and the Philippine National Standards (PNS). The Bureau of Philippine Standards (BPS), under the Department of Trade and Industry (DTI), serves as the national standards body and is responsible for implementing and enforcing PNS and related issues. All products sold in the Philippine market, either local or imported, would need to include the following information in their product labels:

- Registered trademark or brand.
- Registered business information: name and address of manufacturer, importer, re-packer, and others.
- General and active ingredients.
- Content and quality, including weight.
- Country of manufacture.

The Department of Trade and Industry is also responsible for ensuring consumer protection needs are met through activities such as price monitoring, assistance, and effective product certification.

The Bureau of Product Standards updates the list of products under mandatory certification through their website (www.bps.dti.gov.ph) on a bi-annual basis (Box 8.5). In addition, businesses can also access an online portal has been developed to offer information on the various national and international standards, regulations and assessment requirements.

Box 8.5. Standards and Conformance (S&C) Portal in the Philippines

The S&C Portal (www.bps.dti.gov.ph) is a one-stop information centre that provides users with an easy access to a wide range of trade-related technical regulations, standards, and barriers to trade notifications within the Philippines and with major trading partners.

The portal includes a complete catalogue of Philippine National Standards and provides users with the possibility to cross-search multiple databases on line (both foreign and local).

The portal also provides the possibility for users and stakeholders to share comments on proposed technical regulations or standards issued by World Trade Organization (WTO) members (Department of Trade and Industry, 2017[23]).

Source: Department of Trade and Industry (2017), *The S&C Portal*, http://www.bps.dti.gov.ph/index.php?option=com_content&view=article&id=50:the-sac-portal&catid=39:rokstories-samples.

Box 8.6. Supporting product development in the Philippines

Product Development and Design Centre of the Philippines (PDDCP)

The PDDCP offers businesses with resources to help improve product and packaging design and processes. The centre offers seminars and information on the latest development and trends on packaging technologies and related topics.

Brand Equity Development Programme (BrEDP)

Launched in 2017, the BrED programme is aimed at developing and promoting local brands, notably MSMEs from at least one province, in the domestic and international market. The programme is steered by the central DTI office but participants are chosen through the Department of Trade and Industry field offices. The evaluation and selection of beneficiaries are done through the provincial offices. Beneficiaries of the programme will undertake a needs analysis and review of competencies in order to determine the most appropriate intervention. Interventions and activities include brand awareness sessions, capacity building sessions, coaching or mentoring sessions, trademark registration and other promotional activities.

Capacity building under the programme includes training, trips or sessions related to strategic marketing, brand positioning and other brand management activities. In addition, the government supports beneficiaries in facilitating registration of certificates such as the Halal, Food and Drugs Administration, and Hazard Analysis and Critical Control Points (HACCP).

One Town, One Product (OTOP) programme

Launched in 2002, OTOP serves as a stimulus programme for micro, small, and medium enterprises (MSMEs) in the Philippines. The programme encourages communities to identify, develop and grow products and services from their locality. In the recent years, the Department of Trade and Industry had launched OTOP Next Gen, which aims to upgrade the production of MSMEs with "minimum viable products". Beneficiaries of the programme are provided with other assistance packages offered by the DTI.

KAPATID Mentor Micro Entrepreneurs (KMME) programme

KMME is an initiative between the DTI and the Philippine Centre for Entrepreneurship. It is a programme that links MSMEs with other micro, small, and medium entrepreneurs as well as large enterprises and their practitioners from the different *negosyo* centres nationwide. The programme provides MSMEs with the opportunity to scale up their businesses through regular mentoring sessions that focus on the needs of the mentee, e.g. production and marketing strategies and administrative and finance issues. The programme has three components and is focused on: 1) a coaching and mentoring approach between large corporations and MSMEs; 2) providing MSMEs access to Shared Service Facilities (SSF); and 3) an inclusive business model that links MSMEs to large companies' value chains.

SME Roving Academy (SMERA)

SMERA is a progressive learning programme that supports SME development and growth. The project is aimed at integrating business development services of SMEs into the national and local level and creating strong SME networks to ensure a more inclusive promotion programme. SMEs taking part in the programme are guided by an SME counsellor throughout the production process.

Source: Department of Trade and Industry (2017), *Programs and Projects*, www.dti.gov.ph/programs-projects (accessed 14 December 2017).

Regulatory quality management

Regulatory impact assessments

Since 2008, initiatives have been in place to establish regulatory impact assessments in the Philippines. The National Economic and Development Authority (NEDA) has started to work with key development partners through provisions of technical assistance for the RIA pilot programme. Upon the request of NEDA and the Department of Trade and Industry (DTI), the Asian Development Bank (ADB) assessed the institutional framework and possibility of creating the Office of Best Regulatory Practice (OBRP). Following a thorough assessment of the institutions and systems with the support of the ADB, the government identified a number of challenges linked to co-ordination and interface as well as skills and capacity, which made the proposal unviable during this period.

Nonetheless, in 2012, the government decided to carry out pilot tests for regulatory impact assessments through the Department of Tourism (DOT) and the Department of Labour and Employment (DOLE). Some impact statements that have been conducted have focused on business-related issues.

Box 8.7. Regulatory impact assessment (RIA) pilot tests in the Philippines

The Philippines' government has developed a set of regulatory impact assessment (RIA) guidelines to support implementation by line agencies. The guidelines include key steps, assessment issues, and stakeholder consultations. It also provides implementing agencies with several templates to develop preliminary impact assessments (PIA), regulatory impact statements (RIS), and regulatory assessment summaries (RAS).

The Department of Tourism (DOT) and the Department of Labour and Employment (DOLE) are two line agencies that have conducted pilot tests to introduce regulatory impact assessments (RIA) to policy-making processes. Both Departments have developed annual RIA work plans and created dedicated support teams responsible for overseeing its implementation. The agencies have also conducted a number of training and technical learning sessions for local government units.

Since the beginning of the pilots in 2012, DOT has completed four RIS focused on: 1) Rules and Regulations Governing the Conduct of Sports Scuba Diving in the Philippines; 2) Cost Recovery of Hotel Accreditation Fees; 3) Simplification of Hotel Accreditation Fees; 4) Guidelines on Marine Wildlife Tourism. DOT has also begun to introduce RIA to local government units since the fourth quarter of 2017 (Department of Tourism, 2012[14]; Abad Santos, 2017[15]).

Between 2012 and 2016, DOLE has completed eight RIS related to: 1) security of tenure; 2) employment insurance; 3) labour market tests; 4) Magna Carta of seafarers; 5) apprenticeships; 6) private recruitment and placement agencies; 7) public employment service office; and 8) a special programme for the employment of students.

Sources: Department of Tourism (2012), *Philippine RIA Pilot Program*, http://www.tourism.gov.ph/ria_pilot.aspx (accessed on 7 December 2017); Abad Santos, C.B.O. (2017), *Capacity Building on RIA: The Philippines Experience*, Phnom Penh.

Ex post *evaluation*

Ex post reviews of regulations are conducted on a demand-driven basis. There is currently no existing evaluation framework for MSME regulations to be regularly evaluated for their efficiency in meeting specific goals and objectives set out. Nonetheless, the government reviews existing business or SME regulations based on specific priority areas or issues affecting these enterprises.

Stakeholder engagement

Consultations are required for all legislation, department administrative orders and any issuances that directly affect the public. The framework in which consultations take place is defined by the agency. It is the prerogative of the agency formulating the regulations to make their issuance as accessible to the public as possible.

These consultations often take place after the business regulation has been drafted and prior to the approval of the appropriate authorities. Regional or provincial MSME development councils also take part in ensuring that priorities outlined by the National MSME development councils are considered at the local level. MSMEs are consulted when specific regulations are perceived to affect them.

Standard ways of informing the public of a new regulation include letters or notices to affected parties,[2] publications available on the web[3] and in print, and press releases. Some agencies that publish draft legislation or administrative issuances on line also provide stakeholders with the opportunity to share their comments and suggestions. For primary laws, after the comments have been considered and the draft finalised, stakeholders are provided with feedback in the form of legislative hearings or consultations.

In 2011, the Department of Trade and Industry (DTI) introduced One Country, One Voice (OCOV), which is an initiative that aims to engage stakeholders in the process of formulating trade policies. Since its introduction, OCOV has been conducted nationwide for consultations on trade agreements such as the Philippine-European Union (PH-EU) free trade agreement (FTA) and the Regional Comprehensive Economic Partnership (RCEP) (Department of Trade and Industry, n.d.[18]).

There is currently no prescribed timeline for stakeholders to respond to new or amended legislation, whether for general or MSME-specific regulations. In some cases, proposed regulations posted online are open for comments for a few days or a week.

Appeals

The government has made significant efforts to modernise the judicial system in the country, in line with Philippine Development Plan 2017-22 (Chapter 6: Pursuing swift and fair administration of justice) (National Economic and Development Authority, 2017[21]). The eCourt system was launched in 2013 and currently serves as an online case management platform that allows users to file complaints, monitor cases and receive court notices. In cases where appeals do not require legal remedy, MSMEs are encouraged to engage with their local SME Development Council located in their closest MSME assistance centres (Box 8.8).

Box 8.8. Facilitating court appeals in the Philippines

The eCourt system aims to reduce the administrative burden for judicial processes in the country, both at the local and national level. Launched in 2013, the platform provides users with the possibility to track case progress on line. The system puts into a single loop all the case management systems that exist in various court levels and allows for a seamless, electronic transmission of essential case data from lower level courts to the Supreme Council. It also involves the electronic capture, storage, management and retrieval of essential case data and aid judges and court case processors in efficiently handling the volume of cases that flood the jury. Since 2013, the government has continued to improve and expand the system. The government aims to have 297 eCourts across 10 cities by the end of 2017.

The public can access eCourts through a computer or kiosk mounted in a booth inside a court. Through this kiosk, the user can access the database and information on a specific case, including progress and scheduled hearings.

In addition to these basic features, eCourt also has a raffle system, which electronically assigns cases to branches once it has been filed. Parties are automatically informed once this has been done. The system also offers ready templates for court issuances that can be printed on the spot. Overall, the system helps support de-congestion in different courts and helps support employees in ensuring that appeals are addressed in a timely manner (Supreme Court Philippines, 2015[19]; Cabato, 2017[20]).

Sources: Supreme Court Philippines (2015), *Speech delivered by Chief Justice Maria Lourdes P.A. Sereno during Social Good Summit 2015,* http://sc.judiciary.gov.ph/aboutsc/justices/cj-sereno/2015/CJ%20Sereno,%20September%2026,%202015,%20Social%20Good%20Summit%202015,%20Resorts%20World%20Manila,%20Pasay%20City.pdf; Cabato, R. (2017), *Government Rolls Out over 200 eCourts to Promote Transparency,* *http://cnnphilippines.com/news/2017/03/30/200-ecourts-transparency.html.*

SME linkages

Clusters

In 2012, the Philippine government embarked on a three-year journey to develop industry clusters to boost industrial development as well as promote micro, small, and medium enterprises (MSMEs) that are operating within specific industries. The National Industry Cluster Capacity Enhancement Project (NICCEP) aimed to increase the opportunities for enterprises within the same clusters to share knowledge, solutions, technology and resources. The NICCEP also provided the opportunity for the private sector to be actively engaged in the strategic development of the industries in the country, including systematic interaction or dialogues with the local and national government.

The Department of Trade and Industry (DTI) has launched an Industry Cluster Enhancement Programme (ICE) as a way to expand the progress achieved through NICCEP and further upgrade MSME capacities for global competition and integration into global value chains (GVCs). The programme identifies a number of priority industry clusters as targets for specific interventions such as the Shared Service Facilities programme. The Shared Service Facilities programme provides MSMEs with tools, systems and machinery under a shared system.

Box 8.9. Improving MSME productivity through shared facilities in the Philippines

The Shared Service Facilities (SSF) programme aims to improve the competitiveness and productivity of MSMEs nationwide. The SSF provides MSMEs with machinery, equipment and tools under a shared system as a way to address the challenges and reduce the burden that MSMEs face when acquiring or purchasing their own materials (Department of Trade and Industry, 2017[24]).

Target beneficiaries of the SSF project are actual and potential users of SSF, including individuals, co-operatives, associations and other groups of MSMEs. For a facility to be sponsored by the government, the SSF project must meet the following requirements:

- Address processing and manufacturing gaps or bottlenecks of the industry cluster due to the: 1) absence of the needed facility; 2) lack of capacity of an existing facility; 3) high cost of services in an existing facility; and 4) limited technical and administrative services offered to facilitate the growth of MSMEs within the priority industry clusters.
- Increase the productivity of the industry cluster in terms of: 1) product improvement or marketability; 2) price competitiveness; and 3) conformity to standards.
- Support micro-enterprises within the priority industry clusters.
- Improve products that are part of the One Town, One Product (OTOP) project.

There are currently 1 885 SSF across the country, which are well distributed to cater to help in the processing of various products across different regions. A study conducted in 2016 shows around a 20% increase in revenue or sales of SME beneficiaries within selected regions with SSF projects (Medalla et al., 2016[25]).

Sources: Department of Trade and Industry (2017), *Shared Service Facilities (SSF) Projects*, www.dti.gov.ph/programs-projects/shared-service-facilities; Medalla, E. et al. (2016), *Preliminary Assessment of the Shared Service Facilities*, https://dirp3.pids.gov.ph/websitecms/CDN/PUBLICATIONS/pidsdps1618.pdf.

In addition to NICCEP and ICE, the Comprehensive National Industrial Strategy (CNIS) aims to maximise trade and investment by strengthening specific local industries to become globally competitive.[4] The CNIS aims to link and integrate the three industries (agriculture, manufacturing, and services) through innovation and research and development activities, infrastructure investments to enhance and streamline logistics and automation, SME development and other strategic development that facilitate the growth of MSMEs in the global value chains.

Table 8.7. Industry clusters in the Philippines

Product Type	Industry
Agricultural	Bamboo, Banana, Coconut/Coir, Coffee, Dairy, Mango, Milkfish, Palm Oil, Poultry, Rubber, Seaweeds, Tuna, Wood
Manufacturing	Gifts/Decors and Housewares, Mining, Wearables and Homestyle
Services	Health and Wellness, ICT, Tourism

Source: Information provided by the Department of Trade and Industry Bureau of MSMEs, 2017.

Special economic zones (SEZs)

As of November 2017, there are 379 special economic zones in the Philippines, of which 74 manufacturing economic zone are classified as manufacturing economic zones, 262 as information and technology parks or centres, 22 agro-industrial economic zones, 19 tourism economic zones and 2 medical tourism parks (Philippine Economic Zone Authority, 2017[26]).

Special economic zones are guided by Republic Act No. 7916 or the Special Economic Zone Act. A number of activities are permitted within the economic zones and various incentives, both fiscal and non-fiscal, are offered to Philippine Economic Zone Authority (PEZA)-registered enterprises (Annex 8.A).

Non-fiscal incentives in the country include simplified import and export procedures such as the electronic import permit system and automated export documentation system. In addition, foreign nationals also enjoy incentives with regard to labour mobility (Philippine Economic Zone Authority, 2017[27]).

Labour mobility

Labour policy in the country is guided by both in the 1987 Philippine Constitution and the Labour Code of the Philippines. The Philippines continues to align its standards to promote social justice within the workplace. At present, the country has adhered to 37 conventions from the International Labour Organization (ILO), of which 30 are currently in force (International Labour Organization, 2017[28]).

Non-resident foreign nationals may be employed in supervisory, technical or advisory roles in PEZA-registered enterprises. In addition, special non-immigrant visas are also offered for foreign nationals operating in this zone, including dependents such as spouses and unmarried children under 21 years old.

Customs facilitation

In 2014, the Department of Trade and Industry (DTI) re-launched Tradeline Philippines (www.tradelinephilippines.dti.gov.ph), a business intelligence platform dedicated to providing real-time information on trade-related information to current and potential exporters (Tradeline Philippines, 2017[29]). A number of programmes and assistance schemes offered by the DTI to exporters are highlighted in the website.

Box 8.10. Export-assistance schemes and programmes in the Philippines

Start-up Ecosystem Development Programme (SEDP)

SEDP aims to nurture industry and inter-enterprise collaboration among MSMEs. To achieve this, the programme focuses on five strategic areas of development: 1) increasing culture and collaboration; 2) addressing legal and regulatory barriers; 3) offering support through government services, capital and resources; 4) creating a national start-up business council; and 5) establishing a Philippine start-up economic zone.

Regional Interactive Platform for Philippine Exporters (RIPPLES)

As a way to expand the supply base of competitive Philippine exports, RIPPLES supports products and services with high export-potential through strategic interventions such as capacity building, product development and other support mechanisms focused on production, quality, packaging and entry market requirements. Once deemed ready, products and services that are part of this programme are marketed abroad and matched with international partners or buyers.

Philippine Export Competitiveness Programme (PCEP)

PCEP aims to boost the competitiveness of local manufacturers and exporters through seminars and various activities focused on productivity, innovation and specific updates on export.

Doing Business in Free Trade Areas (DBFTA)

Information sessions are organised on a regular basis to inform exporters of the current FTA engagements. These include a handbook as well as a set of flyers to provide users with information on rules of origin, customs procedures, as well as tariff reductions and other incentives in a partner country.

Philippine Halal Export Development and Promotion Programme (PHEDP)

PHDEPT supports the development and promotion of the local Halal industry. The programme aims to establish the regulatory framework and structure to support the export of Philippine Halal products, including ensuring the compliance and quality of the products to national and international standards.

Source: Tradeline Philippines (2017), *Major Programs*, www.tradelinephilippines.dti.gov.ph/web/tradeline-portal/major-programs.

Accreditation is required from all importers and customs brokers for all goods and services, except for importers in special economic zones, partners of Philippine government agencies, and recognised international organisations with diplomatic status. Accredited importers and customs brokers may input import entries online through the Bureau of Customs (BOC) electronic-to-mobile (E2M) system to expedite the process.

The Government of the Philippines is expected to launch an online platform, called TradeNet, to facilitate import and export permits. TradeNet will serve as the Philippines' national single window (NSW) for customs procedures and will be integrated with other ASEAN single windows that are currently in place. TradeNet connects 66 government agencies and 10 economic zones responsible for trade in the country. The system is expected to be integrated into the ASEAN National Single Window in 2018.

Box 8.11. Improving customs procedures in the Philippines

The electronic-to-mobile (E2M) customs system of the Bureau of Customs of the Philippines aims to modernise and improve the revenue collection capacity of the government and reduce the time required to release a cargo or import from three days to thirty minutes.

The E2M customs system aims to automate a number of transactions, including accreditation of importers or customs brokers and other clients, an update of import values, and input of lodgement entries, payment, and cargo release. To support this, the government has aimed to provide suitable IT support facilities and equipment as well as build capacity for the technical staff responsible.

For stakeholders, the project wishes to achieve greater accountability through more transparent and efficient systems, reduce the processing time especially for low-risk transactions, and, overall, help lower the cost of doing business.

Source: Bureau of Customs (2009), *The Basics on the Bureau of Customs e2m-Customs Project.*

Recommendations

- **Consider a regular or systematic review of existing regulations to ensure that proposed regulations continue to meet their intended goals**. The absence of a systematic review process (e.g. sunset clauses) can risk increasing the stock of regulations overtime without lessening the burden imposed on businesses and citizens.
- **Update the business registration toolkit** to ensure that best practices are adapted to the current context and available mediums and technologies.
- **Facilitate the improvements in the Philippine Business Registry to help speed up and reduce the cost of business registration**. Ensure strong and efficient co-ordination across participating agencies with regard to information shared and also promote its use among aspiring and current entrepreneurs.
- **Ensure coherence on the information provided by the different ministries**. It is recommended that websites are regularly updated to ensure that it is in line with any regulatory changes and aligned to avoid overlaps or contradictions in information presented.
- **Establish or assign and oversight body or agency to oversee the mainstreaming of RIA in all regulatory or line agencies and to ensure that RIA is properly implemented.** RIA introduction and implementation could focus on a cross-cutting sectoral issue such as new regulations on SMEs or business registration processes. This can likewise be linked to efforts that reduce regulatory burden in the country, by improving both the stock (quantity) and flow (quality) of regulations.

- **Create a "culture of engagement" that stimulates both the agency and the stakeholders in the consultation process.** For example, by espousing transparency and participation in the regulation-making process, introducing user-friendly web portals, establishing notice-and-comment procedures, and providing plain, clear, and concise draft position papers for public use with adequate time for review and engagement.
- **Consider promoting and informing the public of possible ways to appeal on certain issues or regulations that affect them**. For example, by pursuing regulatory changes in relation to the enforcement of contracts, improving the quality of commercial dispute resolutions systems; or promoting the use of alternative dispute resolutions and arbitration procedures.
- **Consider broadening the options used when improving inspection and enforcement to effectively deliver the objectives of a regulation**. Testing is essential in ensuring that the various interventions are cost-efficient and effective in the long run.
- **Consider aligning national standards and labelling requirements with international or regional (ASEAN) standards**, if it exists, to eliminate duplication and costs related to inspection and encourage more exports.
- **Test and measure if various labelling and standard requirements imposed on businesses are necessary to ensure the quality of products** or if compatible for export, as a measure for value-added for SMEs. Regulatory impact assessments will be useful in helping identify the cost and benefits.
- **Improve backbone services such as financial services and enhance financial literacy** to help SMEs understand and assess financial products and link them to domestic and global markets.
- **Use special economic zones (SEZs) and clusters as an opportunity and platform to effectively introduce more targeted and specific regulations for industries involved**, including initiatives that help improve the quality and scalability of their products and services.
- **Promote and implement technological advancements in cross-border trade to further streamline customs procedures and reduce cost.** Ensure that information and tools are readily available and accessible for SMEs that are interested in exporting their products to specific partner countries or specific destinations.

Notes

[1] Refer to the Joint Memorandum Circular No. 1, 2016: http://blgf.gov.ph/wp-content/uploads/2016/10/dilg_jmcno.1-2016.pdf.

[2] For example, the Department of Trade and Industry's (DTI's) Board of Investments (BOI) issued a Memorandum Circular on the Investments Priorities Plan: http://www.boi.gov.ph/files/2017%20IPP%20GP%20&%20SG%20-%20CTC.pdf.

[3] The Department of Trade and Industry publishes relevant legislations and department issuances via: http://dti.gov.ph/resources/laws-and-policies.

[4] Department of Trade and Industry and Board of Investments (2018), *Comprehensive National Industrial Strategy*, http://industry.gov.ph/comprehensive-national-industrial-strategy/ (accessed on 21 August 2018).

References

Abad Santos, C. (2017), *Capacity Building on RIA: The Philippines Experience*, Phnom Penh. [15]

Bureau of Customs (2009), *The Basics on the Bureau of Customs e2m-Customs Project.* [30]

Cabato, R. (2017), *Government Rolls Out over 200 eCourts to Promote Transparency*, http://cnnphilippines.com/news/2017/03/30/200-ecourts-transparency.html. [20]

Department of Tourism (2012), *Philippine RIA Pilot Program*, http://www.tourism.gov.ph/ria_pilot.aspx (accessed on 7 December 2017). [14]

Department of Trade and Industry (2018), *Press Statement on Ease of Doing Business Reforms by CEODBG Undersecretary Rowel S. Barba*, https://dti.gov.ph/media/speeches#press-statement-on-ease-of-doing-business-reforms-by-undersecretary-rowel-s-barba-may-2018. [3]

Department of Trade and Industry (2017), *Programs and Projects*, http://www.dti.gov.ph/programs-projects (accessed on 14 December 2017). [22]

Department of Trade and Industry (2017), *Republic Act No. 9501: Magna Carta for Micro, Small and Medium Enterprises*, http://www.dti.gov.ph/businesses/msmes/msme-resources/msme-laws. [8]

Department of Trade and Industry (2017), *Shared Service Facilities (SSF) Projects*, http://www.dti.gov.ph/programs-projects/shared-service-facilities. [24]

Department of Trade and Industry (2017), *The S&C Portal*, http://www.bps.dti.gov.ph/index.php?option=com_content&view=article&id=50:the-sac-portal&catid=39:rokstories-samples. [23]

Department of Trade and Industry (2016), *2016 MSME Statistics*, http://www.dti.gov.ph/dti/index.php/2014-04-02-03-40-26/news-room/179-workshop-on-market-access-for-smes-set. [9]

Department of Trade and Industry (2014), *Go Negosyo Act*, http://www.dti.gov.ph/programs-projects/negosyo-center/go-negosyo-act. [13]

Department of Trade and Industry (n.d.), *Stakeholder Consultation*, http://dti.gov.ph/dtiweb3/15-dummy-article/684-stakeholder-consultation. [18]

Development Academy of the Philippines (2017), *Accomplishment Report First Quarter: Modernizing Government Regulations Program.* [17]

Development Academy of the Philippines (2016), *Modernizing Government Regulations: Renewed APEC Agenda for Structural Reform (RAASR) 2016-2020.* [16]

Government of the Philippines (2007), *Anti-Red Tape Act of 2007 (Republic Act No. 9485)*, http://www.csc.gov.ph/2014-02-21-08-28-23/pdf-files/category/234-anti-red-tape-act-of-2007-republic-act-no-9485.html. [1]

International Labour Organization (2017), *International Labour Standards in the Philippines*, http://www.ilo.org/manila/areasofwork/international-labour-standards/lang--en/index.htm. [28]

Medalla, E. et al. (2016), *Preliminary Assessment of the Shared Services Facilities*, https://dirp3.pids.gov.ph/websitecms/CDN/PUBLICATIONS/pidsdps1618.pdf. [25]

MSMED Council (2016), *Micro, Small and Medium Enterprise Development Plan 2017-2022*. [2]

National Competitiveness Council (2017), *The Duterte Administration Strengthens its Efforts on Improving Ease of Doing Business in the Philippines*, http://www.competitive.org.ph/stories/1389 (accessed on 22 February 2018). [4]

National Competitiveness Council Philippines (2017), *Project Repeal: The Philippine Anti-Red Tape Challenge*, http://www.competitive.org.ph/node/1361 (accessed on 7 December 2017). [12]

National Economic and Development Authority (2017), *Philippine Development Plan 2017-2022*, http://www.neda.gov.ph/wp-content/uploads/2017/12/Abridged-PDP-2017-2022_Final.pdf. [21]

Philippine Business Registry (2018), *Philippine Business Registry*, https://www.business.gov.ph/web/guest/bn-search (accessed on 21 February 2018). [11]

Philippine Economic Zone Authority (2017), *Non-Fiscal Incentives to PEZA-Registered Economic Zone Enterprises*, http://www.peza.gov.ph/index.php/eligible-activities-incentives/non-fiscal-incentives. [27]

Philippine Economic Zone Authority (2017), *Operating Economic Zone Map*, http://www.peza.gov.ph/index.php/economic-zones/list-of-economic-zones. [26]

Philippine Statistics Authority (2015), *2015 List of Establishments*. [10]

Republic of the Philippines (2017), *The Executive Branch*, http://www.officialgazette.gov.ph/about/gov/exec/ (accessed on 5 December 2017). [5]

Republic of the Philippines (2017), *The Judicial Branch*, http://www.officialgazette.gov.ph/about/gov/judiciary/ (accessed on 6 December 2017). [6]

Supreme Court Philippines (2015), *Speech delivered by Chief Justice Maria Lourdes P.A. Sereno during the Social Good Summit 2015*, http://sc.judiciary.gov.ph/aboutsc/justices/cj-sereno/2015/CJ%20Sereno,%20September%2026,%202015,%20Social%20Good%20Summit%202015,%20Resorts%20World%20Manila,%20Pasay%20City.pdf. [19]

Tradeline Philippines (2017), *Major Programs*, http://www.tradelinephilippines.dti.gov.ph/web/tradeline-portal/major-programs. [29]

World Bank (2017), *Law Library*, http://www.doingbusiness.org/law-library/ (accessed on 8 March 2018). [7]

Annex 8.A.

Annex Table 8.A.1. Activities and fiscal incentives for registered enterprises in Philippine Economic Zones

Fiscal incentives	Income Tax Holiday (ITH)	Special tax and exemptions	VAT zero rating
Economic Zone Export Manufacturing Enterprise	100% exemption from corporate income tax • Four years for non-pioneer project • Six years for pioneer projects • Three years for expansion projects	• Upon expiry of ITH, 5% special tax on gross income and exemption for all national and local taxes • Tax-Free and Duty-Free importation of raw materials, capital equipment, machinery, etc. • Exemption of wharfage dues, export tax, impost or fees • Exemption from real estate taxes • Exemption from expanded withholding tax	Yes, for all local purchases subject to compliance with Bureau of Internal Revenue (BIR) and Philippine Economic Zone Authority (PEZA)
Information Technology Enterprise	100% exemption from corporate income tax • Four years for non-pioneer project • Six years for pioneer projects • Three years for expansion projects	• Upon expiry of ITH, 5% special tax on gross income and exemption for all national and local taxes • Tax-Free and Duty-Free importation of equipment and parts • Exemption of wharfage dues, export tax, impost or fees • Exemption from real estate taxes • Exemption from expanded withholding tax	Not applicable
Tourism Economic Zone Locator Enterprise	• Four years as qualified under the National Investment Priorities Plan	• Upon expiry of ITH, 5% special tax on gross income and exemption for all national and local taxes • Tax-Free and Duty-Free importation of capital equipment • Exemption from expanded withholding tax	Yes, for all local purchases of goods and services, including land-based telecommunications, electric power, and water bills
Medical Tourism Enterprise	• Four years solely from servicing foreign patients	• Upon expiry of ITH, 5% special tax on gross income and exemption for all national and local taxes • Tax-Free and Duty-Free importation of medical equipment supplies, required for the technical viability and operation of the registered activity/ies of the enterprise • Exemption from expanded withholding tax	Yes, for all local purchases of goods and services, including land-based telecommunications, electric power, and water bills

Agro-Industrial Economic Zone Enterprise	• Four years	• Upon expiry of ITH, 5% special tax on gross income and exemption for all national and local taxes • Tax-Free and Duty-Free importation of production equipment and machinery, breeding stocks, farm implements including spare parts and supplies of the equipment and machinery • Exemption from export taxes, wharfage dues, impost and fees • Exemption from payment of local government fees	Yes, for all local purchases of goods and services, including land-based telecommunications, electric power, and water bills
Economic Zone Logistics Services Enterprise	Not applicable	• Exemption from duties and taxes on raw materials, semi-finished goods for resale to or for packing/covering, cutting, altering for subsequent sales to PEZA-registered export manufacturing enterprises, for direct export or for confinement to PEZA-registered export enterprise	Yes, for all raw materials for checking, packing, visual inspection, storage, and shipping to be sourced locally
Economic Zone Developer or Operator		• 5% special tax on gross income and exemption for all national and local taxes, except real property tax on land owned by the Economic Zone Developer • Exemption from expanded withholding tax	Yes, for all local purchases
Economic Zone Utilities Enterprise		• 5% special tax on gross income and exemption for all national and local taxes, except real property tax on land owned by the Economic Zone Developer • Exemption from expanded withholding tax	Yes, for all local purchases

Source: Philippine Economic Zone Authority (2017), Fiscal Incentives to PEZA-Registered Economic Zone Enterprises, www.peza.gov.ph/index.php/eligible-activities-incentives/fiscal-incentives (accessed 15 December 2017).

Chapter 9. Singapore

Singapore's regulatory reform efforts have focused on improving services and creating space for innovation through its digital strategy. Regulatory reviews, both pre- and post-implementation, are conducted on a regular basis. Public consultation for business-related issues is done through the reaching everyone for active citizenry @ home (REACH) platform or through the involvement of the Pro-Enterprise Panel (PEP) and industry stakeholders. In order to strengthen small and medium-sized enterprise (SME) linkages to the global value chain and encourage innovation, the government has been encouraging private sector collaboration through industry exchanges, the introduction of regulatory sandboxes, and programmes to link government procurement with SMEs.

Regulatory context

Singapore has remained among the top countries with the most appealing business environment (World Bank, 2018[1]). Singapore does not have a specific SME regulatory policy; rather, government efforts focus on improving the regulatory environment for all businesses. To date, many reforms have been undertaken by the government in order to help businesses – including SMEs - better access the different financial and assistance schemes. Many initiatives have been focused on going digital – broadening access to services and allowing SMEs to deal with less paperwork.

Since 2016, the Government has been implementing an Industry Transformation Programme. This is to be achieved through Industry Transformation Maps (ITMs) within 23 selected industries under 6 clusters and is expected to serve as integrated roadmaps to drive industry transformation. Each ITM would contain a growth competitiveness plan, supported by four pillars including trade and internationalisation to support companies (Ministry of Trade and Industry, 2016[2]).

Box 9.1. Industry Transformation Maps (ITMs) in Singapore

The Government of Singapore has committed to taking an industry-centred strategy in a more systematic and co-ordinated way. The Industry Transformation Maps (ITMs) therefore provide a roadmap for the 23 selected key industries within 6 clusters, which represent over 80% of Singapore's gross domestic product (GDP). These clusters include manufacturing, built environments such as construction or real estate, trade and connectivity, essential domestic services, professional services and lifestyle.

The Future Economy Council (FEC), previously known as the Council for Skills, Innovation, and Productivity (CSIP), has assumed responsibility for the implementation of the ITMs. For tighter co-ordination and accountability within the government, a lead government agency would assume overall responsibility for each ITM and co-ordinate efforts among agencies and tripartite partners. Each ITM consists of a growth and competitiveness plan that includes four specific pillars:

- Productivity – supporting companies, especially SMEs, to move to higher value-added activities and increase efficiency.
- Jobs and Skills – equipping people with skills to support greater value creation.
- Innovation – developing new products and services through research and development (R&D).
- Trade and Internationalisation – supporting companies to export and grow abroad.

The implementation of ITMs also calls for the involvement of all relevant stakeholders such as SMEs, research institutions, trade associations and other providers.

Source: Ministry of Trade and Industry (2016), *Media Factsheet – Industry Transformation Maps*, www.mti.gov.sg/MTIInsights/SiteAssets/Pages/ITM/Images/Fact%20sheet%20on%20Industry%20Transformation%20Maps%20-%20revised%20as%20of%2031%20Mar%2017.pdf.

Regulatory governance

Institutional and regulatory setup

Table 9.1. Institutional and regulatory setup

	Government
State structure	Unitary state
Head of state	**President,** who is directly elected by the people and holds veto power over government as stipulated in the Constitution.
Executive	**Prime Minister** appointed by the President is responsible for commanding the majority of the members of parliament. **Cabinet** is responsible for all daily governmental affairs and government policies. It is also accountable to the parliament (Government of Singapore, 2017[3]; Government of Singapore, 2017[4]).
Legislative	Unicameral Parliament 101 seats, with 89 elected members of parliament (MP), 3 non-constituency members of parliament (NCMPs) and 9 nominated members of parliament (NMPs). Both NCMPs and NMPs are nominated (Parliament of Singapore, 2017[5]). • The parliament is responsible for drafting laws, assuming inquisitorial roles in relation to the executive and directing state finances.
Legal system	Common law Full judicial responsibility falls under the Supreme Court (High Court and Court of Appeals) and the State Courts (district courts and magistrate courts). The small claims tribunals handle small claim disputes not exceeding SGD 10 000.
Administrative-territorial structure	Five districts (Community Development Councils, or CDC), which are represented by electoral constituencies and town councils. Each CDC is managed by a council and headed by a mayor with 12-80 members. These are appointed by the Chairman or Deputy Chairman of the People's Association.
Ministry or agency responsible for SMEs or SME-related issues	**SPRING** (Standards, Productivity and Innovation Board) Singapore is a body under the Ministry of Trade and Industry (MTI) that is responsible for the development and growth of enterprises in the country as well as ensuring the highest standards and accreditation for products and services. **International Enterprise** (IE) Singapore, also under MTI, serves as the agency responsible for international trade. SPRING and IE are expected to merge to form **Enterprise Singapore** in the second quarter of 2018.
Other support structures within government on regulatory policy*	• **Accounting and Corporate Regulatory Authority (ACRA)** is the national regulator of business entities, public accountants, and corporate service providers in Singapore. It promotes a trusted and vibrant environment for businesses to thrive and flourish and contribute towards making Singapore the best place for business. • **REACH (reaching for everyone for active citizenry @ home)** serves as the lead agency responsible for facilitating whole-of-government efforts on public and private engagement. • **Pro-Enterprise Panel (PEP)** is a private-public panel chaired by the Head of Civil Service with mainly business leaders as members and supported by a network of senior public offers. The PEP serves as an internal advocate for businesses within the government to enable a more pro-enterprise environment that facilitates the growth of competitive businesses.

* The three entities specified are examples of support structures within government on regulatory policy and are not exhaustive.

Sources: OECD compilation; Government of Singapore (2017), *The Government*, http://www.pmo.gov.sg/the-government (accessed on 29 November 2017); Government of Singapore (2017), *The Cabinet*, www.pmo.gov.sg/the-cabinet (accessed on 29 November 2017); Parliament of Singapore (2017), *Functions*, www.parliament.gov.sg/about-us/parliament-information/functions (accessed on 25 October 2017).

Regulatory process

Before any law (or regulation) is passed, it must first be introduced to parliament through a "bill". A bill is often introduced by a respective minister or any member of the house. These go through three readings through parliament and are then passed to the President before they become an act or law.

Figure 9.1. Law-making process in Singapore

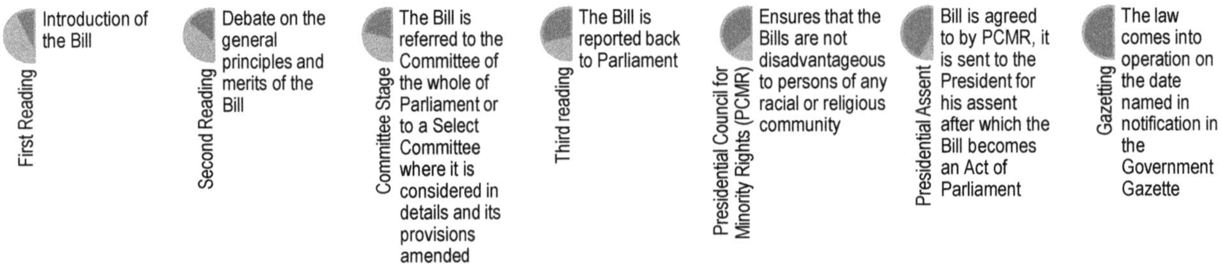

Source: Parliament of Singapore (2017), *Functions*, www.parliament.gov.sg/about-us/parliament-information/functions (accessed on 29 November 2017).

When a new regulation is introduced, line ministries are required to conduct a comprehensive assessment of the regulation, including the benefits gained, costs to stakeholders, and other likely distributional effects. Other alternatives are systematically considered in the process to evaluate the pros and cons of a regulation to businesses, consumers and the government. Alternatives include taxes, standardisation, conformity assessments and self-regulation. Information on this is available to the public prior to its presentation to the parliament. Stakeholders are welcome to submit consultation questions in order to seek clarifications on new or amended regulations. Government agencies or regulators then report the results of their assessments to parent ministries on a regular basis, such as during a mid-term or end-term review.

Business laws and regulations in Singapore

All policy development and implementation in the country occurs at the central level, given Singapore's small size. Similarly, business regulations apply to all firms whether they are big or small. There is no dedicated SME regulatory policy in Singapore (Annex 9.A) (World Bank, 2017[6]).

SMEs in Singapore are defined as enterprises with either an annual sales turnover of less than SGD 100 million or a workforce of fewer than 200 employees. Although this definition has not been gazetted by law, it is nonetheless widely regarded as the national definition for SMEs in the development of national economic plans and assistance programmes as well as in public communications such as budget announcements or ministerial speeches.

SMEs are further classified into several categories, namely: micro, small, medium and large enterprises based on their annual turnover. This classification is used internally among government offices as a way to understand, analyse and report on the SME landscape.

There are approximately 180 000 small and medium-sized (SMEs) in Singapore, which employ around 70% of the workforce and contribute to around 47% of the total GDP in the country.

Business registration and incorporation

Business registration in Singapore is facilitated online by the Accounting and Regulatory Authority of Singapore (ACRA) and can be done within a few hours. In order to incorporate a company, the proprietor(s) would need to prepare the following information and proof: 1) company name; 2) brief description of business activities; 3) shareholders particulars; 4) registered address; 5) company secretary particulars; and 6) constitution.

There are only two steps to incorporation, which includes name registration and actual registration. Name registration of a company normally occurs within an hour and is rejected only under specific circumstances such as repeated names, trademarks, reservations or obscenity. The name is subsequently reserved from the date of application. Once this has been approved and all the paperwork has been submitted, the incorporation can be completed within a few hours. In some cases, authorities can ask for additional information which may prolong the approval process.

Following incorporation, the company would need to open a corporate account in a bank and, if needed, to obtain specific business licences before any operation. If the company's annual revenue is above SGD 1 million, the company is required to register for the Goods and Services Tax (GST). Furthermore, the company would need to ensure that it complies with the Singapore Companies Acts and meet annual filing requirements and formalities.

Highlights of regulatory opportunities and challenges to support SMEs

Administrative simplification

In Singapore, part of simplifying the regulatory process is focused on providing services through one-stop shops. This allows the government to streamline its services and improve co-ordination and alignment across the different concerned ministries and agencies. With the support of Enterprise Singapore, SMEs are provided with easy access to services such as business advisory services and other available government assistance and financing programmes. Some online one-stop shops are also housed in business chambers, associations and community centres. The Accounting and Corporate Regulatory Authority's (ACRA) website BizFile+ and the Government of Singapore's Business licensing portal (LicenceOne) are two such examples (Box 9.2) (ACRA, 2017b[7]; Government of Singapore, 2017[8]).

Other simplification exercises have also focused on improving specific processes to ensure that regulatory objectives are adequately met. As an example, the Monetary Authority of Singapore (MAS) sought to broaden its efforts in promoting financial instruments for enterprise development and simplify the regulatory framework for venture capital (VC) managers (Box 9.3) (Monetary Authority of Singapore, 2017[9]; Monetary Authority of Singapore, 2017[10]).

Efforts have also been undertaken to consolidate services. Enterprise Singapore, for example, serves as both the safety authority for goods as well as the parent agency under which testing, inspection, and accreditation of goods are conducted by the Singapore Accreditation Council (SAC). This arrangement gathers a number of standards, enforcement and inspection processes under one oversight body (Box 9.4).

Box 9.2. Examples of online one-stop shops in Singapore

BizFile+

The Accounting and Corporate Regulatory Authority (ACRA) of Singapore introduced BizFile+, an online business registration and filing portal, as a one-stop facilitator for businesses. BizFile+ offers over 400 e-services, from business registration, submission of statutory documents and retrieval and purchase of information pertaining to business entities registered with ACRA.

LicenceOne

LicenceOne is a one-stop business licensing portal that simplifies the application and payment of licence-related fees and allows business to apply for multiple licences simultaneously across 34 government agencies. Other features of the portal include updating, renewal, and termination of licences.

Sources: ACRA (2017), *BizFile+*, www.bizfile.gov.sg (accessed on 16 November 2017); Government of Singapore (2017), *LicenceOne*, https://licence1.business.gov.sg/ (accessed on 16 November 2017).

Box 9.3. Promoting access to finance in Singapore through regulatory simplification

Venture capital (VC) fund managers play an important role in the ASEAN region's emerging start-up ecosystem. In Singapore, the VC industry has been growing at an unprecedented rate and has been essential in providing seed capital and expertise to local start-ups notably at the early growth stage. As a way to also further promote enterprise development in the country, the Monetary Authority of Singapore (MAS) has sought to further expand the size and scope of available funding.

Prior to simplification, VC managers adhered to the same regulatory frameworks as other fund managers and are subjected to requirements that are not necessarily in line with their operations, which slowed down the application process for new VC fund managers. As a result, the government decided to conduct a public consultation exercise and consulted with relevant stakeholders to help improve the system. The proposed simplification process aimed to improve the extent of contractual safeguards as well as fitness and propriety assessments for VC managers.

Sources: Monetary Authority of Singapore (2017), *Faster Approvals and Lower Requirements for Venture Capital Managers*, www.mas.gov.sg/News-and-Publications/Media-Releases/2017/Faster-approvals-and-lower-requirements-for-venture-capital-managers.aspx; Monetary Authority of Singapore (2017), *Proposed Regulatory Regime for Managers of Venture Capital Funds*, www.mas.gov.sg/~/media/MAS/News%20and%20Publications/Consultation%20Papers/Consultation%20Paper%20on%20Proposed%20Regulatory%20Regime%20for%20Managers%20of%20Venture%20Capital%20Funds.pdf.

Box 9.4. Avoiding duplications in testing and inspections for exported goods from Singapore

The Singapore Accreditation Council (SAC), operating under the aegis of SPRING Singapore, is a is a signatory to Mutual Recognition Agreements (MRA) and Multi-lateral Recognition Agreements (MLA) under the International Laboratory Accreditation Co-operation (ILAC), International Accreditation Forum (IAF), Pacific Accreditation Co-operation (PAC) and Asia-Pacific Laboratory Accreditation Co-operation (APLAC). The MRAs and MLAs provide a global passport for enterprises in Singapore, eliminating the need for duplicative re-testing, re-inspection, or re-calibration of goods upon entry to importing countries (Enterprise Singapore, 2014[11]).

Furthermore, SPRING Singapore functions as a safety authority. There are no labelling requirements for electronic and electrical goods with the exception of Safety Mark for controlled goods, which require the minimum certification procedure based on type testing only. Efforts have been made to streamline these requirements so that there are no requirements for batch inspection, factory inspection and batch testing (Enterprise Singapore, 2014[12]).

Sources: Enterprise Singapore (2014), *Accreditation*, www.spring.gov.sg/Building-Trust/Accreditation/Pages/accreditation-overview.aspx; Enterprise Singapore (2014), *Consumer Protection*, www.enterprisesg.gov.sg/Quality-Standards/Consumer-Protection (accessed on 14 June 2018).

E-government

Since the 1980s, the information and communication technologies (ICT) sector has been driving public sector efficiency and improving the whole-of-government integration. The latest e-government masterplan (2011-15) has focused on strengthening government-private value innovation and economic competitiveness, notably for SMEs. The goal was to shift the delivery of government e-services from a top-down "Government-to-You" system to a "Government-with-You" approach (GovTech, 2016[13]). The e-Gov15's objectives focus on:

- Co-creating for greater value (government as a service and platform provider).
- Connecting for active participation (consulting the public and inviting ideas from the public).
- Catalysing whole-of-government transformation (transforming public sector infrastructure and services through G-Cloud and Singapore Government Enterprise Architecture (SGEA) and transforming the public sector workplace and capabilities).

In 2014, the government introduced the Smart Nation initiative, which aims to harness the growth of ICT and tech-enabled solutions to empower government bodies, businesses, and citizens to address national and global issues and improve the overall welfare of the country.

The Government of Singapore has offered mobile applications of government services for citizens and businesses to access them on the go. Examples of government services going mobile are presented in the Box 9.5.

Box 9.5. Government applications in Singapore

One Service App

In 2015, the Municipal Service Office (MSO) under the Ministry of National Development of Singapore introduced the OneService application, which serves as a platform for citizens to provide feedback to the municipal office on issues such as cleanliness, damaged signs, water quality, sanitation and pest control, among others. The smartphone app allows users to take photos and geo-tag areas of concern for agencies to be able to easily locate and identify the issue. Given the success and popularity of the application, in 2017, the MSO enhanced the application's services by improving the ease of use and providing users with information on the status of their cases. Users are provided are now informed of their feedback with indicators such as acknowledged, working on it, or closed. MSO continues to work with various government agencies to efficiently address issues raised through the application, especially with regard to specific issues that require cross-agency collaboration. The app currently has over 100 000 users with over 130 000 user cases reported (Municipal Services Office, 2017[14]).

ACRA on the Go (Accounting and Corporate Regulatory Authority)

A number of ACRA's services are already accessible on line (www.acra.gov.sg/Online_Services) but the authority has also developed a new mobile application to allow users to access information on ACRA's registry of businesses in Singapore. At the same time, users can also undertake some business registration and filing transactions such as renewing registration for some business entities, filing annual declarations or changing business addresses. An online inquiry service is also made available through the application (ACRA, 2014[15]).

Singapore Budget (Ministry of Finance)

The Budget Mobile App of the Ministry of Finance provides users with information and announcements on Singapore budget and yearly budget statements. Since 2016, the mobile app has also featured a live streaming of the annual budget speeches.

Sources: Municipal Service Office (2017), *One Service, and Engaged Community for a Better Living Environment*, www.mnd.gov.sg/mso/ (accessed on 26 October 2017); ACRA (2014), *Online Services*, www.acra.gov.sg/Online_Services/ (accessed on 26 October 2017).

Singapore also runs a number of programmes intended to help SMEs increase their connectivity by raising awareness of the digital economy benefits and support adoption of digital solutions, as well as provide education and training on the use of digital technology. These programmes are available to SMEs nationwide and are presented in the box below (Box 9.6).

Box 9.6. Encouraging the use of digital platforms for SMEs

SME Go Digital Programme

During the 2017 Budget Speech, the government committed to invest SGD 80 million to launch the SMEs Go Digital Programme. The programme, led by the Info-communications Media Development Authority (IMDA) together with SPRING Singapore and other lead agencies, aims to strengthen SMEs' capability in the use of digital technology. This includes three core components focused on ICT pilots, advice and in-person assistance in SME centres or SME technology hubs, in addition to strengthening data and cybersecurity.

Great Online Shopping Festival (GOSF)

On 2 February 2015, Google, along with Development Bank of Singapore and SingPost, launched a 72-hour long shopping festival. With the support of SPRING Singapore, the festival was aimed at bringing over 60 brands into 1 common platform. SPRING also supported local retailers in adopting digital platforms for sales as a way to cater to a growing digital-savvy population. During the festival, Singpost offered its delivery and returns services to online shoppers, including access to its 90 POPStations or smart locker stations that allow customers to collect, pay or even return purchases at any time of the day.

99% SME Campaign

Launched by DBS and SingTel, the 99% SME campaign was created for SMEs to market their businesses and reach out to more customers via an online platform. This year, the 99% SME eMarketplace was created for SMEs to advertise their products (99% SME, 2017[16]).

Squared Online for SMEs

Google will be working with leading global training providers to equip 1 000 business leaders in SMEs with the knowledge and skills to improve their in-house digital marking capabilities by 2019. This initiative is aligned with the government's SMEs Go Digital Programme (Choudhury, 2017[17]).

SME e-Commerce Accelerator programme

The Singapore Retail Association, with the support of SPRING Singapore and Workforce Singapore has developed an SME e-commerce Accelerator programme to help retailers plan for omni-channel implementation, which is a multichannel or integrated sales strategy. Through the programme, the Singapore government envisions to increase e-commerce sales by 10% by 2020.

Sources: Country response to OECD survey, 2017; 99% SME (2017), *99% SME*, www.99sme.sg/about-99sme/ (accessed 22 November 2017); Choudhury, A. R. (19 April 2017), *Google to Help Train 1,000 SME Business Leaders in Singapore*, www.businesstimes.com.sg/sme/singapore-budget-2017/google-to-help-train-1000-sme-business-leaders-in-singapore (accessed on 22 November 2017).

Regulatory sandboxes

In Singapore, innovation is encouraged through the use of regulatory sandboxes. This involves setting boundaries within which some rules can be suspended to allow greater experimentation for companies, especially SMEs and start-ups.

Box 9.7. Regulatory sandbox: Flexible regulations in Singapore

Regulatory sandboxes have been adopted by Singapore as a way to encourage more innovation from new and emerging industries.

Autonomous vehicles

The Land and Transportation Authority (LTA) had provided more flexibility for autonomous vehicle (AV) trials in the country. The provisions are aimed at providing more time for operators and developers to develop the technology while also providing the time for the government to assess the appropriate regulatory response. The regulatory sandbox has been limited to five years, after which the government would enact a more permanent legislation or re-consider the extension of the sandbox (Channel NewsAsia, 2017[18]).

FinTech

The Monetary Authority of Singapore (MAS) is supporting FinTech innovations by providing start-ups and FinTech players the flexibility to test and improve their products. The MAS holds the authority to relax certain regulations or requirements depending on the experiment. Once the company or entity has successfully carried out the experiment and has exited the sandbox, it must then fully comply with the relevant legal and regulatory requirements (Monetary Authority of Singapore, 2017[19]).

Sources: Channel NewsAsia (2017), *Regulations in Place to Ramp Up Driverless Vehicle Trials in Singapore*, www.channelnewsasia.com/news/singapore/regulations-in-place-to-ramp-up-driverless-vehicle-trials-in-sin-7622038; Monetary Authority of Singapore (2017), *Understanding and Applying to the Sandbox*, www.mas.gov.sg/Singapore-Financial-Centre/Smart-Financial-Centre/FinTech-Regulatory-Sandbox/Understanding-and-applying-to-the-sandbox.aspx.

Regulatory delivery

Regulatory compliance

Compliance with standards

The government encourages the direct use of international standards whenever possible. When there is no appropriate international equivalent, or when there is a need to customise standards to meet domestic requirements, Singapore Standards (SS) are developed in line with the World Trade Organization's Technical Barriers to Trade (TBT) agreement. Alternatively, a provisional standard can also be used, in the form of a technical reference (TR), under certain circumstances as outlined in the box below.

There is a range of mechanisms to facilitate trade between parties, including through Free Trade Agreements (FTAs), Mutual Recognition Agreements (MRAs) and equivalence agreements or arrangements. In addition, it participates in the development of new international standards on various fora, such as the International Standards Organization

(ISO) and International Electro-technical Commission (IEC), as well as regional and international MRAs and Multi-lateral Agreements (MLAs) to establish trade facilitative measures such as mutual recognition of conformity assessment results.

Singapore Standards (SS) are typically reviewed every five years on average to consider whether they should be confirmed, revised, amended, archived or withdrawn; but may be reviewed earlier if the need arises. The development of national standards is co-ordinated by Enterprise Singapore's Standards Division with the guidance of an industry-led Singapore Standards Council.

The Council, which includes representation from private and public stakeholders, formulates strategies on Singapore's standardisation programme. Standards committees responsible for formulating and establishing national standards have representatives from government, industry, professional and tertiary institutions, and consumer associations. As part of the standards development process, members of the public and SMEs are also invited to provide public comments on draft Singapore Standards for development, review and publication (Enterprise Singapore, 2018[20]).

Box 9.8. Shared standards building in Singapore

Standards serve as an important benchmark for best practices across different industries – from product design to manufacturing and export. Enterprise Singapore, Singapore's national standards body, helps to meet optimal industry standards that are well-aligned with international standards by working closely with Singapore Standards, representatives from the public and private sector, research organisations, academia and consumers (Enterprise Singapore, 2018[21]).

In cases where there are no existing international standards, Enterprise Singapore helps develop new standards via two processes:

1. Singapore Standard (SS), which a voluntary standard that is subjected to a full consensus process and a two-month long public review. A Singapore Standard becomes mandatory when it is either cited or included in the legislation.
2. Technical reference (TR), which is a fast-track document without the public review, and is only used for the following purposes:
    - as a test, before it is implemented in the whole industry, e.g. technical reference for Electric Vehicle (EVs) Charging System in Singapore to support the test of EVs
    - as a way to meet urgent demands, e.g. Technical Reference on Cloud Computing for the use of public computing services
    - as a temporary standard, in case of an urgent need for a formal reference standard.

Source: Enterprise Singapore (2018), *Standards*, www.enterprisesg.gov.sg/quality-standards/standards (accessed on 14 June 2018).

At the regional level, Enterprise Singapore represents Singapore at the ASEAN Consultative Committee for Standards and Quality (ACCSQ), which addresses Technical Barriers to Trade (TBTs) in ASEAN through the harmonisation of standards and technical requirements, development of MRAs on conformity assessment results and harmonisation of regulatory regimes.

Compliance with intellectual property

As of July 2017, approximately 17 000 SMEs in Singapore (8% of the total SME population in the country) have registered their intellectual property (IP) rights in Singapore. Many companies, including SMEs, also own IP in the form of copyright and trade secrets, which do not require registration. Singaporean companies which are registered overseas can also own IP for their overseas operations. To facilitate this process, the government has actively introduced a number of initiatives (Box 9.9).

Box 9.9. Strengthening intellectual property for SMEs in Singapore

The Ministry of Law and Intellectual Property Office of Singapore (IPOS) recognises that SMEs need assistance to understand and utilise IP to their advantage. IPOS leverage trade and business associations to organise activities like IP innovation seminars. Singapore enterprises can also sign up for IP and IP management courses run by IPOS' training subsidiary, IP Academy. IPOS will be launching a business portal with guides and diagnostic toolkits on IP to help SMEs understand their IP needs. In addition, IPOS' subsidiary, IP ValueLab, provides local companies with subsidised one-on-one assistance for IP audit and IP strategy development (Ministry of Law Singapore, 2017$_{[22]}$).

Furthermore, IPOS runs IP legal and business clinics for SMEs, where they can seek preliminary advice from IP experts and lawyers for free. The advice sought can include advice on IP disputes and enforcement.

The Intellectual Property Intermediary (IPI) was also established to assist SMEs to assess their technology gaps and help them find the IP that is best suited for their needs. (Enterprise Singapore, 2018$_{[23]}$).

Enterprise Capability Upgrading Programme

The Agency for Science, Technology and Research's (A*STAR) Technology for Enterprise Capability Upgrading programme asigns its researchers to SMEs to help them develop in-house R&D capabilities. Its Headstart programme enables SMEs to licence A*STAR's IP on preferential terms. To date, more than 650 researchers have been attached to SMEs and more than 60% of A*STAR's licences have been dedicated to SMEs (Enterprise Singapore, 2018$_{[24]}$).

Capability Development Grant

The Capability Development Grant (CDG) is a financial assistance programme that helps SMEs build capabilities across ten key business areas, which include intellectual property protection (Enterprise Singapore, 2018$_{[24]}$). An IP project may typically encompass one or more of the following areas:

- Audit an existing IP management framework and develop an IP management roadmap.
- Develop an IP management system.
- Conduct IP research and intelligence analysis.

The grant defrays up to 70% of qualifying project costs.

Innovation and Capability Voucher

The Innovation and Capability Voucher (ICV) is a simple-to-apply, easy-to-use voucher to encourage SMEs to develop their business capabilities (Enterprise Singapore, 2018[25]). SMEs can use the voucher to upgrade and strengthen their core business operations through consultancy in the areas of productivity, human resources, financial management and innovation. The voucher can be used to offset the cost of the following IP management projects:

- Intellectual Property Legal Diagnostic to help businesses identify key IP assets and strategies to protect and commercially exploit them.
- Intellectual Property Management (IPM) diagnostic to help businesses assess the strengths and weaknesses of their IP deployment and management system.

Sources: Ministry of Law Singapore (2017), *Written Answer by Minister for Law, Mr K Shanmugam, to Parliamentary Question on Local SMEs Owning Intellectual Property Rights*, www.mlaw.gov.sg/content/minlaw/en/news/parliamentary-speeches-and-responses/written-answer-by-minister-for-law--mr-k-shanmugam--to-parliamen8.html; Enterprise Singapore (2018), *Intellectual Property*, https://spring.enterprisesg.gov.sg/Growing-Business/Grant/development-areas/Pages/intellectual-property.aspx; Enterprise Singapore (2018), *Grants*, www.enterprisesg.gov.sg/Financial-Assistance/Grants (accessed on 14 June 2018); Enterprise Singapore (2018), *Innovation and Capability Voucher*, www.smeportal.sg/content/smeportal/en/moneymatters/grants/innovation-capability-voucher-icv.html.

Enforcement and inspections

Singapore adopts several approaches to regulatory enforcement to ensure that business-related regulations are efficiently carried out (Box 9.10). Singapore Customs, for example, adopts a multi-pronged approach of strengthening self-compliance, timely detection of violations, deterrence through effective enforcement and penalties, regular monitoring of compliance status and risk reviews in order to achieve a high level of compliance of Singapore's trade and customs law. A highly compliant trading community will enable Singapore Customs to better facilitate the flow of legitimate trade while targeting control measures to detect the minority of fraudulent traders, without raising compliance cost for traders in general or unduly inconveniencing them with onerous regulatory requirements.

Box 9.10. Various Approaches to regulatory enforcement in Singapore

Accreditation and quality standards compliance

An accreditation of an enterprise entails that it has been assessed against internationally recognised standards. Accreditation is granted to calibration and testing laboratories, certification bodies, inspection bodies and proficiency testing providers. In Singapore, the national authority responsible for independent accreditation of conformity assessment bodies is the Singapore Accreditation Council (SAC) (Enterprise Singapore, 2016[26]).

Risk-based approach

Risk-based approaches, often in the form of random sampling and inspections, are applied by some government ministries or agencies. For example, the Inland Revenue Authority of Singapore uses risk-based approaches in carrying out compliance actions, by outlining areas of audit and specifically focusing on common errors committed by taxpayers when filing (Inland Revenue Authority of Singapore, 2017[27]).

Peer reviews

Peer reviews are conducted based on monitoring and complaints, and other audit activities for disciplinary processes. Disciplinary processes may also refer to the strict code of professional conducts and ethics in certain professions. Any breach on the code, from complaints or other forms, can lead to an investigation and disciplinary process.

Disclosure frameworks

Disclosure frameworks are aimed at improving the effectiveness of information disclosures by creating an overarching or standard framework. As an example, for companies, selecting the best audit firms suited to their size and complexity can often be challenging. Audit firms can vary in structure, strategies and priorities and the difference may result in complex accounting issues. As a way for listed companies to better evaluate and select right auditors, the Accounting and Regulatory Authority (ACRA) of Singapore had released an Audit Quality Indicators (AQIs) Disclosure Framework. The AQI framework includes eight audit quality indicators for audit committees to use as a common measurement by which audit quality can be assessed (ACRA, 2015[28]).

Rewards and sanctions

Source: Enterprise Singapore (2016), *Getting Accreditation*, www.smeportal.sg/content/smeportal/en/bizguides/quality-and-standards/2015/getting-accreditation_g.html; Inland Revenue Authority of Singapore (2017), *IRAS' Focus on Taxpayer Compliance*, www.iras.gov.sg/irashome/About-Us/Taxes-in-Singapore/Helping-and-Encouraging-Compliance/IRAS--Focus-on-Taxpayer-Compliance/; ACRA (14 October 2015), *Audit Quality Indicators Disclosure Framework*, www.acra.gov.sg/Publications/Guides/Audit_Quality_Indicators_Disclosure_Framework/.

Regulatory quality management

In Singapore, business regulatory policies are applied to all relevant enterprises. Formal assessments of business-related regulatory policies are conducted by the respective government agencies at their discretion. Assessments include regional and international benchmarking, where possible.

Singapore does not have a central oversight body or ministry with the sole function of looking into regulatory policies; nonetheless, respective government ministries and agencies are tasked to develop and review the regulations under their purview. Reviews of regulations are both demand-driven and conducted proactively. However, industry feedback does play a key role in providing agencies with the information on areas to review.

Government agencies are free to set the mode, frequency or type of regulatory review it undertakes as needed. These reviews can either focus on individual regulations that affect a business, a whole sector or a policy area, according to the jurisdiction covered by a specific ministry. These impact assessments are used to evaluate the effects of regulatory policies on specific target groups (such as businesses, consumers, or third-party stakeholders) as well as on the economy.

Monitoring and evaluation activities are also regularly conducted by respective government agencies to ensure that the key objectives of regulations are met. Various Key Performance Indicators (KPIs) are attached to regulatory policies and respective government agencies would report back to parent ministries on a regular basis in order to consolidate and verify the information, which is then published after each financial year.

Stakeholder engagement

Public consultations are regularly launched by the Government of Singapore to request for feedback on newly proposed or amended regulations or on existing government programmes and initiatives. Many of these public consultations focus on reducing administrative burden and improving the ease of doing business in the country. As part of the announcement for new or amended regulations, a suitable timeline would be provided for business owners to comply with the regulations so that businesses would have adequate time to adapt. Compliance rates are monitored when reviewing the regulations. Individual assessments on regulations are evaluated *ex post* and compared with outcomes. Businesses would also be informed of the necessary steps to comply with new regulations. Once the regulations take into effect, companies that are still unable to comply with any of the requirements would need to face penalties.

The relevant government agencies are responsible for communicating the benefits and costs of business regulatory policies to the general public. This is done through national outreach events such as seminars, conferences and workshops and public announcements both in paper or online media using platforms such as the press, government websites and social media platforms. In addition, major regulatory policies which may affect a range of sectors or industries in the economy are announced during annual budget announcements or National Day rally speeches.

Public agencies proactively review and update their rules, and these efforts can be boosted by ideas from businesses that are often best placed to tell the government how the rules can be formulated and implemented better to create a more pro-business and customer-centric environment, Singapore had established its Pro-Enterprise Panel (PEP).

The PEP ensures that government rules and regulations remain relevant and supportive of a pro-business environment. Businesses, notably SMEs, that would like to raise their concerns regarding specific regulations or regulatory decisions, are welcome to submit their feedback or appeal to PEP for consideration. Since its inception in 2000, more than 1 800 suggestions have been received and more than half of these have led to changes in rules or regulations.

Box 9.11. Improving transparency and ease of doing business in Singapore through stakeholder consultation

In 2016, the Accounting and Corporate Regulatory Authority (ACRA) and the Ministry of Finance (MOF) launched two rounds of public consultations on the proposed amendments to the Companies Act and Limited Liability Partnerships Act. First enacted in 1967, the Companies Act had already undergone several reviews to ensure that the corporate regulatory regime continued to be robust and supportive of Singapore's growth as a global hub for businesses and investors. The proposed amendments in 2016 sought to reduce the regulatory burden and improve the ease of doing business, as well as enhance the transparency of business entities with the aim of reducing burden for businesses and improving transparency (Ministry of Finance Singapore, 2017[29]; ACRA, 2017[30]). A summary of the feedback received from stakeholders was published online to reflect discussions from the consultation process (Ministry of Finance Singapore, 2017[31]). Based on the feedback received, MOF and ACRA made some revisions to the proposed amendments.

Revisions after the first round of consultations included the introduction of an inward re-domiciliation regime that allows corporations to transfer its registration from its home jurisdiction to another. This way, foreign corporations wishing to relocate to Singapore could be incorporated as a Singaporean company subject to the local Companies Act.

Revisions after the second round focused on reducing regulatory burden and improving the ease of doing business by: 1) simplifying the requirements for private companies to hold annual general meetings and file annual returns; and 2) removing the requirement for common seals and introducing an alternative of signature by authorised persons.

Another key revision following consultations sought to improve corporate transparency by requiring companies to disclose specific information on ownership and control of businesses in line with international standards for combatting money laundering and the financing of terrorism. An amendment to the Accountants Act clarified that a breach of the Ethics Pronouncement 200 would be grounds for disciplinary action under the act.

Sources: Ministry of Finance Singapore (2017), *MOF and ACRA Publish Responses to Public Feedback on Proposed Changes to the Companies Act, Limited Liability Partnerships Act, and Accountants Act*, www.mof.gov.sg/news-reader/articleid/1710/parentid/59/year/2016?category=Press%20Release (accessed 20 November 2017); Ministry of Finance Singapore (2017), *OF and ACRA Invite Public Feedback on Proposed Changes to the Companies Act, Limited Liability Partnerships Act, and Accountants Act*, https://app.mof.gov.sg/Public-Consultation/Public-Consultation-Closed/2017/MOF-and-ACRA-Invite-Public-Feedback-on-Proposed-Changes-to-The-Companies-Act-Limited-Liability-Partnerships-Act-and-Accountants-Act.

Prior to any public consultation exercise, government agencies are highly encouraged to submit a consultation paper to REACH (reaching everyone for active citizenry @ home). REACH's website serves as an online discussion forum to gather responses from the public on a particular government policy or programme (Government of Singapore, 2017[32]).

Box 9.12. Strengthening citizen engagement in Singapore

Government agencies in Singapore have continuously sought to improve public service by reaching out to stakeholders, notably in relation to proposed regulations or programmes. As a way to streamline and consolidate public engagement efforts, the Government of Singapore has set up REACH (reaching everyone for active citizenry @ home), an agency responsible for the whole-of-government approach to citizen engagement.

Before a government agency decides to conduct or organise a public consultation through REACH, they would need to consider the following:

- Public consultations should have a purpose, e.g. to consult about policies or implementation plans at the early stages of the policy-making process.
- Participating agencies should be informative and provide sufficient information to ensure the public understands the issues, in order for them to be able to provide informed responses.
- Participating agencies should be responsible for sharing findings to be uploaded on the same page as the original consultation in a timely fashion, by explaining the responses received and how these responses have informed the policy process.

Once the government agency has decided to proceed with the consultation exercise, it must submit a consultation paper to REACH. The paper includes a brief summary of the regulation, details of the consultation such as proposed changes or amendments made to the regulation, feedback channels (email, mail or phone) and any supporting documents that they wish to disclose to the public. An online discussion forum is used to gather responses from the public, through the REACH website. Stakeholders that are consulted are open to share their views and comments or seek clarifications on the proposed amendments to existing regulations or bills, with supporting evidence provided when required. Consultations usually last for approximately four weeks. After the consultations have been conducted, a summary of the responses is published on the REACH website, which is made available to the public.

Source: Government of Singapore (2017), *REACH*, www.reach.gov.sg (accessed on 15 November 2017).

Box 9.13. Making legislation simple and accessible in Singapore

As part of the effort to make local laws easier to understand, Singapore's Attorney-General's Chambers (AGC) has improved its Statutes Online (SSO) website. The website serves as the official and free online repository for all legislation passed in the country. The improvements aimed to make the written laws more accessible to different users, from parliamentarians to civil society.

Following two rounds of public consultant surveys (November 2013 and September 2016), the AGC had rolled out a beta version of the website to provide users time to adjust to the new features and to allow them to provide feedback before its official launch in 2017.

Part of the simplification process also includes progressively improving law drafting in the country, as a way to present complex information to a varied set of users. This includes shortening phrases and using simpler English terms, simplifying provisions and adopting gender-neutral requirements.

Source: Government of Singapore (2015), *Singapore Statutes Online*, http://statutes.agc.gov.sg/aol/home.w3p (accessed on 17 November 2017).

New or amended regulations may also be published via other means, including government statements on various government agencies' website and press releases. As an example, recent amendments to the Consumer Protection Fair Trading Act (CPFTA) were published on MTI's website. The CPFTA provides for civil actions which may be taken against errant retailers who persist in unfair practices. In addition, it aims to simplify onerous measures that can impose unnecessary costs to businesses that may then be passed on to consumers.

Following substantial feedback from stakeholders, the Attorney-General's Chambers (AGC) has recently revamped its Singapore Statutes Online (SSO) website to make it more available to the public. Furthermore, as a way to encourage public engagement, the Attorney-General's Chambers (AGC) of Singapore is currently simplifying the language and presentation of Singapore's statutes in order to make regulatory requirements clearer and more comprehensive (Government of Singapore, 2015[33]).

SME linkages

Public and private sector collaboration

Singapore has introduced a number of initiatives and programmes to foster growth among SMEs as well as encourage collaboration between the private and public sector (Box 9.14). The Government itself plays an active role in procuring goods and services from SMEs. Each year, over 80% of government contracts (roughly half of total government contract value) go to SMEs. By number of contracts, more than 40% were won by companies with revenue of less than SGD 10 million. Of these contracts, almost half were won by micro-enterprises with revenue of less than SGD 1 million.

Box 9.14. Government initiatives to improve public-private collaboration

PACT and Gov-PACT

The Partnerships for Capability Transformation (PACT) is an initiative that encourages enterprises to collaborate for mutual benefits. Under PACT, lead enterprises collaborate with smaller SMEs in projects related to capability development and joint business development. Capability development projects include areas such as supplier upgrading, co-innovation and knowledge transfer. Joint business development projects include areas such as the formation of business alliances or embarking on projects related to shared resources.

In 2017, a Government Partnerships for Capability Transformation (Gov-PACT) programme was launched to help SMEs without a track record participate in government procurement. Gov-PACT provides grants to SMEs and start-ups to collaborate with and undertake innovative projects initiated by government agencies. SMEs and start-ups will be funded at various stages of product and solution development for these innovative projects.

Example of a Gov-PACT project:

- The Housing and Development Board (HDB) worked with SMEs to develop the business and deployment model for a Smart Elderly Monitoring and Alert System. The system allowed families to monitor the safety of the elderly at home and to receive alerts when a mobile panic button is pressed during an emergency, or when unusual living patterns are detected. HDB helped to pair SMEs with telecommunication companies to operationalise the system, which is now being piloted in Yuhua.

Public-Private Co-Innovation Partnership

The Public-Private Co-Innovation Partnership (PPCIP) set up in 2010 aimed to encourage innovation between the government and the private sector, and provide opportunities for companies commercialise future-ready solutions in sectors such as urban solutions, ICT, healthcare and education. By the time the PPCIP concluded in 2016, numerous government agencies had also started to put in place similar initiatives to support public-private co-innovation and collaboration.

Examples of PPCIP projects:

- Jurong Town Corporation (JTC) Open Innovation Call, which aimed to seed, drive and replicate innovation projects
- Ministry of Health's (MOH) Care-at-Home Grant, which aimed to encourage greater innovation and adoption of technologies that are both productive and cost-effective among home care service providers.

Crowdsourcing

Government agencies are making use of crowdsourcing methods to identify innovative solutions to social, economic and technological challenges. Crowdsourcing is an effective way for the government to partner with businesses, community and individuals.

Examples of a government crowdsourcing campaigns:

- At the recent Designathon 2017, organised by the Design Singapore Council, there was a focus on developing solutions for persons with disabilities. The winning team comprised of students from the Singapore University of Technology and Design, who developed a device for converting a manual wheelchair into an electric wheelchair at a fraction of the price of a regular electric wheelchair.
- The Housing and Development Board (HDB) rolled out a competition called the HDB's Cool Idea Challenge, which solicited ideas for a safer gas hob. Fires caused by unattended cooking cause a significant portion of fires in residential buildings; as a result, students from Republic Polytechnic and Anglo Chinese Junior College proposed a gas hob with a safety device that cuts off the gas supply when the flame goes out – ultimately preventing fires. The team subsequently worked with City Gas and Aerogaz, two gas companies in Singapore, to commercialise the idea and then eventually released it to the market in 2015.

Accreditation@IMDA scheme

The Accreditation@IMDA scheme helps promising and innovative Singapore-based technology start-ups establish their credentials. To date, the scheme has helped around 59 companies by providing assistance to strengthen their products and provide advice on fundraising and business pitches. Seventeen of these companies have been accredited, out of which 13 have won contracts. They will benefit from the SGD 60 million of government pipeline opportunities that have been generated to date.

Example of a company that has benefited from Accreditation@IMDA:

- SenseInfosys is a company founded in 2013 that focuses on data fusion, analytics and fraud detection in military-grade intelligence products in the security and maritime domains. Their products enable enterprises to analyse data to gain timely and accurate insights for improving their operational processes and making more informed decisions. After SenseInfosys was accredited through the Accreditation@IMDA scheme in 2016, the company went on to win six government projects despite being a newcomer without a significant prior track record. Last year, the company successfully raised SGD 2 million from investors to help accelerate the company's growth.

Source: Country response to OECD survey, 2017.

Government agencies help ensure that tenders are appropriately sized to give SMEs a chance to compete for them. About 90% of contracts called by the government agencies each year are below SGD 100 000 in value. There were more than 30 000 of such contracts in 2016. Only about 5% of government contracts are above SGD 1 million. For some larger products, if suitable, the government may call separate tenders for different parts of the project, giving smaller companies an opportunity to participate. Some smaller companies have also formed consortiums with others to tender for larger and more complex projects.

Online platforms have also been developed by the government in collaboration with the private sector to encourage and facilitate small players to take part in bids for government contracts. For example, GeBIZ Mall is a platform for suppliers that are interested in selling to government agencies. Through this platform, suppliers are given electronic "shelf space" to sell their goods and services. Each supplier can list ten items on their online shelf for free. Government agencies can then buy directly from these suppliers if the purchases are below SGD 5 000 or they can request for quotations. Over the last 5 years, an average of 5 000 orders per year has been placed through the platform, which amounts to approximately SGD 3.5 million per year. The government continues to encourage and promote the use of this platform among SMEs. Another platform called GovBuy allows government agencies to post small projects or tasks for IT programmers to work on. No track record is required to participate in this platform.

Labour mobility

Although labour policies and legislation are applicable to the overall workforce and do not differentiate between small and medium enterprises and other business entities, the human resource schemes introduced by the government to strengthen the labour market in Singapore are expected to help SMEs adapt to the changes in the global economy (Box 9.15). The Ministry of Manpower can also exercise temporary manpower policy adjustments during periods of transition, including allowing companies to reduce the number of work permits, use temporary foreign workers while recruiting and training locals, and pool foreign expertise at the industry level that can help foster knowledge for the local workforce.

Box 9.15. Strengthening the labour market in Singapore

P-Max programme

The P-Max programme provides funding to help SMEs better recruit, manage and retain newly-hired Singaporean citizens or permanent residents that fall under the category of professionals, managers, executives and technicians (PMETs). P-Max aims to enable SMEs to adopt progressive human resource practices through training and basic human resources (HR) toolkits.

Under this programme, SMEs will benefit from a one-time SGD 5 000 grant if they successfully implement the recommended HR processes and retain PMETs hired under the programme for at least 6 months. SMEs can concurrently receive salary support if they place and train eligible Singaporean PMETs under the Career Support Programme or Professional Conversion Programmes.

Lean Enterprise Development (LED) scheme

The LED scheme aims to help progressive SMEs transform and grow in the new manpower-lean landscape. The objective is to support SMEs that want to be pioneers and early adopters of change: becoming more productive, more innovative and more manpower-lean. This will help create stronger business growth and offer better jobs and careers to Singaporeans and permanent residents.

With the LED scheme, SMEs will be supported in:

- Becoming more manpower-lean: higher productivity and faster innovation is essential to achieve this.
- Building a stronger Singaporean core: the restructuring process should result in better jobs, pay and careers for Singaporeans.
- Developing better quality workers: such employees, including foreign workers, should be more skilful and have more relevant expertise and/or experience.

Source: Country response to OECD survey, 2017.

Customs facilitation

Often in collaboration with SPRING Singapore, International Enterprise Singapore (IE Singapore)[1] serves as the government agency that promotes international trade and supports Singapore companies in going global. Through its Plug and Play Network, Enterprise Singapore aims to ease entry for Singapore SMEs into markets such as China, India and Southeast Asia (Shafeeq, 2017[34]).

Box 9.16. Plug and Play Network (PPN) Singapore: Helping SMEs expand overseas quickly

Enterprise Singapore found that six out of ten SMEs find it challenging to find contacts or suitable partners to expand overseas. In line with this, the agency launched the Plug and Play Network (PPN) in July 2017 to provide business advisory services, business matching and market setup through co-working spaces. The PPN, with its 9 partners including consultancy forms and co-working space providers, helps SMEs access markets in more than 45 cities across China, India and Southeast Asia.

Source: Shafeeq, S. (2017), *IE Singapore Sets Up Network for SMEs to Expand Overseas Quickly - The Business Times*, https://ie.enterprisesg.gov.sg/Media-Centre/News/2017/7/IE-Singapore-sets-up-network-for-SMEs-to-expand-overseas-quickly.

Various Customs-related initiatives have also been launched to address challenges faced by SMEs relating to cross-border trade. Examples include initiatives within Singapore such as TradeNet, TradeXchange, and the National Trade Platform (NTP), along with initiatives pursued together with other ASEAN countries, such as the ASEAN Single Window (Box 9.17).

Box 9.17. Customs initiatives in Singapore

TradeNet

TradeNet is Singapore's National Single Window for trade declaration. Launched in January 1989, it allows various parties from the public and private sectors to exchange trade information electronically. TradeNet integrates import, export and transhipment documentation processing procedures and enables the trade and logistics communities to fulfil their trade formalities. Through TradeNet, Singapore Customs and other competent authorities monitor the movement of goods and enforce health, safety and other regulatory requirements. TradeNet reduced the cost and time to prepare, submit and process trade documents. It expedites the clearance of cargo and allows fees and taxes to be deducted electronically (Koh, 2017[35]).

TradeXchange

TradeXchange is a neutral and secure trade platform that facilitates the exchange of information within the trade and logistics community. Launched in 2007, TradeXchange provides seamless inter-connectivity among commercial and regulatory systems for the Singapore trade and logistics community. In addition, it offers a single electronic window for integrated workflow, submissions and enquiries to the Sea Ports, Airports, Maritime Authorities, Customs and Competent Authorities. TradeXchange is a multi-agency initiative led by Singapore Customs, the Economic Development Board and the Infocomm Development Authority of Singapore (IDA) (GovTech Singapore, 2018[36]).

National Trade Platform

Singapore is building the NTP as a trade and logistics IT ecosystem connecting businesses, community systems and platforms, and government systems. When completed, the NTP will replace TradeNet as the National Single Window for permit declaration and TradeXchange as the platform connecting trade and logistics community. As the next generation platform, the NTP will be designed as an open innovation platform, which businesses and service providers can tap on to develop new applications to support evolving business needs (Singapore Customs, 2017[37]).

Sources: Koh, J. (2017), *Singapore TradeNet: Single Windows & Regional Interoperability – Trends and Consideration*, www.unescap.org/sites/default/files/26%20Apr%202017%20-%20Singapore%20Experience.pdf; GovTech Singapore (2018), change, https://www.tech.gov.sg/Programmes-Partnerships/Programmes-Partnerships/Initiatives/TradeXchange; Singapore Customs (28 September 2017), *Building the National Trade Platform (NTP)*, www.customs.gov.sg/about-us/national-single-window/national-trade-platform.

Recommendations

- **Consider adopting formal regulatory approaches**, such as regulatory impact assessments (RIA), to standardise practices across ministries when conducting evaluation or assessments.
- **Consider linking existing online platforms into one portal.** For example, LicenceNet can also be integrated into the GeBiz portal, as a way to ensure a single portal for all business transactions.
- **Streamline all public consultation procedures in the REACH platform and link it with efforts conducted by the Pro-Enterprise Panel.** Use this as an opportunity to encourage more feedback on specific regulations or programmes and provide information on how feedback received has been used to inform future policies, especially for business-related policies.
- **Consider best practice sharing and implementation of new and innovative approaches to improving enforcement and compliance when regulating new and emerging industries,** such as through the use of behavioural insights. Agencies that have already implemented or tried such approaches should share it across the government so that the public service can collectively reduce compliance costs for businesses.

Notes

[1] With effect from 1 April 2018, Enterprise Singapore would serve as the agency which promotes international trade and supports Singapore to go global.

References

3E Accounting (2017), *Visa and Work Pass*, https://www.3ecpa.com.sg/resources/human-resource-immigration/visa-and-work-pass/. [38]

99% SME (2017), *99% SME*, https://www.99sme.sg (accessed on 22 November 2017). [16]

ACRA (2017), *Companies Act Reform*, https://www.acra.gov.sg/Legislation/Companies_Act_Reform/ (accessed on 26 October 2017). [30]

ACRA (2015), *Audit Quality Indicators Disclosure Framework*, http://www.acra.gov.sg/Publications/Guides/Audit_Quality_Indicators_Disclosure_Framework/. [28]

ACRA (2014), *Online Services*, https://www.acra.gov.sg/Online_Services/ (accessed on 26 October 2017). [15]

ACRA (2017b), *BizFile*, https://www.bizfile.gov.sg/ (accessed on 16 November 2017). [7]

Channel NewsAsia (2017), *Regulations in Place to Ramp Up Driverless Vehicle Trials in Singapore*, http://www.channelnewsasia.com/news/singapore/regulations-in-place-to-ramp-up-driverless-vehicle-trials-in-sin-7622038. [18]

Choudhury, A. (2017), *Google to Help Train 1,000 SME Business Leaders in Singapore*, http://www.businesstimes.com.sg/sme/singapore-budget-2017/google-to-help-train-1000-sme-business-leaders-in-singapore. [17]

Enterprise Singapore (2018), *Grants*, https://www.enterprisesg.gov.sg/Financial-Assistance/Grants (accessed on 14 June 2018). [24]

Enterprise Singapore (2018), *Innovation and Capability Voucher*, https://www.smeportal.sg/content/smeportal/en/moneymatters/grants/innovation-capability-voucher-icv.html. [25]

Enterprise Singapore (2018), *Intellectual Property*, https://spring.enterprisesg.gov.sg/Growing-Business/Grant/development-areas/Pages/intellectual-property.aspx. [23]

Enterprise Singapore (2018), *Standards*, http://www.enterprisesg.gov.sg/quality-standards/standards (accessed on 14 June 2018). [21]

Enterprise Singapore (2018), *Standards Committees & Partners*, https://www.smeportal.sg/content/smeportal/en/bizguides/quality-and-standards/2015/standards-committees---partners_g.html. [20]

Enterprise Singapore (2016), *Getting Accreditation*, https://www.smeportal.sg/content/smeportal/en/bizguides/quality-and-standards/2015/getting-accreditation_g.html. [26]

Enterprise Singapore (2014), *Accreditation*, https://www.spring.gov.sg/Building-Trust/Accreditation/Pages/accreditation-overview.aspx. [11]

Enterprise Singapore (2014), *Consumer Protection*, https://www.enterprisesg.gov.sg/Quality-Standards/Consumer-Protection (accessed on 14 June 2018). [12]

Government of Singapore (2017), *LicenceOne*, https://licence1.business.gov.sg/ (accessed on 16 November 2017). [8]

Government of Singapore (2017), *REACH*, http://www.reach.gov.sg (accessed on 15 November 2017). [32]

Government of Singapore (2017), *The Cabinet*, http://www.pmo.gov.sg/the-cabinet (accessed on 29 November 2017). [3]

Government of Singapore (2017), *The Government*, http://www.pmo.gov.sg/the-government (accessed on 29 November 2017). [4]

Government of Singapore (2015), *Singapore Statutes Online*, https://sso.agc.gov.sg/ (accessed on 17 November 2017). [33]

GovTech (2016), *eGov Masterplans*, https://www.tech.gov.sg/About-Us/Corporate-Publications/eGov-Masterplan. [13]

GovTech Singapore (2018), *TradeXchange*, https://www.tech.gov.sg/Programmes-Partnerships/Programmes-Partnerships/Initiatives/TradeXchange. [36]

Inland Revenue Authority of Singapore (2017), *IRAS' Focus on Taxpayer Compliance*, https://www.iras.gov.sg/irashome/About-Us/Taxes-in-Singapore/Helping-and-Encouraging-Compliance/IRAS--Focus-on-Taxpayer-Compliance/. [27]

Koh, J. (2017), *Singapore TradeNet: Single Windows & Regional Interoperability - Trends and Considerations*, http://www.unescap.org/sites/default/files/26%20Apr%202017%20-%20Singapore%20Experience.pdf. [35]

Ministry of Finance Singapore (2017), *MOF and ACRA Invite Public Feedback on Proposed Changes to the Companies Act, Limited Liability Partnerships Act, and Accountants Act*, https://www.mof.gov.sg/Public-Consultation/Public-Consultation-Closed/2017/MOF-and-ACRA-Invite-Public-Feedback-on-Proposed-Changes-to-The-Companies-Act-Limited-Liability-Partnerships-Act-and-Accountants-Act. [29]

Ministry of Finance Singapore (2017), *MOF and ACRA Publish Responses to Public Feedback on Proposed Changes to the Companies Act, Limited Liability Partnerships Act, and Accountants Act*, https://www.mof.gov.sg/Newsroom/Press-Releases/MOF-and-ACRA-Publish-Responses-to-Public-Feedback-on-Proposed-Changes-to-The-Companies-Act-Limited-Liability-Partnerships-Act-and-Accountants-Act. [31]

Ministry of Law Singapore (2017), *Written Answer by Minister for Law, Mr K Shanmugam, to Parliamentary Question on Local SMEs Owning Intellectual Property Rights*, https://www.mlaw.gov.sg/content/minlaw/en/news/parliamentary-speeches-and-responses/written-answer-by-minister-for-law--mr-k-shanmugam--to-parliamen8.html. [22]

Ministry of Manpower (2017), *Work Passes and Permits*, http://www.mom.gov.sg/passes-and- [39]

permits (accessed on 22 November 2017).

Ministry of Trade and Industry (2016), *Media Factsheet - Industry Transformation Maps*, https://www.mti.gov.sg/MTIInsights/SiteAssets/Pages/ITM/Images/Fact%20sheet%20on%20Industry%20Transformation%20Maps%20-%20revised%20as%20of%2031%20Mar%2017.pdf. [2]

Monetary Authority of Singapore (2017), *Faster Approvals and Lower Requirements for Venture Capital Managers*, http://www.mas.gov.sg/News-and-Publications/Media-Releases/2017/Faster-approvals-and-lower-requirements-for-venture-capital-managers.aspx. [10]

Monetary Authority of Singapore (2017), *Proposed Regulatory Regime for Managers of Venture Capital Funds*, http://www.mas.gov.sg/~/media/MAS/News%20and%20Publications/Consultation%20Papers/Consultation%20Paper%20on%20Proposed%20Regulatory%20Regime%20for%20Managers%20of%20Venture%20Capital%20Funds.pdf. [9]

Monetary Authority of Singapore (2017), *Understanding and Applying to the Sandbox*, http://www.mas.gov.sg/Singapore-Financial-Centre/Smart-Financial-Centre/FinTech-Regulatory-Sandbox/Understanding-and-applying-to-the-sandbox.aspx. [19]

Municipal Services Office (2017), *One Service, and Engaged Community for a Better Living Environment*, https://www.mnd.gov.sg/mso/ (accessed on 26 October 2017). [14]

Parliament of Singapore (2017), *Functions*, http://www.parliament.gov.sg/about-us/parliament-information/functions (accessed on 25 October 2017). [5]

Shafeeq, S. (2017), *IE Singapore Sets Up Network for SMEs to Expand Overseas Quickly - The Business Times*, https://ie.enterprisesg.gov.sg/Media-Centre/News/2017/7/IE-Singapore-sets-up-network-for-SMEs-to-expand-overseas-quickly. [34]

Singapore Customs (2017), *Building the National Trade Platform (NTP)*, https://www.customs.gov.sg/about-us/national-single-window/national-trade-platform. [37]

World Bank (2018), *Doing Business 2018: Reforming to Create Jobs*, http://www.doingbusiness.org/~/media/WBG/DoingBusiness/Documents/Annual-Reports/English/DB2018-Full-Report.pdf. [1]

World Bank (2017), *Law Library*, http://www.doingbusiness.org/law-library/ (accessed on 8 March 2018). [6]

Annex 9.A.

Annex Table 9.A.1. Business-related laws in Singapore

Type	Description
Banking and credit laws	Banking Act, Asian Development Bank Act, Bills of Exchange Act, Bills of Sale Act, Deposit Insurance Act 2005, Development Fund Act, Development Loan Act 1987, Development Investment Fund Act, Currency Act, Exchange Control Act, External Loans Act, Finance Companies Act, Financial Procedure Act
Bankruptcy and collateral laws	Bankruptcy Act (revised 2009)
Commercial and company laws	Commercial and Industrial Security Corporation act, Common Gaming Houses Act, Companies Act, Competition Act, Co-operative Societies Act, Copyright Act, Corrosive and Explosive Substance and Offensive Weapons Act, Consumer Protection (Fair Trading) Act, Consumer Protection (Trade Descriptions and Safety Requirements) Act, Contact Lens Practitioners Act, Contracts (Right of Third Parties) Act, Control of Essential Supplies Act, Control of Manufacture Act, Control of Plants Act, Control of Vectors and Pesticides Act, Defamation Act, Dentists Act, Employment Agencies Act, Distress Act, District Cooling Act, Economic Development Board Act, Environmental Pollution Control Act. Electrical Workers and Contractors Licensing Act, Electronic Transactions Act, Energy Market Authority of Singapore Act, Factories Act, Feeding Stuffs Act. Dangerous Fireworks Act, Hire-Purchase Act, Free Trade Zones Act, Frustrated Contracts Act, Gas Act, Geographical Indications Act, Fire Safety Act, Fisheries Act, Explosive Substances Act, Films Act, Apportionment Act, Apportionment of Rents Act, Appraisers and House Agents Act, Agri-Food and Veterinary Authority Act., Air Navigation Act, Animals and Birds Act, Sale of Goods (United Nations Convention) Act, Trust Companies Act, Limited Liability Partnerships Acts 2005, Sale of Commercial Properties Act, Architects Act, Arms and Explosives Act, Accountants Act, Accounting and Corporate Regulatory Authority Act, Biological Agents and Toxins Act 2005, Boundaries and Survey Maps Act, Bretton Woods Agreement Act, Broadcasting Act, Chemical Weapons (Prohibition) Act, Chit Funds Act, Cinematograph Film Fire Duty Act, Civil Aviation Authority of Singapore Act, Betting Act, Betting and Sweepstakes Duty Act, Business Registration Act, Business Trusts Act, Carriage by Air Act., Carriage of Goods by Sea Act, Casino Control Act 2006, Cattle Act, Central Provident Fund Act, Charities Act, Companies Act (revised 2014)
Labour law	Employment Agencies Act, Employment of Foreign Workers Act, Employment Act, Central Provident Fund Act, Industrial Relations Act, Workmen's Compensation Act. Workplace Safety and Health Act 2006, Trade Disputes Act, Trade Unions Act. Tripartite Guidelines on Mandatory Retrenchment Notification
Land and building laws	Land Acquisition Act, Land Revenue Collection Act, Land Surveyors Act, Land Titles (Strata Act), Land Titles Act, Sale of Commercial Properties Act, Property Tax (Surcharge) Act, Property Tax Act, Building and Common Property (Maintenance and Management) Act, Building and Construction Authority Act, Building and Construction Industry Security of Payment Act, Building Control Act, Building Maintenance and Strata Management Act 2004, Executive Condominium Housing Scheme Act, Foreshores Act, Conveyancing and Law of Property Act, Workplace Safety and Health Act 2006
Securities laws	Commodity Trading Act, Financial Advisers Act, Futures Trading Act, Government Securities Act, Exchanges (Demutualization and Merger) Act, Securities and Futures Act, Trustees Act
Tax laws	Stamp Duties Act, Property Tax Act, Property Tax (Surcharge) Act, Internal Revenue of Singapore Act, Audit act, Charities Act, Goods and Services Tax Act, Fees Act, Entertainment Duty Act, Estate Duty Act, Income Tax Act, Economic Expansion Incentives (Relief from Income Tax) Act
Trade laws	Endangered Species (Import and Export) Act 2006, Customs Act, Countervailing and Anti-Dumping Duties Act, Hazardous Waste (Control of Export, Import, and Transit) Act, Geographical Indications Act, Foreshores Act, Carriage of Goods by Sea Act, Merchant Shipping Act, Registration of Deeds Act, Regulation of Imports and Exports Act
Insolvency law	Companies Act 2017

Source: World Bank (2017), *Law Library*, www.doingbusiness.org/law-library/ (accessed 8 March 2018).

Chapter 10. Thailand

Thailand is reforming its regulatory environment to help facilitate the growth of businesses in the country. Since 2017, the government has focused on reducing administrative burdens to improve the business environment by improving the licensing process and developing online platforms to further facilitate e-commerce. In 2017, the Thai government has committed to improving the regulatory process in its revised constitution. Thailand has also developed a new 4.0 Strategy aimed at transforming the country into a first world nation with the development of future industries. To help small and medium-sized enterprises (SMEs) link up with global value chains (GVCs), the government has established dedicated industry clusters to support the growth and development of priority industries domestically and abroad.

Regulatory context

Thailand's commitment to improving service delivery is rooted in the Royal Decree on Criteria and Procedures in Good Governance (B.E. 2546) passed in 2003. The decree was introduced by the government as a way to improve the quality and performance of public administration across the different ministries, agencies and state institutions in the country and lift up the quality of services provided to citizens and businesses.

The government also recognises the importance of reviewing the suitability and feasibility of legislation. In this regard, it has enacted the Royal Decree on Revision of Law B.E. 2588, which has been in force since 9 September 2015. The law requires that the relevant authority conduct a review of the appropriateness of the law every five years since its implementation.

In parallel, the government enacted the Licensing Facilitation Act, B.E. 2558 in 2015 to help reduce the administrative burden on licensing procedures. The act requires each authority to review the laws concerning their respective licensing requirements and determine whether such licensing requirement should be repealed or replaced by another measure every five years since the licensing requirement has come into force.

To affirm this commitment to good regulatory practices, Section 77 of the new Thai Constitution passed in 2017 clearly outlined the use of good regulatory practice tools in the enactment, revision and repeal of laws. This includes the need to conduct assessments on a mandatory basis as well as stakeholder consultation throughout the regulatory process.

Every five years, Thailand develops two national SME strategies, reflected in the SMEs Promotion Plan or Master Plan, which lays down the foundation for SME activities for the next five years, and the Action Plan, which is issued after the master plan and serves as an implementation plan and guidance – based on the master plan – for Office of the SME Promotion (OSMEP) and all involved agencies.

The most recent SMEs promotion plan (No. 4) (2017-21) aims to increase the contribution of SMEs to more than 50% of gross domestic product (GDP) in 2021. The current promotion plan is well-aligned with Strategy 3 of the National Economic and Social Development Plan, which highlights the importance of creating a strong, sustainable and competitive economy by developing a strong entrepreneurial environment conducive to SMEs and community and social enterprises. Strategy 3 also emphasises the importance of registering SMEs to encourage participation in the formal economy.

Sub-strategy 3 of the 4th SME Promotion Master Plan also aims to promote SME access to domestic and international markets and stipulates the importance of creating and developing new export products and services by organising activities to strengthen the knowledge needed to conduct international business, such as customs, laws, regulations and related matters to enhance the knowledge of SMEs who have no experience in exporting or have just started exporting.

Regulatory governance

Institutional and regulatory setup

Table 10.1. Institutional and regulatory setup

	Government
State structure	Unitary state
Head of state	King
Executive	**Prime Minister** is elected in the lower house and officially appointed by the king. The Prime Minister serves as the head of the government and leads the Cabinet of Thailand. **Cabinet** or the Council of Ministers is composed of 35 state and deputy ministers.
Legislative	Bicameral 630 members The **Senate** has 150 members, in which 76 are elected from the 75 provinces and the metropolitan area of Bangkok. The rest go through a selection committee and are either appointed or elected. It has limited legislative oversight but is responsible for oversight and the appointment of members forming the judiciary and independent government agencies. The **House of Representatives** has 500 members, 375 are elected and 124 are selected according to representation and party list. It serves as the main legislative chamber and holds authority over the appointment or dissolution of the executive.
Legal system	Civil law The **Courts of Thailand** is the largest court system and represents the majority of the courts (Court of First Instance, Court of Appeals, Supreme Court of Justice). **Administrative Court is** responsible for settling litigations between the state, including its ministries and agencies and private citizens. **Constitutional Court** is responsible for all matters referring to the constitution.
Administrative-territorial structure	76 provinces, which are each led by an appointed governor. Each province is further divided into districts, which is led by a district chief who is appointed by the central government. There are currently 878 districts in the country.
Ministry or agency responsible for SMEs or SME-related issues	**Office of Small and Medium Enterprise Promotion (OSMEP)** is the central SME agency responsible for co-ordinating SME policies and propelling SMEs in the domestic and international level. It is also responsible for drafting the five-year SME promotion plans.
Other support structures within government on regulatory policy	• **Office of the Public Sector Development Commission (OPDC)** is responsible for supporting public sector development and the delivery of public services (Office of the Public Sector Development, 2017[1]). • **Office of the Council of State (OCS)** holds consultative functions for the executive branch and is responsible for: 1) drafting laws, by-laws, rules and regulations as requested by the executive body; 2) providing legal advice to the state agencies or enterprises; 3) submitting opinions to the Council of Ministers for new legislation or amendment or repeal of existing regulations (Office of the Council of State, 2017[2]). • **The Federation of Thai Industries (FTI)** is composed of private sector representatives and serves as the representative for industrial operators in the country for issues related to the promotion and development of the Thai industry (The Federation of Thai Industries, 2015[3]).

Sources: OECD compilation; Office of the Council of State (2017), *Philosophy, Mandate, and Organisation Chart*, www.krisdika.go.th/wps/portal/general_en/!ut/p/c5/04_sb8k8xllm9msszpy8xbz9cp0os3g_a2czq0ctq89apyana0__eioaqgdxawm_y30_j_zcvp2cbedfafgmrsc!/dl3/d3/l2djqsevuut3qs9zqnz3lzzftjbdnjfbndfjuujsqjbjt1qwuffdrtawvja!/; Office of the Public Sector Development (2017), *History*, https://www.opdc.go.th/content.php?menu_id=2&content_id=3491 (accessed on 22 December 2017); The Federation of Thai Industries (2015), *About F.T.I.*, https://www.fti.or.th/2016/eng/ftiaboutfti.aspx (accessed on 20 December 2017).

Regulatory process

The formulation of new laws and regulations pertaining to SMEs are held by both the executive and the legislative bodies of the government. Line ministries are responsible for drafting regulations within their respective domain.

On the executive side, the Council of Ministers is endowed with the authority to propose either a normal bill or a draft emergency decree to the National Assembly. The normal bill requires the approval of the National Assembly and the signature of the king as well as a formal publication in the Government Gazette before it becomes an act that comes into force. Majority of the bills passed by the Government of Thailand are classified as normal bills (Office of the Council of State, 2017[4]).

In case of emergencies related to maintaining national public safety or economic security as well as calamity-related events, the council holds the power to draft an emergency decree which can be passed on directly to the king without any prior review or approval from the National Assembly. However, since the decree is enacted based on immediate threat or danger, the council would then need to present the decree to the National Assembly without delay in the next National Assembly. If approved, the decree will permanently have the force of law; otherwise, if not, it will be considered as lapsed (Office of the Council of State, 2017[4]).

Figure 10.1. Legislative process in Thailand

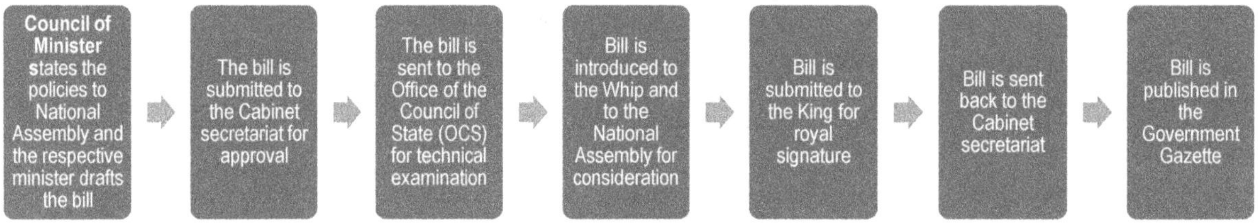

Source: Office of the Council of State (2017), *Thai Legislative Process*, http://www.krisdika.go.th/wps/portal/general_en/!ut/p/c4/04_sb8k8xllm9msszpy8xbz9cp0os3g_a2czq0ctq08jb0tta09zqw83c58wywt_q_2cbedfakmaacy!/.

Business laws and regulations in Thailand

There are 3 004 679 registered small and medium-sized enterprises (SMEs) in the country, which account for 99.7% of the total number of enterprises in the country. SMEs also represent around 78.48% of total employment; however, there is currently no distinction between part-time and full-time employment within SMEs.

Given the importance of the SME sector in Thailand, the Government of Thailand passed the SME Promotion Act, B.E. 2543 in 2000. The Act aims to promote and strengthen SMEs in Thailand and align them with international standards. The Act also provides Office of the Small and Medium Enterprise (OSMEP) with the authority to define the SME criteria based on present economic and social conditions. Currently, micro, small, and medium enterprises (MSMEs) in Thailand are defined by the number of employees and fixed assets (Table 10.2). Micro-enterprises are bulked together with small enterprises, as there is currently no available definition for micro-enterprises.

Table 10.2. Definitions of MSMEs in Thailand

	Micro and small enterprises		Medium enterprises	
	No. of employees	Fixed assets (THB)	No. of employees	Fixed assets (THB)
Manufacturing	≤ 50	≤ 50 million	51-200	> 50 to 200 million
Trading (wholesale)	≤ 25	≤ 50 million	26-50	> 50 to 100 million
Trading (retail)	≤ 15	≤ 30 million	16-30	> 30 to 60 million
Service	≤ 50	≤ 50 million	51-200	> 50 to 200 million

Source: Information provided by the Office of Small and Medium Enterprise Promotion (OSMEP) Thailand, 2018.

All efforts and programmes on SME policy development and promotion are carried out under the guidance and supervision of the Office of the SME Promotion (OSMEP) through its master plans. Other than what is specified in the master plan, SMEs are subjected to all business regulations, including those provided in the table below (World Bank, 2017[5]).

Table 10.3. Business-related laws and regulations in Thailand

Type	Description
Banking and credit laws	Commercial and Banking Act, B.E. 2505
Bankruptcy and collateral laws	Bankruptcy Act (No. 7), B.E. 2547
Commercial and company laws	Act Determining Offences Relating to the Register Partnership, Limited Partnership, Limited Company Association and Foundation, B.E. 2499, Licensing Facilitation Act, B.E. 2558
Land and building Laws	Engineer Act, B.E. 2542, Architect Act, B.E. 2543
Insolvency law	Order of the National Council for Peace and Orders No. 21/2017, Order No. 21/2560 on Amendment of Laws to Facilitate Ease of Doing Business
Secured transactions law	Business Collateral Act, B.E. 2558

Source: World Bank (2017), *Law Library*, www.doingbusiness.org/law-library/ (8 March 2018).

Business registration in Thailand is done through the Department of Business Development of the Ministry of Commerce, but the extent to which certain agencies are involved also depends on the type of business. Most non-Thai individuals are in the country are engaged in a partnership or company. Although a non-Thai individual is not prohibited from engaging in a sole proprietorship in Thailand, specific labour laws and other legal issues limit the ease of engaging in this type of business (Ministry of Commerce, 2018[6]).

Table 10.4. Registration requirements in Thailand

	Commercial	Partnership	Company
Description	Individual or group of individuals (ordinary partnership), with exceptions	Business owned by at least two individuals	At least three persons signing together
Registration areas	Office of Finance, Bangkok Metropolitan Administration, Bangkok District Office	Department of Business Development (DBD) office	
Registration requirements	• Request for registration • Commercial registration certificate • Sign of business name	• Name of partnership • Objective of partnership • Location of office and/or branches • Name, address, nationality, occupation and items that are invested • Managing partner information • Limitation of managing partner's power • Partnership seal	• Promoters must be ordinary person, 12 years or more, and must reserve to buy at least 1 share • Company name • Location of head office • Objective of the company • Registered capital • Name, address, age, occupation and number of shares that persons who start the company reserve to buy share • Name, address, and age of two witnesses
Setup fee	THB 50 (+ additional costs depending on the service)*	THB 1 000 (+ additional costs depending on the service)*	THB 500 (+ additional costs depending on the service)*
Continuity of the business entity			Perpetual succession unless wound up
Closure of business		By partners' cessation or dissolution	Winding up or striking off

* A list of the costs can be found here:
http://www.dbd.go.th/dbdweb_en/ewt_news.php?nid=3974&filename=index (sole proprietorships);
http://www.dbd.go.th/dbdweb_en/ewt_news.php?nid=3973&filename=index (partnerships);
http://www.dbd.go.th/dbdweb_en/ewt_news.php?nid=3966&filename=index (company).
Source: Ministry of Commerce (2018), *Department of Business Development*, www.dbd.go.th/dbdweb_en/main-php?filename=index (accessed on 12 March 2018).

At the same time, non-Thai individuals engaged in partnerships and companies also face some limitations with regard to the type of business they can be engaged in. For example, they are not allowed to engage in the following activities: 1) media, including print, radio or television broadcasting; 2) rice, arable, or orchard farming; 3) livestock rearing; 4) forestry and related products; 5) fishery in relation to marine life and special economic zones; 6) extraction of Thai medicinal herbs; 7) auctioning of local historical artefacts; 8) manufacture of Buddha image and alms bowls; 9) real property trading.

Highlights of regulatory opportunities and challenges to support SMEs

Administrative simplification

An implementation plan to review and simplify business-related legislation that impacts on SMEs is underway. Nonetheless, the government has been proactive in continuously improving the business environment. In 2017, the government launched an administrative burden reduction programme to improve the regulatory environment for businesses. The reform aims to change the process, legal acts and back office efficiency as a way to reduce the costs and risks of regulations for businesses and citizens and improve the country's international ranking for ease of doing business.

Furthermore, the Licensing Facilitation Act was passed to improve accountability and transparency and reduce regulatory burden on businesses that apply for licences. Box 10.1 elaborates on the specific objectives of the law (Khampee, 2016[7]).

Box 10.1. Improving licensing procedures in Thailand

In 2015, the Thai government introduced The Licensing Facilitation Act, B.E. 2558, which mandates each authority responsible for licensing to review and evaluate their respective licensing act or procedure every five years and determine if it has to be repealed or replaced by an alternative measure. This review is carried out by the issuing authority, with the support of the Law Reform Commission under the Office of the Council of State and is subsequently submitted to the Council of Ministers. The implementation process is overseen by the Public Sector Development Commission.

The licensing act targets four specific tools and services:

Licensing manual

In the event licensing is required, the responsible authority would need to prepare a licensing manual. The manual would need to explicitly state all the information needed by the applicant such as the rules, terms, conditions, channels and duration of the services, fees, and other requirements. The manual would need to be available, accessible and distributed to the public or applicants. This is done by establishing a Service Link centre in each responsible authority. At present, around 8 000 manuals have been published on www.info.go.th.

One-stop service and online service

As a way to further facilitate the licensing process, the responsible government is also mandated to establish a One-Stop Service Centre to carry out the licensing process and expand its e-service channel.

Application acceptance

This means that no applications can be refused by the government. Instead, the officer responsible for the application procedure must provide suggestions in any case the application does not meet the necessary requirements. In case that the requested requirements cannot be met, both the applicant and the officer-in-charge would need to sign a memo agreeing to the case.

Officer's procedures

The officer would need to abide by the processing time specified in the manual. In any case that the application process exceeds the suggested timeline, the officer must provide a notice to the applicant and the Office of the Public Sector Development every seven days until it the application has been resolved. The applicant may file a civil action against the officer in case of delay.

Sources: Khampee, K. (2016), *Workshop on New Approaches in Measuring and Reinforcing Trust in Public Institutions*, www.opdc.go.th/english/files/MeasuringandReinforcing.pdf; Government of Thailand (2015), *Licensing Facilitation Act, B.E. 2558*, http://www.opdc.go.th/uploads/files/2558/LICENSING_FACILITATION_ACT_2015.pdf.

Through the Licensing Facilitation Act, government agencies responsible for granting licences are provided with the authority to establish a one-stop service centre to administer this process (Government of Thailand, 2015[8]).

Box 10.2. One-stop shops in Thailand

Examples of one-stop services setup based on the Licensing Facilitation Act in Thailand include:

One Start One-Stop Investment Centre (OSOS)

OSOS is operated by the Thailand Board of Investment (BOI) and serves as Thailand's first comprehensive service centre for investors. Available services include advisory services, registration, applications for investment-related permits and licences, and applications for public utilities.

www.osos.boi.go.th

One-Stop Service Centre (OSSC) for visa and work permits

An OSSC has been established by the Bureau of Immigration to process visa and work permits for non-nationals. However, not all are entitled to use OSSC services and is only available for applications who are requesting for an extension of their temporary stay, change in address, a re-entry permit or a change in visa status. This is also applicable for non-nationals concerned by the following laws: Immigration Act, Petroleum Act, Board of Investment Act and Industrial Estate Authority of Thailand.

www.bangkok.immigration.go.th

One-Stop Service (OSS) for SMEs

The One-Stop Service Centre for SMEs is managed by the Office of Small and Medium Enterprise Promotion (OSMEP) and provides services to SMEs, including:

- Help desks for needs and requirements of SMEs.
- Free consultancy services for the development of products and services, marketing planning, financial management and company upgrading.
- SMEs registration desks.
- Assistance for internationalisation and promotion, as well as matchmaking with large companies.

Other existing service centres include that of the Food and Drug Administration, Express Authority (EXAT), Thailand Film Office, etc. To date, the services are only available in Thai.

www.oss.sme.go.th/oss

Source: Government of Thailand (2015), *Licensing Facilitation Act, B.E. 2558*, www.opdc.go.th/uploads/files/2558/LICENSING_FACILITATION_ACT_2015.pdf.

In recent years, various laws have been introduced to facilitate e-commerce in the country (Table 10.5). Several e-commerce promotion programmes that aim to strengthen the capacities of Thai businesses have also been spearheaded by various government agencies (Ministry of Commerce, 2018[6]) (Box 10.3).

Table 10.5. Laws and decrees supporting e-commerce in Thailand

	Law No.	Description
Consumer Protection Act	B.E. 2522 (1979)	Law that intends to protect consumers against unfair practices, false or misleading information, and other consumer protection issues
Electronic Transactions Act	B.E.2544 (2001)	Law that supports the legal effects of electronic address information including civil and commercial activities and state activities, which have legal effect when done in electronic data format
Royal Decree on Regulating Electronic Payment Services	B.E. 2551 (2008)	Law that regulates electronic payment offerings
Royal Decree on Security Procedures for Electronic Transactions	B.E. 2544 (2010)	Law that supports secure electronic transactions

Source: Information provided by the Ministry of Commerce, 2018.

Box 10.3. Fostering e-commerce in Thailand

Department of Business Development (DBD)

The *E-market Expansion Programme* aims to build and develop Thai businesses and encourage them to expand using e-commerce.

The *Offline 2 Online Community Product Development Programme* aims to create an online marketing channel and establish distribution channels for Thai entrepreneurs through the online platform.

Electronic Transactions Development Agency (ETDA)*

ETDA has rolled out a number of programmes to support SMEs, namely: the *Thailand E-commerce Sustainability programme*, SMEs *Go Online programme,* and the *Electronic Market Promotion and Development programme for SMEs*.

* The list is not exhaustive. Additional projects and programmes can be found on the following website: https://www.etda.or.th/promotion.html.
Source: Ministry of Commerce (2018), *Department of Business Development*, www.dbd.go.th/dbdweb_en/main-php?filename=index (accessed on 12 March 2018).

The Department of International Trade Promotion (DITP) of the Ministry of Commerce has a number of programmes and activities in place to support the export of local products from the country. For example, DITP had introduced an online platform for local businesses to connect with domestic and foreign suppliers. In addition, the Electronic Transactions Development Agency (ETDA) is responsible for the use and development of electronic transactions in the country, both at the corporate and public sector level. To help achieve this, ETDA has introduced a number of platforms to support consumers and businesses to help improve the use of online transaction systems and platforms (Electronic Transactions Development Agency, 2012[9]).

Box 10.4. Thailand's online platforms for SMEs

Thaicommercestore.com

Thaicommercestore serves as an online platform for SMEs to sell their products domestically. The website is operated by the Department of Business Development (DBD) of the Ministry of Commerce. Sellers can register for free and can sell as many products as they wish. In addition, users of the platform can also access information and participate in workshops on market development and management of online products and shops.

Thaitrade.com

Launched in 2013, thaitrade.com has been playing an important role in promoting and bringing Thai products to the local and domestic market. Thaitrade is a business-to-business (B2B) online marketplace established by the Ministry of Commerce. It allows local suppliers to post their products on line with detailed descriptions as well as certifications. Products that are endorsed on the website are verified and approved by the DITP. Interested and potential buyers can also search for sellers or after-sales requests on the website and access deals and promotions.

Membership is free of charge. Members of the platform are able to access a wide range of benefits and privileges, including discount and special rates from banks and shipping costs. In addition to serving as a channel for trade negotiations, the website also provides users with market information, updates and relevant news for Thai entrepreneurs and clients to access. Announcements for training and workshops organised by the government or partners in the private sector can also be found in the platform.

Thaitrade.com has been extended to tap online retailing. For example, Thaitrade.com's Small Order OK (SOOK) is a business-to-consumer (B2C) e-marketplace targeting retail shoppers around the world that are interested in purchasing in smaller quantities (Department of International Trade Promotion, 2017[10]).

Thaiemarket.com

Thaiemarket.com is an information system or centre for e-commerce operators in Thailand – serving as a learning channel to facilitate knowledge sharing and best practices across users. It also serves as a database that keeps track of the volume and value of electronic transactions and provides a platform for handling complaints and co-ordinating with relevant agencies on issues relating to e-commerce operations.

Online complaint centre

The online complaint centre provides a platform to respond to issues from consumers and businesses with online transaction problems. The centre also promotes user confidence by providing guidelines or criteria when receiving and addressing complaints.

Sources: Department of International Trade Promotion (2017), *Thaitrade*, www.thaitrade.com/home (accessed 3 January 2018); Electronic Transactions Development Agency (2012), *Highlight Projects*, www.etda.or.th/promotion.html (accessed on 15 June 2018).

Regulatory quality management

Regulatory impact assessment

Article 77 of the revised constitution (2017) requires government agencies to conduct assessments of newly introduced regulations. Other than that, there is no formal requirement to assess SME impacts of newly-introduced regulations.

When regulatory impact assessments are conducted for new regulations and are passed to the Cabinet for consideration, the responsible ministry or agency is required to present the negative and positive impacts of the new regulation. As a supplement to the guidelines (Box 10.5), a checklist for examining the necessity of a legislative enactment must also be filled up by the responsible entity (Government of Thailand, 2017[11]).

Currently, training and workshops are regularly organised by the government to improve the understanding of regulatory impact assessments and encourage its application. The government has also developed a set of guidelines for the assessment process.

The Department of Business Development notifies the result of the impact assessments and regulatory requirements through the department's website or the Office of Small and Medium Enterprise Promotion.

Box 10.5. Guidelines for drafting legislation in Thailand

All draft legislation must:

- Comply with and not be contrary or inconsistent with the Constitution and Organic Acts.
- Comply with and not be contrary to or inconsistent with the National Strategy and National Reform Plans.
- Have regard to or consider the compliance with the principles and substance of the Facilitation of the Licensing Facilitation Act, B.E. 2558 (2015) and the Royal Decree on the Criteria and Procedures for Good Governance, B.E. 2546 (2003) and the Royal Decree on Revision of Law, BE. 2558 (2015).
- Comply with the principles of Section 77 of the Constitution.
    - For example, for a permit system, the legislation must: 1) have clear objectives; 2) have the rules, time period and framework for the issuance and denial of the permit clearly provided in the draft; 3) have evidence of the implementing agency's readiness and capability to examine and comply with the legislation; 4) have a well-defined reason for its necessity and period of validity; and 5) use information technology to facilitate the system and achieve objectives.

A more detailed version of the requirements can be found online.

Source: Government of Thailand (2017), *Cabinet Resolution B.E. 2560,* www.lawreform.go.th/index.php/post/506 (accessed on 12 March 2018).

Ex post *evaluation*

In 2003, the government launched the Process Improvement Project based on the Royal Decree on Criteria and Procedures for Good Governance. The project aimed to reduce the time required to deliver services. 144 government agencies participated in the process improvement as part of the evaluation phase of the project (Khampee, 2016[7]).

Building on the work that has been achieved, the sub-committee on the Reform of Business Activity Regulations of the Thai government had initiated a joint initiative with the private sector to do an inventory and review of eight selected indicators[1] and to improve or simplify policies and processes that constrain the growth of businesses or help curb corruption.

Box 10.6. Doing business reform programme in Thailand

In 2017, a public-private joint initiative, also referred to as the "guillotine project", was launched to improve the business environment in the country. This reform aims to change processes, legal acts and back office efficiency as needed to move Thailand to top 20 in the 2019 World Bank Doing Business rankings. This is carried out through a careful case-by-case review to ensure that regulations needed in Thailand to protect health, safety and environment, such as appropriate health, safety and environmental rules, are maintained and strengthened, even as unnecessary requirements that distract regulators and businesses from the important protective regulations are removed.

The programme's goal is to:

- Substantially reduce the costs and risks of regulations affecting businesses and citizens by simplifying or abolishing rules affecting the doing business procedures and produce concrete and visible results in 2017.
- Improvement in international rankings to signal Thailand's reforms to the international community.
- Provide credibility and full transparency in the reform process by setting targets for improvements and reporting publicly on improvements in regulations by regulatory agency overtime.
- Stimulate small businesses and entrepreneurship by removing barriers to starting up and expanding businesses.
- Reduce corruption and business uncertainty resulting from complex and discretionary procedures.

As a result of these efforts, in November 2017, Thailand's rank in the World Bank's latest Doing Business indicators rose to 26 from 48 (World Bank, 2017[12]).

Source: World Bank (2017), *Thailand Moves Up in Global Doing Business Ranks*, www.worldbank.org/en/news/press-release/2017/11/01/thailand-moves-up-in-global-doing-business-ranks.

In 2015, the Thai government passed a sunset law (Royal Decree on Revision of Law, B.E. 2558), which requires all government agencies to review the suitability and feasibility of the existing or planned law and determine whether it should be kept, revised or repealed. Since 2015, government legislation passed by the Ministry of Commerce have been reviewed at least once.

Stakeholder engagement

In addition to requiring assessments for newly introduced regulations, Article 77 of the new Constitution of Thailand requires stakeholder consultation. The government has developed a set of guidelines for the consultation process accordingly.

Consultations are mostly conducted through physical public meetings prior to the drafting of the legislation and then passed to the Cabinet.

Box 10.7. Consultation process for draft legislation in Thailand

1. The agency would need to arrange a public consultation to gather opinions for the preparation of the legislation. The public hearing must be announced, at the very minimum, on line or through other platforms such as www.lawamendment.go.th. All public hearings must be held for more than 15 days.
2. The agency would need to announce the procedures, period of commencement, and termination. I should also disclose information on the legislation, such as: a) the current problems and causes; b) the necessity of the legislation to address the problem; c) the substantive principles; and d) specific issues which require opinion or the draft act for the public consultation.
3. After the consultation, the state agency is required to prepare a report to conclude the results of the consultations. The report must contain: a) the method for conducting the public hearing; b) the number of sessions and period of time for each session; c) target groups; d) issues and opinions discussed and raised; e) dissent or opinion of state agencies and parties involved; f) statement of reason for each issue; g) decision and results of public hearing in the legislation.
4. The state agency should prepare a statement according to the checklist to examine the necessity of the legislative enactment and submit it to the Cabinet Secretariat for the proposal of the draft legislation. The results of the consultation must also be attached to the proposal.
5. The Cabinet Secretariat shall analyse the results of the consultation and the impact that may arise from the legislation according to the criteria outlined in the checklist. If necessary, the Cabinet Secretariat can request more information the agency or request for additional consultation. Once addressed, the draft must be returned to the Secretariat.
6. The Council of Ministers then passes the draft to the Office of the Council of State for consideration. The Office of the Council of State reviews the impact assessment and consultation. If needed, it may request the state agency to provide more information or additional consultation or may conduct it itself. A report shall then be prepared by the Office of the Council of State following the modifications to or approval of the draft.
7. If an amendment is to be made, the Office of the Council of State would need to notify the agency of the revisions and submit a statement in accordance with the criteria prescribed in the checklist.

Source: Government of Thailand (2017), *Cabinet Resolution B.E. 2560*, www.lawreform.go.th/index.php/post/506 (accessed on 12 March 2018).

A number of the consultation processes related to business issues are conducted with representatives from the private sector, such as the Thai Chamber of Commerce (TCC) and the Federation of Thai Industries (FTI).

Two websites (www.lawamendment.go.th and www.dbd.go.th) publish all ongoing consultations with stakeholders. Recently, the Office of Small and Medium Enterprise Promotion (OSMEP) has conducted a public consultation for the draft legislation on Social Enterprise Promotion, as a way to promote the growth of enterprises that also aims to improve the quality of life of the Thai population (www.lawamendment.go.th, 2017[13]).

Regulatory delivery

Civil service framework

Regulations are delivered through the different state agencies. Various mechanisms are used to ensure that SME regulations are carried out efficiently. Implementation of SME regulations is carried out by the respective ministries and local governments. When applying regulations, agencies adhere to the legal definition but often tailor this according to the local conditions.

Although policy reviews are not carried out on a regular basis, the government, through the Office of the Public Sector Development Commission (OPDC), continues to make significant efforts to improve the business environment and provide better quality services to citizens and businesses via ongoing public sector reform initiatives (Box 10.8) (Office of the Public Sector Development, 2017[14]).

Box 10.8. Improving service delivery in Thailand

Public Sector Management Quality Award (PMQA) is an award provided on an annual basis to government agencies or state institutions that adopt good governance practices. Performance of ministries, agencies, or institutions is measured using seven categories.

Ministerial and Provincial Rightsizing is being carried out by the government to strengthen roles, missions and rightsizing, and improve the overall competitiveness of public servants in a fast-changing, global environment.

Blueprint for Change is a change management system that aims to increase the efficiency within the public sector. This includes adopting new patterns, techniques, frameworks and processes as a way to continuously improve the management aspects of public service.

Participatory Public Administration is a new policy that encourages government officials to reach out to the stakeholders in the decision-making process, both directly and indirectly. This can be achieved through referendums, public hearings and other platforms.

Source: Office of the Public Sector Development (2017), *Public Sector Reform Initiatives*, www.opdc.go.th/english/content.php?url=view&cat_id=2 (accessed on 22 December 2017).

Regulatory compliance

Compliance with standards and intellectual property

SMEs and potential start-ups face certain issues in relation to intellectual property (IP) registration, which may be attributed to the limited capacity and expertise for the approving agency to operate more efficiently and take decisions on specific applications. The government continues to adjust staff and operations of IP registration to suit the current demand; however, specific bottlenecks that prolong the process limit the possibility for SMEs to seize the existing opportunities.

Labelling and other non-tariff barriers are issues faced by Thai SMEs to be able to compete within the global value chain. For example, although some certification processes are harmonised, SMEs face issues in relation to numerous accreditation bodies that operate under different standards.

As a way to address these issues, the government has introduced several programmes and activities, including some focused on developing skills and knowledge for entrepreneurs to create value added in their products and services. These activities include branding and product development or packaging development to meet new trends and needs in the international market.

Box 10.9. Promoting intellectual property in Thailand

IP Mart (www.thaiipmart.com) serves as an online centre of intellectual property trading for various artefacts and for people interested in buying goods, exchanging ideas or setting up meetings with IP Mart as an intermediary. Since 2017, IP Mart has been improving the credibility of information posted on the website and further increasing accessibility, operability and efficiency by exploring other channels and platforms such as mobile applications. IP Mart was set up as a way to encourage innovation and business expansion, as well as help reduce the import of technology from abroad (Ministry of Commerce, 2018[15]).

Source: Ministry of Commerce (2018), *IP Mart*, www.thaiipmart.com/home (accessed on 18 June 2018).

SME linkages

Clusters

In September 2015, the Thai government introduced a cluster policy, which aims to increase the industrial competitiveness of specific sectoral and geographical areas. These clusters help link producers or manufacturers, suppliers, research institutions and other supporting organisations involved within an industry. Through these clusters, the government is able to properly target a wide range of development projects and reforms that can facilitate investment and growth.

Other projects carried out by the Department of Industrial Promotion focus on specific programmes that link entrepreneurs to foreign companies in industries such as medicine and health, aircraft development and automatic engines and robotics.

As a way to further link and enhance the performance of Thai entrepreneurs to the supply chain, the Thai government, through the Department of Industrial Promotion of the Ministry of Industry, is conducting several activities to support the development and increase added value of the exported products, including:

- A potential super cluster programme.
- A development programme for entrepreneurs and industrial enterprises in automatic engines and robotics.
- An automotive parts development programme.

Beyond product development, the Board of Investment (BOI) has been supporting entrepreneurs, notably SMEs, to integrate into the global value chains. The BOI Unit for Industrial Linkage Development (BUILD) helps link SMEs with major companies domestically and internationally through matchmaking events such as a central market for trading materials and parts, buyer meets seller, sourcing services and international exhibitions. The Department of International Trade Promotion's (DITP) website provides the possibility for SMEs to look for Thai suppliers working in different industries.

In addition to clusters, the Government of Thailand is has also developed new growth hubs through the Eastern Economic Corridor (EEC), which covers 13 000 square kilometres between Chachoengsao, Chonburi and Rayong provinces. The government aims to accelerate the growth in these provinces and establish them as centres for trade, investment and regional transportation.

Thailand 4.0

The Thai government has also launched Thailand 4.0, a new economic model that aims to strengthen the country's potential in addressing challenges such as the inequality, imbalance and the middle-income trap (Box 10.10). Thailand 4.0 aims to encourage the growth of specific industries by providing investors with incentives to participate in the development of target industries (Royal Thai Embassy, 2017[16]).

Box 10.10. Highlights of the Thailand 4.0 strategy

The Thailand 4.0 strategy aims to achieve four objectives: economic prosperity, social well-being, raising human values and environmental protection. To achieve these objectives, the government has prepared five agendas:

Prepare Thais for Thailand becoming a First World nation

The model aims to transform Thai citizens into competent citizens through: 1) reforming the education system; 2) setting up a skills development programme; and 3) introducing measures to support refill and reform strategy by improving their status and potential through provision of financial support, social opportunities and other area-based mechanisms.

Develop technology clusters and future industry

Thailand aims to develop ten future industries as a way to attract high-value investments in the country. The government provides benefits to investors in the ten industries classified under first S-curves and new S-curves. The first S-curves are industries that have a solid foundation but require more innovation and research and development (i.e. next generation automotive technology; smart electronics; affluent, medical and wellness tourism; agriculture and biotechnology; food for the future). On the other hand, the new S-curves focus on new industries that can improve competitiveness and innovation in the country (robotics, aviation and logistics, biofuels and biochemical, digital, and medical hub). In brief, the country aims to build on five groups of technology and targeted industries, namely: 1) food, agriculture, and biotech; 2) health, wellness, and biomedical; 3) smart devices and robotics; 4) digital, internet of things (IoT), artificial intelligence, and embedded technology; and 5) creativity, culture, and high-value services. As a way to propel the growth of these industries, the government aims to focus on the demand for knowledgeable and highly skilled manpower and the need to reform the Thai research system.

Incubate entrepreneurs and develop networks of innovation-driven enterprise

The focus on the five groups of technology and targeted industries intends to support entrepreneurs and networks through: 1) shifting traditional farmers to "smart farmers"; 2) transforming traditional SMEs into "smart SMEs"; 3) switching from traditional services to "high-value services"; and 4) promoting the development of start-ups.

Strengthen the internal economy through the mechanisms of 18 provincial clusters and 76 provinces

The aim is to ensure that the benefits of economic growth are spread to all regions and that there is an equal distribution of economic benefits. To do this, the government aims to strengthen the economic structure and internal market system by creating a database on trade and connectivity across all levels of government and setting up an appropriate regulatory regime to support growth and access of SMEs and social enterprises to the market. Furthermore, several strategies and guidelines have been developed for 19 provincial clusters to develop them as strategic economic region, e.g. Upper Northern Region 1 as the creative cluster and agricultural good innovation hub while the southern region serves as the southern agricultural trading centre for rubber, oil palm and fruit. An innovation hub is also expected to be established in each region.

Integrate with ASEAN and connect Thailand to the global community

Thailand aims to position itself as a trading nation and one of Asia's business centre by: 1) encouraging multinational corporations to establish international headquarters and trading centres in Thailand; 2) developing the Eastern Economic Corridor; 3) developing industrial clusters to promote high potential bases for targeted industries or the so-called superclusters; and 4) establishing special border economic zones in 10 provinces. Thailand also aims to bridge trade with neighbouring countries (Cambodia, Laos, Myanmar and Viet Nam) and aims to adopt a service sector policy and strategy to enhance the competitiveness of Thai service providers abroad.

Source: Royal Thai Embassy, *Thailand 4.0*, http://thaiembdc.org/thailand-4-0-2/ (accessed on 2 January 2018).

Labour mobility

Labour policy for foreigners in Thailand is guided by the Royal Decree on Recruitment of Foreigners, which was recently introduced in 2017. The decree sets the extent and limitation of foreign recruitment.

Non-resident foreign nationals may be employed in supervisory, technical or advisory roles, notably in special economic zones or priority clusters identified by the Board of Investment.

Information and networking

The Board of Investment regularly updates its business guide, which provides information for investors investing in the country. The business guide includes information on the different regulations that may affect them as well as incentives and assistance schemes (full ownership, tax incentives, etc.) that can be availed of when investing in specific priority areas.

Promotional events are regularly organised by the government, through the Department of International Trade Promotion (DITP). To do this, DITP has been introducing various schemes to support trade. Some promotional programmes are also organised by the Department of Foreign Trade through embassies abroad. These activities include trade promotions and other activities as a way to expand trade, border investment and participation in special economic zones.

Table 10.6. Export promotion schemes in Thailand

	Scheme
Schemes in accordance with government strategic issues	• Digital commerce scheme to develop and promote SMEs internationally • Schemes to promote the development of services and expand the network of logistics service providers
Schemes in accordance with the international trade strategy	• ASEAN trade development and promotion scheme • Thailand's promotion scheme to be the world's leading gem and jewellery hub • Scheme to promote Thailand as an ASEAN hub for trade and investment • Scheme on Thai logistics to create trade opportunities and services in the strategic trade route • Promotional scheme for Thailand to be the business leader of the East • Scheme to develop and promote food, agricultural products, food processing and halal product industries.

Source: OECD (forthcoming), *ASEAN SME Policy Index 2018: Boosting Competitiveness and Inclusive Growth in ASEAN*, OECD Publishing, Paris.

Customs

Thailand has introduced several programmes to improve customs procedures, including an integrated tariff database and an e-Tracking System (Box 10.11). The government has also been pursuing activities and reforms that help facilitate rules of origin. These include improving the systems that focus on: 1) issuing certificates of origin; 2) licensing and issuing certificates on general import-export goods; 3) costing for products; 4) self-registration; 5) database on the rules of origin; 6) digital signature; and 7) electronic signature and seal.

Box 10.11. Improving customs procedures in Thailand

Integrated tariff database

The database allows users to access information on import and export tariff rates as well as related information on exemptions of duty or special privileges. The database also includes information to related acts, e.g. the Customs Act, the Customs Tariff Act and other notifications from the Customs Department and the Ministry of Finance.

e-Tracking System

The system provides users with online customs clearance tracking services, such as account information, invoices and shipment status.

Sources: Thailand Customs Department (2018), *Official integrated tariff database, Thailand 4.0*, http://igtf.customs.go.th/ (accessed on 24 August 2018); Thailand Customs Department (2018), *E-tracking system*, http://e-tracking.customs.go.th (accessed on 24 August 2018).

Thailand's National Single Window system has been officially in place since October 2014. Since then, government agencies have been collaborating to further facilitate import, export and other logistical operations (The Thai Customs Department, 2016[17]).

Table 10.7. Agencies linked to the Thai National Single Window

	Agency
Complete electronic data linkage for all goods and documents	The Thai Customs Department; Department of Industrial Works; Department of Mineral Resources; Department of Disease Control Royal Forest Department; The Board of Investment of Thailand; Department of Medical Sciences; Office of the National Broadcasting and Telecommunications Commission; Department of Primary Industries and Mines; Department of Mineral Fuels; Department of National Parks, Wildlife and Plant Conservation; Department of Land Transport; Marine Department; Rubber Authority of Thailand; Electrical and Electronics Institute; Office of the Cane and Sugar Board; National Bureau of Agricultural Commodity and Food Standards; Department of Internal Trade; Excise Department; Thai Industrial Standards Institute; Food and Drug Administration; Office of Atoms for Peace; Department of Energy Business; Fine Arts Department (26)
Electronic data linkage for some goods	Defence Industry Department; Department of Agriculture; Department of Fisheries; Department of Foreign Trade; Department of Livestock Development (5)
Electronic data linkage with paper-based documents	Department of Provincial Administration; The Thai Chamber of Commerce and Board of Trade of Thailand (2)

Source: The Thai Customs Department (2016), *The Progress Report on the Development of Thailand National Single Window*, www.thainsw.net/INSW/Ent/DisplayDocumentDetailServlet?act=SRH&docCde=765&nswLang=E.

At present, 26 agencies have completed data linkage for all types of goods and customs information and formalities. The statuses of other agencies connected to the system are outlined in the table above.

Recommendations

- **Use the administrative burden reduction programme as an opportunity to further improve the stock of regulations and further identify issues that affect SMEs.** Consider expanding the programme to cover specific issues or industries of concern.
- **Enhance implementation of regulatory impact assessments (RIA) and involve businesses, especially SMEs, in the development of new regulations.**
- **Consider broadening the range of stakeholders involved in the deliberation of SME regulations and programmes.** Encourage more participation from industry leaders in the ASEAN region and beyond to help align policies and programmes with initiatives introduced at the regional and international level.

Notes

[1] The eight priority indicators in the World Bank Doing Business Indicator as well as Thailand's rank in each include: dealing with construction permits (Rank 42); registering property (Rank 68); getting credit (Rank 82); protecting minority investors (Rank 27); paying taxes (Rank 109); trading across borders (Rank 56); enforcing contracts (Rank 51); resolving insolvency (Rank 23).

References

Department of International Trade Promotion (2017), *Thaitrade*, https://www.thaitrade.com/home (accessed on 3 January 2017). [10]

Electronic Transactions Development Agency (2012), *Highlight Projects*, https://www.etda.or.th/promotion.html (accessed on 15 June 2018). [9]

Government of Thailand (2017), *Cabinet Resolutions B.E. 2560*, http://www.lawreform.go.th/index.php/post/506 (accessed on 12 March 2018). [11]

Government of Thailand (2015), *Licensing Facilitation Act, B.E. 2558*, http://www.opdc.go.th/uploads/files/2558/LICENSING_FACILITATION_ACT_2015.pdf. [8]

Khampee, K. (2016), *Workshop on New Approaches in Measuring and Reinforcing Trust in Public Institutions*, https://www.opdc.go.th/english/files/MeasuringandReinforcing.pdf. [7]

Ministry of Commerce (2018), *Department of Business Development*, http://www.dbd.go.th (accessed on 12 March 2018). [6]

Ministry of Commerce (2018), *IP Mart*, http://www.thaiipmart.com/home (accessed on 18 June 2018). [15]

OECD (forthcoming), *ASEAN SME Policy Index 2018: Boosting Competitiveness and Inclusive Growth in ASEAN*, OECD Publishing, Paris. [18]

Office of the Council of State (2017), *Philosophy, Mandate, and Organisation Chart*, http://www.krisdika.go.th/wps/portal/general_en/!ut/p/c5/04_SB8K8xLLM9MSSzPy8xBz9CP0os3g_A2czQ0cTQ89ApyAnA0__EIOAQGdXAwM_Y30_j_zcVP2CbEdFAFGmRSc!/dl3/d3/L2dJQSEvUUt3QS9ZQnZ3LzZfTjBDNjFBNDFJUUJSQjBJT1QwUFFDRTAwVjA!/. [2]

Office of the Council of State (2017), *Thai Legislative Process*, http://www.krisdika.go.th/wps/portal/general_en/!ut/p/c4/04_SB8K8xLLM9MSSzPy8xBz9CP0os3g_A2czQ0cTQ08jb0tTA09zQw83c58wYwt_Q_2CbEdFAKMAAcY!/. [4]

Office of the Public Sector Development (2017), *History*, https://www.opdc.go.th/content.php?menu_id=2&content_id=3491 (accessed on 22 December 2017). [1]

Office of the Public Sector Development (2017), *Public Sector Reform Initiatives*, http://www.opdc.go.th/english/content.php?url=view&cat_id=2 (accessed on 22 December 2017). [14]

Royal Thai Embassy (2017), *Thailand 4.0*, http://thaiembdc.org/thailand-4-0-2/ (accessed on 2 January 2017). [16]

Thailand Customs Department (2018), *E-tracking System*, http://e-tracking.customs.go.th (accessed on 24 August 2018). [20]

Thailand Customs Department (2018), *Official Integrated Tariff Database, Thailand 4.0*, [19] http://igtf.customs.go.th/ (accessed on 24 August 2018).

The Federation of Thai Industries (2015), *About F.T.I.*, https://www.fti.or.th/2016/eng/ftiaboutfti.aspx (accessed on 20 December 2017). [3]

The Thai Customs Department (2016), *The Progress of Thailand National Single Window*, http://www.thainsw.net/INSW/Ent/DisplayDocumentDetailServlet?act=SRH&docCde=765&nswLang=E. [17]

World Bank (2017), *Law Library*, http://www.doingbusiness.org/law-library/ (accessed on 8 March 2018). [5]

World Bank (2017), *Thailand Moves Up in Global Doing Business Ranks*, http://www.worldbank.org/en/news/press-release/2017/11/01/thailand-moves-up-in-global-doing-business-ranks. [12]

www.lawamendment.go.th (2017), *Summary of the Results of the Hearing on the Draft Social Enterprise Promotion Act*, http://www.lawamendment.go.th/index.php/laws-department/item/1130-2017-08-29-03-57-28. [13]

Chapter 11. Viet Nam

Viet Nam has undertaken impressive efforts to improve the efficiency of its administration and administrative processes, including streamlining business and investment regulatory frameworks. The government has introduced mandatory regulatory impact assessments in the development of legal documents and lawmakers are required to identify the likely distributional effects of new regulations, especially through the consultation process. Impact evaluations of existing regulations have also been conducted in the past years, although not systematically. Viet Nam has recently introduced a new small and medium-sized enterprise (SME) support law in 2017, which consolidates and overwrites all previous laws and regulations related to SMEs. A dedicated SME Development and Promotion Council is responsible for co-ordinating inputs from various ministries and agencies involved in SME development, as well as advising the Prime Minister related policies and instruments. The government is also making good progress in building its e-customs portals and National Single Window towards convergence with the Association of Southeast Asian Nations (ASEAN) Single Window.

Regulatory context

The regulatory context for businesses in Viet Nam has undergone a remarkable transformation over the past three decades as the country transitioned from a state-led command economy to a market-oriented economy. In 1986, Viet Nam launched a broad economic reform package called "Doi Moi", or "renovation", which focused on opening up Viet Nam's economy and improving its business environment. A few years later, Viet Nam introduced the Law on Private Enterprises and Companies Law in 1990 to allow Vietnamese citizens to establish private businesses for the first time. This was an important milestone for Viet Nam, despite the fact that the requirements and procedures required by this new law were complicated and prohibitive to most entrepreneurs. Only 34 000 privately owned businesses were established between 1990 and 2000.

A subsequent Law on Enterprise in 1999 significantly reduced the administrative procedures relating to starting businesses. Many other reforms have since been made to policies and regulations related to credit, land, taxes, customs, standards and more. Large-scale reforms to reduce government control and improve the efficiency of state-owned enterprises (SOEs) through privatisation, or "equitisation", are also underway.

Reform efforts to streamline business procedures, reduce administrative burden, increase transparency and improve access to resources and services have benefitted businesses of all sizes, including micro and SMEs, which account for 97% of all businesses registered in Viet Nam and 37% of total employment in the country (General Statistics Office, 2016[1]). As of 2016, there are around 590 000 active micro, small, and medium enterprises (MSMEs) in Viet Nam, of which 68% are micro-enterprises (Can, 2017[2]).

Most business laws and regulations in Viet Nam apply to enterprises of all sizes, although some may provide special provisions for SMEs (for example, lower rates of corporate income tax). However, given the importance of SMEs in the Viet Nam economy, the government has also introduced SME-specific development plans and regulatory policies to give SMEs preferential treatment.

The first piece of regulation explicitly targeting SMEs was introduced in 2001 and it laid the foundation for establishing a dedicated SME Agency under the Ministry of Planning and Investment (MPI) (Decree 90/2001/ND-CP). Decree No. 90 also introduced a five-year SME Development Plan, which has been renewed since. The latest SME Development Plan covers the period 2011-15 (Box 11.1). Decree No. 90 was later replaced by Decree No. 56/2009/ND-Development and Promotion and most recently by the Small and Medium Enterprise Support Law No. 04/2017/QH14 in July 2017 (hereafter "SME Support Law").

Viet Nam has increasingly aligned its regulatory frameworks to facilitate integration into international markets. As part of the World Trade Organization (WTO) accession process, Viet Nam has significantly reformed much of its legal and regulatory frameworks to be more transparent and compliant with international standards. It has made revisions to a number of major business-related laws and regulations to improve the investment environment in Viet Nam, some of which have special provisions for SMEs. Viet Nam became a WTO member in 2007.

Considerable efforts also have been made to align or adapt national regulations with regional (ASEAN) or international standards. The introduction and adoption of regulatory impact assessments (RIA) is an example of this, as is the implementation of the standard cost model under a National Project on Administrative Reform (Project 30) (Box 11.6).

In order to benchmark the performance of Viet Nam's business regulatory environment and to continue advancing business reforms, the government refers to the World Bank's Doing Business Indicators, the Global Competitiveness Report of the World Economic Forum, the ASEAN SME Policy Index and the World Intellectual Property Organization (WIPO) indicators on intellectual property, among many international resources.

Box 11.1. Viet Nam Government Action Plan on SME Development 2011-15

The most recent five-year Government Action Plan on SME Development was issued for the period of 2011-15 (Vietnam Law and Legal Forum, 2012[31]). This development plan aims to increase the number of SMEs by 350 000 between 2011 and 2015, and create 3.5 to 4 million associated jobs over the same period. In order to achieve these targets, the plan outlines a number of support measures:

1. Complete the legal framework for SME entry, operation and withdrawal from the market.
2. Support access to capital and credit and improve the efficiency of capital use for SMEs.
3. Support innovation and application of new technology for SMEs.
4. Develop human resources, particularly on improving administrative capacity.
5. Establish industrial co-operation between linked groups and industrial parks, as well as increase land access for SMEs.
6. Provide supportive information to facilitate market expansion for SMEs.
7. Develop an assistance system for SMEs.
8. Manage the implementation of the SME Development Plan, particularly specific measures such as establishing an SME support fund, intensifying technology application and innovation.

Source: Vietnam Law and Legal Forum (2012), *Decision No. 1231/QD-TTG: Development Plan for Small- and Medium-sized Enterprises during 2011-2015*, http://vietnamlawmagazine.vn/decision-no-1231-qd-ttg-development-plan-for-small-and-medium-sized-enterprises-during-2011-2015-3167.html.

Regulatory governance

Institutional and regulatory setup

Table 11.1. Institutional and regulatory setup in Viet Nam

	Government
State structure	Single Party Socialist Republic
Head of state	**President**
Executive	The executive power in Viet Nam is vested in the **President** and the **Government of Viet Nam**. The President is responsible for national defence and foreign relations. The President can recommend the election of the Vice President, Prime Minister, Chief Justice and Chief Prosecutor to the National Assembly. The President can directly appoint Deputy Prime Ministers, Ministers and other government members. The President also serves as the commander-in-chief of the Viet Nam People's Armed Forces, as well as the Chairman of the Council for Defence and Security. • The government is headed by the **Prime Minister**, who presides over several Deputy Prime Ministers as well as other ministers in charge of specific activities. The **Office of the Government** is responsible for co-ordinating with ministries, provincial-level People's Committees and concerned agencies and organisations in preparing draft legal documents as well as reviewing and commenting on them before they are submitted to higher level institutions.

	• **Line Ministries** are responsible for initiating and drafting law and regulation proposals. They also oversee the implementation of regulations in their fields of competence. • **Ministry of Justice** is in responsible for quality control of all laws and regulations.
Legislative	**Unicameral legislature** The constitutional and legislative powers in Viet Nam are vested in the **National Assembly**. Only the National Assembly can formulate and amend the constitution as well as laws, according to the Constitution and the Law on the Organisation of the National Assembly. The National Assembly is also responsible for making decisions pertaining to national affairs and exercising supreme control over the activities of the state.
Legal system	• The **Supreme Court** is the highest judiciary power. As Viet Nam abides by a one-party political system, the judiciary including all judges and procurators are members of the Communist Party of Viet Nam. The Supreme Court is accountable to the National Assembly. • Three levels of **People's Courts** exist below the Supreme People's Court: 1) the superior people's courts, which are appellate courts responsible for the northern, central and southern regions of Viet Nam; 2) provincial-level people's courts which are trial and appellate courts; 3) district level people's courts which are trial courts only. • A **Central Military Tribunal** is subordinate to the Supreme People's Court, and it presides over a system of military tribunals at various levels of the People's Army in Viet Nam. • The top prosecutorial authority in Viet Nam is the **Supreme People's Procuracy**. These authorities are responsible for supervising and inspecting judicial compliance by government agencies and officials. Every people's court has its own people's procuracy.
Administrative-territorial structure	5 municipalities and 58 provinces, which are further subdivided into urban districts, towns, provincial cities, and rural districts.
Ministry or agency responsible for SMEs or SME-related issues	**SME Development Council** headed by the Minister of MPI and the **Agency for Enterprise Development** under the Ministry of Planning and Investment (MPI)
Other support structures within government on regulatory policy	• **SME Development and Promotion Council** helps to SME development initiatives and programmes, as well as advise the Prime Minister on policies and instruments that encourage SME development • **Directorate for Standards, Metrology and Quality (STAMEQ)** is the national standardisation agency. It issues national standards and helps develop international standards. STAMEQ is housed under the Ministry of Science and Technology. • **State Bank of Viet Nam** is the national banking regulator. • Various non-government bodies including **Viet Nam Chamber of Commerce and Industry (VCCI)** and **Viet Nam SME Association (VINASME)** are important institutions that help advocate for more enabling and favourable regulatory policy framework for SMEs

Viet Nam's legislative process

The legislative process begins when the government proposes draft laws to the National Assembly and draft ordinances to the Standing Committee of the National Assembly. According to Article 100 of the Constitution, the executive branch is responsible for issuing, reviewing and handling legal documents, including supporting decrees and circulars, according to their duties and authorities (UNDP, 2012[4]).

The Ministry of Justice (MOJ) is in charge of quality control of all laws and regulations. It also monitors their implementation. The MOJ performs the state management on development and implementation of laws and regulations, post-review of legal normative documents, control of administrative procedures and legal dissemination and education; state management on execution of civil and administrative judgments, judicial-administrative activities, judicial affairs support, state compensation in administrative management and execution of judgments and other justice works nationwide; management of the implementation of laws and regulations on handling of administrative violations; and public services provision in the areas under the ministry's state management (Government of Viet Nam, 2013[5]).

Figure 11.1. Viet Nam's legislative process

Note: The National Assembly assigns the Law Committee, the Ministry of Justice and other relevant agencies to produce a report explaining opinions and revisions to the draft legislative programme.
Source: UNDP (2012), *Legislative Processes and Procedures of the National Assembly, Research Report*, Hanoi.

Regulatory process for business-related laws

The Ministry of Planning and Investment (MPI) is the relevant line ministry for putting forth draft laws and ordinances relating to business and investments. The MPI is also in charge of SME dedicated laws and regulations. The Agency for Enterprise Development (AED) under the MPI serves as the central SME Agency in Viet Nam. The agency supports the government in formulating policies and regulations related to SME and in designing and implementing SME support programmes.

The MPI is responsible for implementing the business- and investment-related laws and regulations that have been approved by the National Assembly. In addition, an SME Development and Promotion Council have been set up to help implement Decree No. 56 and multiple initiatives and programme on SME development. Since Decree No. 56 has been replaced by the SME Support Law in 2017, it is expected that the council will continue to help implement the new law. The council also advises the Prime Minister on policies and instruments that encourage the development of SMEs. Members of this council include:

- Minister of Planning and Investment (Chairman).
- Director General of the Enterprise Development Agency (Standing Secretary).
- Leaders of the Ministry of Planning and Investment, Industry and Trade, Finance, Justice, Agriculture and Rural Development, Construction, Transport, Science and Technology, Natural Resources and Environment, Education and Training, Labour - War Invalids and Social Affairs, and Steering Committee for Enterprise Development and Reform.
- Leaders of provincial People's Committee of Hanoi, Ho Chi Minh City, Hai Phong, Da Nang and Can Tho.
- Leaders of the Chamber of Commerce and Industry (VCCI), the Viet Nam Co-operative Alliance (VCA), the Viet Nam Association of Small and Medium Enterprises (VINASME), and of some business associations in Viet Nam.
- Selected experts in the fields of economics, science and technology upon request from relevant ministries.

The Ministry of Justice (MOJ) is responsible for monitoring the implementation of laws by the relevant ministries. The People's Procuracy is responsible for supervising and inspecting judicial compliance by government agencies and officials.

Laws and regulations relevant for SMEs

In Viet Nam, most business regulations and regulatory policies are designed and formulated for all businesses irrespective of their size. These general regulations and regulatory policies cover many areas of business operations including incorporation, corporate governance, credit, customs, labour, land and technology. Key business-related laws include:

- Labour Law
- Land Law
- Civil Code (includes provisions for intellectual property rights)
- Law on Corporate Income Tax
- Law on Competition
- Law on Securities
- Law on Competition (2004)
- Law on Enterprise (1999)
- Investment Law.

Some general business laws and regulations also include special provisions for SMEs. Such regulations relate to simplified accounting standards, reduced corporate income tax rate and reduced frequency of financial as well as tax report submissions. For example, according to the Law on Corporate Income Tax, SMEs are entitled to a lower corporate tax rate of 20% compared to 22% for larger companies.

To benefit from special state support for SMEs, Vietnamese businesses must fall under the categories outlined in Table 11.2. Micro, small and medium enterprises are categorised according to employment numbers and total capital in various sectors, depending on the nature of the relevant sector. For example, trade and services tend to use less labour and capital than the other sectors but yield higher sales and revenue. The categorisation of MSMEs in Table 11.2 is consistent with the categories used by the General Statistical Office (GSO), which collects and compiles data and statistics for policy analyses, policymaking and policy advocacy purposes.

Table 11.2. Definition of micro and SMEs in Viet Nam

Sector	Micro-enterprises	Small-sized enterprises		Medium-sized enterprises	
	No. of labourers	Total capital (VND)	No. of labourers	Total capital (VND)	No. of labourers
1. Agriculture, forestry and fishery	10 or fewer	20 billion or less	10 to 200	20 to 100 billion	200 to 300
2. Industry and construction	10 or fewer	20 billion or less	10 to 200	20 to 100 billion	200 to 300
3. Trade and service	10 or fewer	10 billion or less	10 to 50	10 to 50 billion	50 to 100

Source: Decree No. 56/2009/ND-CP on SME Support and Promotion.

There have also been several laws dedicated to supporting SMEs enacted since 2001, all of which have been overwritten by the latest Small and Medium Enterprise Support Law

No. 04/2017/QH14 in July 2017 (hereafter "SME Support Law") since January 2018. The SME Support Law aims to support SME growth, make Vietnamese businesses globally competitive, and reduce the administrative burden for investors and entrepreneurs (Box 11.2) concurrent with other ongoing economy-wide reforms. Three implementation decrees to guide the implementation of the law are currently being drafted and are expected to be adopted by the early of 2018.

Box 11.2. Priorities of the Viet Nam SME Support Law 2017 and its prevailing regulatory policies

General priorities:

- Increase the number of active SMEs to 1 million by 2020.*
- Improve the legal environment and policy framework for SMEs in all regulatory areas including business registration, permit and licences, taxes, customs, access to finance.
- Improve SME access to credit and different types of funds and capital.
- Support business start-ups and innovation.
- Support SMEs in accessing land and office space, particularly in industrial zones and high-tech parks.
- Support market access and linkages with domestic as well as international supply chains.
- Support formal business registration for household businesses and micro-enterprises according to the Enterprise Law.
- Improve the quality of support programmes and policies for SMEs.

Key provisions:

- SMEs are eligible for a lower corporate income tax (CIT) rate for a finite period.*
- Companies investing in distribution chains in which at least 80% of supplied goods are produced by SMEs in Viet Nam are eligible for CIT exemption and reduction.
- SMEs can opt for a simplified accounting system as stipulated in the relevant accounting regulations.
- Provincial People's Committees could support local SMEs located in industrial or high-tech zones with land leases.
- Ministries and provincial People's Committees are obligated to support and/or co-operate with SMEs in research and development, technology development including technology training and transfer, intellectual protection and in establishing common technology clusters.
- SME start-ups and SMEs participating in value chains may be eligible for additional incentives.

* The law does not specify the rate of reduction of CIT, although an earlier draft in May proposed a rate reduced by 5% for a maximum duration of five years. It is expected that the rate and eligibility period will be specified in a forthcoming guiding regulation (PwC, 2017[6]).

Source: PwC (2017), *PWC Vietnam News Brief: Lower Corporate Income Tax Rates and Other Incentives for Small and Medium Enterprises*, http://www.pwc.com/vn/en/publications/2017/170721-pwc-vietnam-newsbrief-law-sme-en.pdf.

Highlights of regulatory opportunities and challenges to support SMEs

Regulatory clarity

Viet Nam has set out clear principles for the development of regulatory policy, legal and normative documents. Such rules and processes applicable to the making of laws and regulations are stipulated in the Law on the Making of Laws and Legal Normative Documents ("Law on Laws"), introduced in 2008 and amended in 2015 (Box 11.3). The process outlined in the Law on Laws applies to all policies, laws and regulations including those pertaining to SMEs.

Box 11.3. Law on the Making of Laws and Legal Normative Documents (Law on laws)

The main principles of the regulatory policy, legal and normative documents in Viet Nam are stipulated at the Law No. 80/2015/QH13 regarding the Promulgation of Legal and Normative Documents dated 22 June 2015 (often known as the Law on Laws) (Government of Viet Nam, 2015[7]). According to Article 5 of the law, key principles of regulatory policies, legal and normative documents in Viet Nam include the following:

- Ensure the constitutionality, legitimacy, and uniformity of legal normative documents in the legal system.
- Comply with regulations of law on authority, manner and procedures for formulating and promulgating legal normative documents.
- Ensure transparency of legal normative documents.
- Ensure the feasibility, frugality, effectiveness, promptness, accessibility and practicality of legal normative documents;
- Integrate gender equality issues in legal normative documents; ensure simplification of administrative procedures.
- Ensure national defence and security, environmental protection without obstruction of implementation of the international agreements to which the Socialist Republic of Viet Nam is a signatory.
- Ensure publicity and democracy in receipt of and response to opinions, complaints from agencies, organisations and individuals during the process of formulating and promulgating legal normative documents.

Source: Government of Viet Nam (2015), *Law No. 80/2015/QH13 regarding Promulgation of Legal and Normative Documents*.

Some specific policy targets are set out in both Viet Nam's SME Development Plan and SME Support Law, along with some provisions to support their achievement. The SME Development Plan aims to register 80% of SMEs by 2020 (20 years after the passing of the law) and ensure that 50% of small companies have financial accounts by 2025. The SME Support Law aims to reach 1 million active SMEs by 2020 (Box 11.2). However, there are no accompanying indicators with which to measure or track progress towards achieving these targets.

Regulatory delivery

Regulatory compliance

Regulatory compliance is acknowledged to be a particular challenge for SMEs in terms of time and cost. In a given year, production factories are subject to many inspections by various government agencies to check compliance with regulations in environmental standards, workplace health and safety, taxation and reporting, labour standards and working conditions. Inspections often take place individually, according to the administering agency and, as such, are not systematically considered or grouped together to limit possible duplication.

Regulatory requirements relating to importing input products can also be especially challenging for SMEs to understand. Some key customs procedures – such as Harmonised System (HS) codes - are not yet consistently applied. This can sometimes result in the charging of different tariffs for the same product. Customs procedures and regulations, including import-export tax procedures, remain highly challenging for SMEs.

As part of the WTO accession process, Viet Nam has significantly reformed a number of regulatory and trade facilitation measures to comply with international standards. Efforts have been made to implement agreements on intellectual property, investment measures, customs valuation, sanitary and phytosanitary measures, import licensing provisions, anti-dumping and countervailing measures, and rules of origin.

The Directorate for Standards, Metrology and Quality (STAMEQ) is the national standardisation agency. It issues national standards and helps develop international standards. STAMEQ is housed under the Ministry of Science and Technology. Considerable efforts also have been made to align or adapt national regulations with regional (ASEAN) or international standards. However, there are no current plans or programmes to harmonise or streamline sanitary and phytosanitary requirements (i.e. requirements certification, licensing/product certification, labelling requirements, inspections and testing, etc.) at the national or regional levels.

Enforcement and inspection

Viet Nam has adopted a rewards and sanction approach to regulatory enforcement. Many regulations feature a separate section which stipulates that rewards and sanctions are subject to the prevailing regulations, leaving their implementation vague. Rewards and sanctions may be implemented at the ministry, government, President or National Assembly level.

Vietnamese customs authorities apply the principle of risk management, which aims to help facilitate export and import activities while reducing costs and shortening clearance time (Box 11.4). For example, according to Resolution 19/2016/ NQ-CP, the government has requested ministries to change management methods, specialised inspections and other management principles on the basis of risk assessment, international practices and a substantial change to the post-clearance audits; apply electronic management of procedures; and share information among functional agencies, organisations, specialised inspections agencies and customs agencies. However, while many ministries have issued legal documents to apply risk management principles in customs supervision and management, full implementation is still in progress (Government of Viet Nam, 2014[8]).

Box 11.4. Principles of risk management in customs operations in Viet Nam

- Customs authorities shall apply the principle of risk management in deciding on customs inspection and supervision of goods and vehicle, and shall support the tackling of smuggling and illegal cross-border trafficking of goods.
- Risk management in customs operations shall include the collection and processing of customs information; establishment of criteria for and evaluation of customs declarants' adherence to the law, and classification of risks; and implementation of appropriate measures for customs management.
- For the purposes of serving the application of risk management to customs operations, customs authorities shall manage and apply a communication system that automatically integrates and processes data.
- The Minister of Finance shall establish criteria for evaluation of customs declarants' adherence to the regulations of law, classify risks and apply risk management to customs operations.

Source: Government of Viet Nam (2014), *Law on Customs, National Assembly No. 54/2014/QH13*, www.wipo.int/edocs/lexdocs/laws/en/vn/vn081en.pdf.

Regulatory delivery – including compliance, enforcement and inspection - is regularly reviewed by the Ministry of Justice (MOJ) and the National Assembly, although there are no official statistics on compliance rates.

Administrative simplification

Administrative simplification is a priority for the Viet Nam government. Since its first administrative simplification policy in 1994 (Resolution 38/CP), the government has continued to implement various policies and plans aimed at improving Viet Nam's business environment and making the administrative system simpler, more transparent, efficient and easily understood. Between 2001 and 2010, Viet Nam implemented a Public Administration Reform Master Programme, which included many measures to streamline government procedures and reduce administrative burden. As part of this Master Programme, Viet Nam gradually introduced one-stop shops across the country (Box 11.5).

Between 2007 and 2010, Viet Nam implemented a Master Plan to Simplify Administrative Procedures, also known as Project 30 (Box 11.6). Project 30 draws its name from its target to simplify at least 30% of administrative procedures as well as reduce administrative costs by 30%. It also aimed to modernise the domestic regulatory system and bring it closer in line with WTO and international trade agreements. The project benefitted from strong government support and co-ordination, successfully delivering a comprehensive inventory of administrative procedures on an online database along with reviews of the necessity, legality and user-friendliness of these procedures. Project 30 also proposed 2 sets of simplification measures. In 2011, the OECD reviewed the progress of Project 30 and proposed recommendations on implementing its findings.

Box 11.5. One-stop shops in Viet Nam

The first one-stop shop in Viet Nam was piloted in Ho Chi Minh City in 1995. Since then, Viet Nam has introduced one-stop shops all over the country to consolidate the delivery of government services to support business start-ups, including information about regulations and their requirements, licensing and permit issuance.

The implementation of one-stop shops was first stipulated by law in the Public Administration Reform Master Programme 2001-10. Roll out of this model began in 2003. By 2007, the one-stop shop initiative was scaled up to all departments and procedures at local levels as well as made mandatory at the central level. By the end of 2015, 88% of departments at the provincial level, 99% of departments at the district level and 97% of departments at the commune, ward and township level had introduced nearly 13 000 one--stop shops across Viet Nam (Blunt et al., 2017[9]).

However, services provided by one-stop shops do not necessarily span different ministries or across levels of government. As a result, businesses may still have to visit multiple one-stop shops in order to complete all necessary administrative procedures (Blunt et al., 2017[9]).

Source: Blunt, M. et al (2017), *One-stop Shops in Vietnam: Changing the Face of Public Administration for Citizens and Businesses through a Single Door to Multiple Services*, http://documents.worldbank.org/curated/en/509861498753741062/One-stop-shops-in-Vietnam-changing-the-face-of-public-administration-for-citizens-and-businesses-through-a-single-door-to-multiple-services.

Box 11.6. Regulatory simplification process and outcomes from Project 30

Project 30 catalogued more than 5 000 administrative procedures and more than 9 000 legal normative documents in a database. Reviews of these procedures and documents were undertaken by ministries, local and foreign businesses, according to the administrative simplification process as follows:

1. Prepare an inventory of administrative procedures.
2. Conduct a self-review of the necessity of the administrative procedure, including from the community's perspective.
3. Expert review of difficult administrative procedures by special task force.
4. Recommendations on whether to keep, simplify or abolish procedure.

By the end of Project 30 in late 2010, the government had issued 25 special resolutions requesting ministries to simplify 4 723 administrative procedures. This significantly reduced administrative burden for citizens and businesses and was estimated to save some USD 20 million a year in invoicing procedures and some USD 50 million in tax declaration and collection (Vo and Nguyen, 2016[10]).

Source: Vo, T. and C. Nguyen (2016), *Towards Responsive Regulatory Management Systems: Country Report for Viet Nam*, http://www.eria.org/ERIA-DP-2016-22.pdf.

The government has continued its commitment to reduce administrative burden in Viet Nam. In January 2018, the Ministry of Industry and Trade issued Decree No. 08/2018/ND-CP to remove 55% of all business and investment criteria for 8 sectors under its management: petroleum, tobacco, franchise, e-commerce, electricity, chemicals, industrial explosive materials and food trade (675 out of 1 216 business criteria) in a sweeping reform of Viet Nam's business sector. The ministry also announced a plan to remove some 58% of goods codes (420 out of 720) subject to pre-clearance inspection. This followed from a Resolution No. 01/NQ-CP issued in late 2017 which set out the government's aim to reduce business criteria in various ministries by 50%. As of the end of 2017, five ministries had put forth plans to remove more business criteria under its scrutiny (Vietnam News, 2017[11]).

Regulatory quality management

Lawmakers are required to identify the likely distributional effects of the regulation, especially through the consultation process (with the public and with other line ministries, agencies and the business community). In some cases, public consultations of draft regulations with business associations have been useful in identifying the likely distributional effect of regulations. For example, a recent consultation on the draft decree on conditional business lines and business conditions helped regulators realise that proportionally, it costs much more for a small business to obtain a food safety certificate or a permit to trade in liquefied gas than for a large business.

Ex post *evaluation*

The government has also conducted *ex post* assessment of the impacts of several SME regulatory policies, including Decrees No. 90 and No. 56, which helped to formulate the SME Support Law. However, more than 80% of SME support policies and programmes have not had their progress monitored and evaluated, as noted by the Report on the Implementation of Policies and Programmes to assist SMEs in the framework of Decree 56/2009/ND-CP on SME support.

Regulatory impact assessment

The Law on Laws introduced the obligation to conduct regulatory impact assessments (RIA) in the development of legal documents of almost all levels including: laws, ordinances, resolutions of the National Assembly, decrees of the government, decisions of the Prime Minister, ministry circulars and also resolutions by the People's Council at the provincial level (Box 11.7). The Law on Promulgation also stipulates that the National Assembly and all of its commissions, the government, all ministries and provincial People's Committees are responsible of the implementation of RIA when they draft the regulations that are in their authority.

RIA has been used extensively in the making of the SME Support Law between 2015 and 2017, helping to improve the quality of the law. For example, RIA helped quantify the costs and benefits of different proposed policy measures, such as the reduction of corporate income taxes applicable to SMEs, household support for registration, support to SMEs to innovate and to become part of industry clusters or global value chains. RIA has also helped to enrich debates and consultations on the draft law at provincial, ministry and National Assembly level.

Box 11.7. RIA of proposed regulatory policies as stipulated in Article 35 of the Law on the Promulgation of Legal Normative Documents, 2015

- Agencies and organisations which are responsible for drafting regulatory policy shall assess the impact of each proposed policy. Deputies of the National Assembly shall assess the impact of each proposed policy or request a competent authority to do so.
- During the process of drafting, appraising, inspecting, considering and commenting on law/ordinance proposals and draft regulations, if new policy issues are proposed to be included in the draft, the submitting agency must assess the impact of such draft regulations and proposals.
- The assessment of each proposed policy in must articulate the following: issues to be addressed; objective of the policy; solutions to the issues to be included in the policy; positive and negative impacts, cost and benefit of the policy actions and solutions; comparative analysis of costs and benefits of the proposed solutions; selected solution and reason for such selection; impact assessment of administrative procedure which might arise due to the policy; impact assessment on gender-related issues (if any).
- When assessing the impact of proposed policies, agencies, organisations and deputies of the National Assembly must carry out impact analysis and draft the report on impact assessment; seek opinions and feedback about the draft report and revise the draft report.

Source: Government of Viet Nam (2015), *Law No. 80/2015/QH13 regarding Promulgation of Legal and Normative Documents*.

A Technical Guide on Regulatory Impact Assessment has been developed by MOJ with support from USAID. Benchmarks against regional or international practices were frequently referred to in the development of the technical guide.

International good practices, such as the *OECD Guiding Principles on RIA* and examples from Australia, South Korea and the United Kingdom are increasingly referred to in formal assessments of the impacts of SME regulatory policies as well as in public communications on their costs and benefits.

E-government

Several online databases for regulations have been introduced in Viet Nam (Box 11.8).

Box 11.8. Online databases for regulations in Viet Nam

The official regulation database in Viet Nam is the E-Gazette. The E-Gazette is run by the government and financed by the state budget. It covers regulations by sector. The E-Gazette is the most comprehensive regulation database in the country and is regularly updated at http://congbao.chinhphu.vn/.

The Ministry of Justice also provides a comprehensive database of laws and regulations at the national as well as provincial level. The laws and regulations are classified by the issuing agencies (National Assembly, government, ministries, etc.) http://vbpl.vn/Pages/portal.aspx.

Some law databases have also been set up by companies for commercial purposes, for example, the Online Law Library by Lawsoft. This database is regularly updated and can provide many types of regulations for payment. The library is at the following address: https://thuvienphapluat.vn/.

Some ministries and provinces also feature regulation databases on their websites, usually for regulations under their authority. For example the law database of the Ministry of Finance: http://vbpq.mof.gov.vn/ or that of Ho Chi Minh City: http://vbpl.vn/thanhphohochiminh/Pages/Home.aspx

The Ministry of Planning and Investment runs an e-regulations website that presents step-by-step user guides on investment procedures in seven provinces in Viet Nam: Binh Dinh, Da Nang, Hai Duong, Hanoi, Ho Chi Minh City, Phy Yen and Vinh Phuc https://vietnam.eregulations.org/.

E-customs

E-customs has been introduced in Viet Nam, starting from pilots in selected units. The implementation of e-customs procedures in Viet Nam will help shorten clearance time and reducing the requirements for declarations. Viet Nam is also building Viet Nam's National Single Window (NSW) to facilitate trade. Under the Customs' Reform Strategy of Modernisation through 2020, Viet Nam's National Automated Cargo and Port Consolidated System (NACCS) and Viet Nam's Customs Intelligence Information System (CIS) have been applied to all customs departments and sub-departments nationwide. The use of NACCS and CIS has also motivated the use of information technologies in other related areas including electronic tax payment (e-payment), electronic manifest (e-manifest), electronic invoice (e-invoice) and electronic permit (e-c/o and e-permit).

Through e-customs, Viet Nam is currently working to simplify its system of licences and certificates, including those concerning exports and imports, certificates of origin (c/o), quarantine and food safety. These efforts are demonstrated through the eCoSys (online c/o system) as well as through automatic import licensing.

Regulations on e-commerce and e-payments are not yet well understood by general businesses.

Stakeholder engagement

Article 34 of the Law on Laws (2008) introduced a general obligation to conduct public consultations during the regulatory drafting process. Public feedback may be collected in the form of "direct comments and suggestions, circulation of the draft decree for comments and suggestions, organising consultation workshops, making use of websites of the government and the leading drafting agency or mass media" (Government of Viet Nam, 2008[12]).

Public consultations of draft regulations are frequently discussed with business associations including the Viet Nam Association of Small and Medium Enterprises

(VINASME), Viet Nam Chamber of Commerce and Industry (VCCI) and the Young Business Association, among others.

In 2016, the Prime Minister personally chaired a meeting with the business sector focused on improving government management, business rights and obligations, advancing administrative reform and applying global standards in accounting (Dao, 2016[13]). The government also participated in a Viet Nam Private Sector Forum organised by the Viet Nam Young Entrepreneurs' Association (VYEA) and Mekong Business Initiative (Customs News, 2017[14]).

The government works closely with international partners to support the development of SME regulatory policy and regulations. Support activities including studies, workshops, and training and capacity building programmes to address the substantive contents of regulatory policy as well as legal and regulatory processes. An SME Partnership Group (SMEPG) supports donor-government collaboration and consultation in the formulation of SME policies and regulations.

Appeals

Formal appeals against a regulatory decision by an individual business – SME or otherwise – is highly unusual. It is possible to make an appeal through the commercial court system, although this is also uncommon (Government of Viet Nam, 2011[15]).

SME linkage policies

Viet Nam has significant linkages into the global value chain, with among the highest number of foreign companies and highest foreign direct investment (FDI) in ASEAN. Viet Nam has 283 industrial and export processing zones that have attracted over 4 100 FDI projects with investment capital amounting to nearly USD 60 billion (Ernst and Young, 2014, p. 20[16]). Traditionally, FDI has primarily gone to low-productivity sectors, such as clothing, and vertical linkages between local suppliers and foreign firms have been limited, in part due to the weak absorptive capacity of local firms (OECD, forthcoming[17]). However, Viet Nam is increasingly prioritising high-productivity tech and clean sectors.

There are three high-tech zones in Da Nang, Hao Lac (Hanoi) and Ho Chi Minh focusing on microelectronics, biotech, IT, nanotech, robotics and new energy.

Viet Nam has 18 economic zones that offer incentives such as free tariffs for selected items, lower personal income tax, reduced rents and fees. As of May 2017, Viet Nam plans to establish three new economic zones with special status in North Van Phong (Khanh Hoa province), Phu Quoc (Kien Giang province) and Van Don (Quang Ninh province). These three SEZs will have their own Law on Special Administrative-Economic Zones which might supersede local regulation without being contrary to the Constitution and Viet Nam's international commitments. A draft of the law submitted by the Ministry of Planning and Investment has proposed simplified administrative structures for the new SEZs, as well as guaranteed level playing field between domestic and foreign investors in the SEZ. Additionally, parties engaging in foreign civil, commercial or business contracts will have the option to apply foreign laws or international practices rather than Vietnamese law. The draft law also reduces the number of conditional business lines for investors from the 243 in the Investment Law to 108 in the SEZs, among other procedural simplifications. The draft law is awaiting approval by the National Assembly as of January 2018 (Vietnam Law and Legal Forum, 2018[18]).

Box 11.9. Appeal process for regulatory decisions in Viet Nam

According to Article 7 of the Law No. 02/2011/QH13 dated 11 November 2011 on Appeals, the appeal processes for regulatory enforcement decisions, administrative or judicial are as below:

1. Where there are grounds to believe that administrative decisions or administrative acts are unlawful or directly infringe upon their legitimate rights and interests, the complainants shall make first-time complaints to the persons who have issued the administrative decisions on the decisions, or initiate the initiates an administrative lawsuit in court according to the provisions of the Law on Administrative Proceedings.
   Where the complainants disagree with the first settlement decision, or the complaint is not resolved after the prescribed time limit, the complainant may file a second complaint to the immediate superior head of the person competent to handle the first-time complaints or may initiate the administrative lawsuits at courts according to the provisions of the Administrative Laws Law.
   Where the complainants disagree with the second complaint settlement decision or if at the expiration of the prescribed time limit, the complaint remains unresolved, the complainant may initiate an administrative lawsuit in court according to the provisions of the Law on Administrative Proceedings.
2. For administrative decisions or administrative acts of ministers, heads of ministerial-level agencies or heads of government-attached agencies (hereinafter collectively referred to as ministers), the complainants shall file complaints to the ministers or the heads of the agencies under the Government, or shall initiate administrative lawsuits at courts according to the provisions of the Administrative Proceedings Law.
   Where the complainants disagree with the complaint settlement decision of the Minister or the complaint is not settled within the prescribed time limit, the complainant may initiate an administrative lawsuit at the Court according to the provisions of the Law on Administrative Proceedings.
3. For administrative decisions or administrative acts of presidents of provincial/ municipal People's Committees (hereinafter collectively referred to as provincial-level People's Committees), the complainants shall make first-time complaints to the People's Committee Chairpersons Provincial people or initiate an administrative lawsuit in court according to the provisions of the Law on Administrative Proceedings.
   Where the complainants disagree with the decision on the first-time settlement of the complaint by the provincial-level People's Committee president or the complaint is not settled within the prescribed time limit, he/she may file a second complaint to the minister in charge of the sector/industry or initiate an administrative lawsuit in court according to the provisions of the Law on Administrative Procedure.
4. If the complainant disagrees with the second resolution of the Minister or the complaint is not resolved by the end of the prescribed time limit, he/she may initiate an administrative lawsuit in court according to the provisions of the Law on Administrative Proceedings.

Source: Government of Viet Nam (2011), *Law on Appeals, National Assembly No. 02/2011/QH13*.

Recommendations

- **Consider methods to better quantify or complement existing review structures,** such as regulatory impact assessments (RIA), to standardise practices across ministries when conducting evaluation or assessments.
- **Consider strengthening linkages across existing online platforms into one portal.** Existing platforms like LicenceOne, TradeNet and others could be streamlined further to allow even greater ease for businesses to interface with the government. More agencies could also be inducted into these platforms, towards digitising government to business transactions for greater ease of compliance.
- **Consider best practice sharing and implementation of new and innovative approaches to improving enforcement and compliance or when regulating new and emerging industries**, such as through the use of behavioural insights. Agencies that have already implemented or tried such approaches should share them across the government so that the public service can collectively reduce compliance costs for businesses.

References

Blunt, M. et al. (2017), *One-stop Shops in Vietnam: Changing the Face of Public Administration for Citizens and Businesses through a Single Door to Multiple Services*, http://documents.worldbank.org/curated/en/509861498753741062/One-stop-shops-in-Vietnam-changing-the-face-of-public-administration-for-citizens-and-businesses-through-a-single-door-to-multiple-services. [9]

Can, V. (2017), *SME Development: Vietnamese Experience*, http://www.pecc.org/resources/trade-and-investment-1/2421-smes-development-vietnamese-experience/file. [2]

Customs News (2017), *Vietnam Private Sector Forum: 65% of Enterprises Wish a Government in Action*, http://customsnews.vn/vietnam-private-sector-forum-65-of-enterprises-wish-a-government-in-action-4200.html. [14]

Dao, T. (2016), *PM-chaired Meeting Flooded with Foreign Investors' Policy Recommendations*, https://e.vnexpress.net/news/news/pm-chaired-meeting-flooded-with-foreign-investors-policy-recommendations-3395407.html. [13]

Ernst and Young (2014), *Doing Business in Vietnam*, http://www.ey.com/Publication/vwLUAssets/Doing_Business_in_Vietnam/$FILE/Doing_Business_in_Vietnam_16000319.pdf. [16]

General Statistics Office (2016), *Statistical Database*, http://www.gso.gov.vn/Default.aspx?tabid=706&ItemID=13412. [1]

Government of Viet Nam (2015), *Law No. 80/2015/QH13 Regarding Promulgation of Legal and Normative Documents*. [7]

Government of Viet Nam (2014), *Law on Customs, National Assembly No. 54/2014/QH13*, http://www.wipo.int/edocs/lexdocs/laws/en/vn/vn081en.pdf. [8]

Government of Viet Nam (2013), *Decree No. 22/2013/ND-CP on the Functions, Tasks, Powers, and Organisational Structure of the Ministry of Justice*. [5]

Government of Viet Nam (2011), *Law on Appeals, National Assembly No. 02/2011/QH13*. [15]

Government of Viet Nam (2008), *Law on the Promulgation of Legal Documents of the National Assembly, No.17/2008/QH12*, http://www.moj.gov.vn/vbpq/en/lists/vn%20bn%20php%20lut/view_detail.aspx?itemid=10500. [12]

OECD (forthcoming), *Inclusive Investments in GVCs: Opportunities for ASEAN SMEs*, OECD Publishing, Paris. [17]

PwC (2017), *PWC Vietnam News Brief: Lower Corporate Income Tax Rates and Other Incentives for Small and Medium Enterprises*, http://www.pwc.com/vn/en/publications/2017/170721-pwc-vietnam-newsbrief-law-sme-en.pdf. [6]

UNDP (2012), *Legislative Processes and Procedures of the National Assembly, Research Report*, [4]

Hanoi.

Vietnam Law and Legal Forum (2018), *Draft Law on Special Economic Zones Offers Maximum Incentives*, http://vietnamlawmagazine.vn/draft-law-on-special-zones-offers-maximum-incentives-6138.html. [18]

Vietnam Law and Legal Forum (2012), *Decision No. 1231/QD-TTG: Development Plan for Small- and Medium-sized Enterprises during 2011-2015*, http://vietnamlawmagazine.vn/decision-no-1231-qd-ttg-development-plan-for-small-and-medium-sized-enterprises-during-2011-2015-3167.html. [3]

Vietnam News (2017), *Gov't Cuts MoIT Regulations*, http://vietnamnews.vn/economy/421274/govt-cuts-moit-regulations.html#Ta9Yu7eL90Mumad4.97. [11]

Vo, T. and C. Nguyen (2016), *Towards Responsive Regulatory Management Systems: Country Report for Viet Nam*, http://www.eria.org/ERIA-DP-2016-22.pdf. [10]

ORGANISATION FOR ECONOMIC CO-OPERATION AND DEVELOPMENT

The OECD is a unique forum where governments work together to address the economic, social and environmental challenges of globalisation. The OECD is also at the forefront of efforts to understand and to help governments respond to new developments and concerns, such as corporate governance, the information economy and the challenges of an ageing population. The Organisation provides a setting where governments can compare policy experiences, seek answers to common problems, identify good practice and work to co-ordinate domestic and international policies.

The OECD member countries are: Australia, Austria, Belgium, Canada, Chile, the Czech Republic, Denmark, Estonia, Finland, France, Germany, Greece, Hungary, Iceland, Ireland, Israel, Italy, Japan, Korea, Latvia, Lithuania, Luxembourg, Mexico, the Netherlands, New Zealand, Norway, Poland, Portugal, the Slovak Republic, Slovenia, Spain, Sweden, Switzerland, Turkey, the United Kingdom and the United States. The European Union takes part in the work of the OECD.

OECD Publishing disseminates widely the results of the Organisation's statistics gathering and research on economic, social and environmental issues, as well as the conventions, guidelines and standards agreed by its members.

OECD PUBLISHING, 2, rue André-Pascal, 75775 PARIS CEDEX 16
(42 2018 36 1 P) ISBN 978-92-64-30542-7 – 2018

www.ingramcontent.com/pod-product-compliance
Lightning Source LLC
Chambersburg PA
CBHW061207240926
51846CB00006B/1141
* 9 7 8 9 2 6 4 3 0 5 4 2 7 *